NATIONAL
GEOGRAPHIC

SECRETS OF THE
NATIONAL
PARKS

SECOND EDITION

THE EXPERTS' GUIDE TO THE BEST
EXPERIENCES BEYOND THE TOURIST TRAIL

D0167428

NATIONAL GEOGRAPHIC
WASHINGTON, D.C.

CONTENTS

Page 1: Newfound Gap, Great Smoky Mountains National Park
Opposite: Square Tower House, Mesa Verde National Park

INTRODUCTION

Our national parks are known for their iconic vistas. From Yosemite's Half Dome to the Everglades' "river of grass" to the vast expanses of the Grand Canyon, these majestic sites are in large measure what inspired previous generations to protect these lands.

For many of us, though, the value of our parks is more personal. They are brought to life by glimpsing the early morning light on the water, by strolling through a stand of old-growth pine, or by witnessing the drama of a thunderhead breaching a mountain pass.

At the National Park Trust, we work every day to acquire inholdings and adjacent lands to complete and to expand our national parks and to introduce our parks to our children, so they might have their own transformative adventures and be inspired to continue our mission. Let me share some of my own encounters and the secrets they have uncovered through the years.

One need not travel far to find a national park. Like many cities, Washington, D.C., is blessed by easy access to our parks, including one of my favorites, Shenandoah National Park.

An early morning departure from the city puts me at the Nethers trailhead in time to tackle the circuit hike to the pinnacle of Old Rag Mountain. Lunch on the open, rocky summit provides expansive views of the Blue Ridge, and an after-lunch hike down the circuit loop allows me to depart for the city by dinner. For the adventurous, take the circuit hike in winter; in the crisp air you'll have the trail to yourself, allowing for even more dramatic vistas.

Each park provides stories that fascinate. The first rangers who patrolled our parks were often homesteaders, hunters,

"When citizens have an understanding of the national parks, they will be inspired and will want to join the army of stewards to care for these inherited places. That will be the ultimate savior of these resources—citizens' caring. Parks are truly places of learning."

—ROBERT G. STANTON
Former Director, National Park Service

or trappers who knew the land. At Glacier National Park, Dan Doody was one of these early guardians. Across the Middle Fork of the Flathead River, one can still see the remains of Doody's log lodge, where Dan and his wife, Josephine, greeted outdoor adventurers from around the country. In her spare time, Josephine—known as the Bootleg Lady of Glacier Park—kept the Great Northern trainmen supplied with moonshine. Look across the river and you'll see where the trains would pull off and signal with a whistle for a fresh supply!

Every park visit offers new surprises. Hiking down from Glacier Point in Yosemite late one afternoon, we failed to reach the valley before sunset. As the sun lowered, pinpoints of light sprang out all over the face of El Capitan—the flashlights of rock climbers spending the night on the sheer face of this rock wall brought the stars to Earth.

Our best known parks are famous for their historic lodges, including the Old Faithful at Yellowstone, the Ahwahnee (formerly the Majestic) at Yosemite, and El Tovar at the Grand Canyon. Yet there are fascinating lodges to be found in less traveled parks.

In Voyageurs, look for the Kettle Falls Hotel. It's accessible only by water and takes one back to an earlier era. At Lassen Volcanic, seek out the Drakesbad on Hot Springs Creek at the head of Warner Valley. This rustic collection of log cabins and a guest ranch, accessible by a rutted forest road, has been here in one form or another for over a century. The thermal pool, Drake's Bath, provides a soothing soak at the end of a day of hiking.

We at the National Park Trust feel fortunate in our task to preserve many of these natural and historic places for the enjoyment of all, as we work every day with the National Park Service and a constellation of other partners.

It is our mission to ensure that these opportunities not only continue but are known and accessible by all in our richly diverse nation. Please enjoy this book and use it as your point of departure for discovering your own park secrets.

—F. WILLIAM (BILL) BROWNELL
Chair, Board of Trustees
National Park Trust

Manzanita Lake, Lassen Volcanic National Park

ABOUT THIS BOOK

This is a book of secrets—hundreds of items of information designed to help you get the most out of exploring America's true treasures, our national parks.

For this guide, the editors of National Geographic called on some of the best nature writers and most experienced travelers to visit parks across the nation. Their mission? Tell us about hidden gems in places off the well-beaten tourist tracks, those lesser known experiences that can make a trip to a national park truly special, exciting, and memorable.

Yes, there are still secrets to be found in such long-traveled parks as the Grand Canyon, Death Valley, Petrified Forest, Haleakalā, and Wind Cave (to name only a few). Our writers-at-large talked to park rangers, outfitters, and

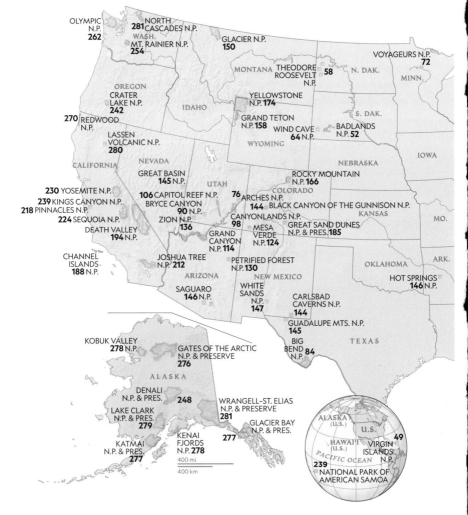

local guides, among others, to uncover the least crowded beaches, barely tramped trails, hard-to-find sights, and more. They then organized the secrets into easy-to-read narratives to help you plan and enjoy your national park adventures.

Each park description includes inspiring photos of the scenery and wildlife awaiting you on your visit, plus National Geographic maps to orient you to the areas, though you'll want to grab detailed park maps at visitor centers showing roads, trails, and other features before you set out to explore on your own.

The book is organized geographically, making it easier to tackle the parks in small chunks or to focus on a specific destination. We arrange our secrets starting with the iconic spots, moving out to less-visited areas. A highly opinionated "Not To Be Missed" listing accompanies each entry, and the favorite sites of the real insiders—members of the National Park Trust, local park staff, frequent visitors, and experienced outfitters—are offered throughout.

Sit back and learn about the less-known sides of our national parks, then head out on a trip to one or more. We hope soon you'll discover your *own* secrets in America's national parks.

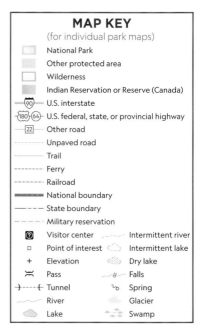

MAP KEY
(for individual park maps)

	National Park
	Other protected area
	Wilderness
	Indian Reservation or Reserve (Canada)
90	U.S. interstate
180 64	U.S. federal, state, or provincial highway
22	Other road
	Unpaved road
	Trail
	Ferry
	Railroad
	National boundary
	State boundary
	Military reservation
Ⓩ Visitor center	Intermittent river
▫ Point of interest	Intermittent lake
+ Elevation	Dry lake
≍ Pass	Falls
─┤····├─ Tunnel	Spring
River	Glacier
Lake	Swamp

NOTE: *Bold numbers indicate the pages on which the parks are featured within this book.*

1 | EAST

Sweet Bay Pond at sunrise, Everglades National Park, Florida

"*How lucky are we to have the national parks that are accessible to all? There is a sense of renewal that comes from a walk in the woods where our senses are alerted to the sights, sounds, and smells of nature. What could be better than that?*"

—DORO BUSH KOCH
FOUNDER, BB&R WELLNESS CONSULTING,
AND HONORARY CHAIR, BARBARA BUSH FOUNDATION

Sailing from Bar Harbor, off Mount Desert Island

ACADIA

Long before parts of it became a national monument in 1916 (and a national park three years later), Maine's Mount Desert Island was attracting visitors eager to savor its mountains, forests, lakes, and, especially, its stunning coastline. These included many of America's wealthiest families, who built opulent summer homes in the Bar Harbor area, as well as tourists who filled more than two dozen island hotels.

Some of Mount Desert's well-to-do residents, alarmed that the very scenic qualities they loved were threatened, pushed for the creation of a national park, donating land and money for that purpose. Over the years, Acadia National Park has grown to encompass more than 40 percent of the island, as well as areas on nearby Schoodic Peninsula and Isle au Haut.

Although Acadia is one of the nation's top ten most-visited national parks, there are still secret spots to be found if you know where to look.

on Bar Island, situated less than 0.5 mile out from shore. Surprisingly enough, you can actually walk to the island, as long as you begin and end your hike during the period 1.5 hours on either side of low tide (visitor centers have tide schedules).

You'll have plenty of company on your walk, so here's an alternative: Rent a canoe or kayak in Bar Harbor and paddle to Bar Island during the other nine hours of the tidal cycle. You may not be alone on the island, but you'll enjoy its view in far greater solitude.

Although this is a short trip on a fairly protected part of the bay, you'll still be on the ocean, so know your abilities, such as swimming, and check the weather forecast before setting out.

THE EAST SIDE

If on your visit to Acadia you encounter occasional road traffic or a crowded scenic spot, bear in mind that without the foresight of island lovers more than a century ago the first national park east of the Mississippi would never have existed, and Mount Desert would be far less accessible to travelers than it is today.

The center of much island activity is the town of Bar Harbor, which sits on the northeastern shore.

1 Bar Island There's a great view of town and the mountains of eastern Mount Desert Island from a high point

2 Park Loop Road This 27-mile road was designed in part by landscape architect Frederick Law Olmsted, Jr., who wanted to showcase scenery that he described as having "a certain bigness of sweep."

The route provides access to many of Acadia's most popular spots, including **Sand Beach, Otter Cliff, Jordan Pond,** and **Cadillac Mountain.** As such, it

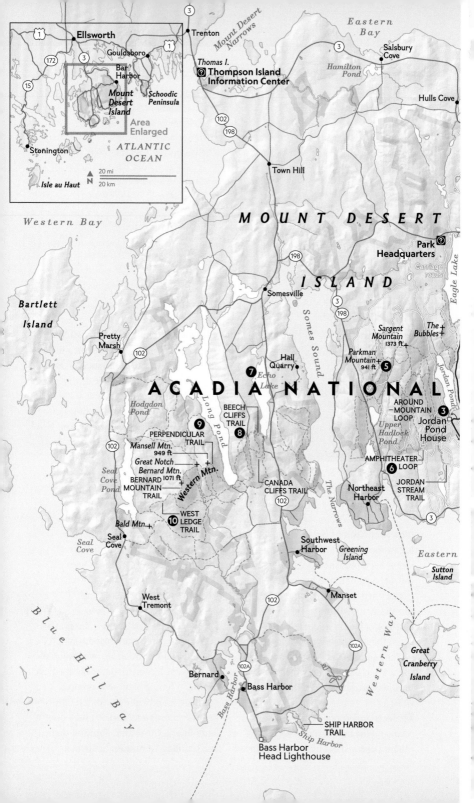

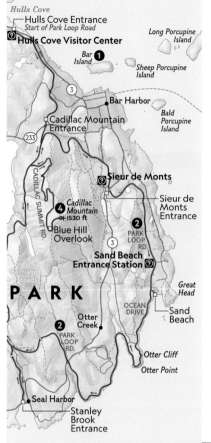

Frenchman

Bay

Hulls Cove

Hulls Cove Entrance
Start of Park Loop Road
Hulls Cove Visitor Center

Long Porcupine
Island

Bar
Island **1**

Sheep Porcupine
Island

3

Bar Harbor

Bald
Porcupine
Island

Cadillac Mountain
Entrance

233

Sieur de Monts

Sieur de
Monts
Entrance

4 Cadillac
Mountain
1530 ft

CADILLAC SUMMIT RD.

Blue Hill
Overlook

2
PARK
LOOP
RD.

3

**Sand Beach
Entrance Station**

Carriage
roads

P A R K

Great
Head

OCEAN
DRIVE

Sand
Beach

2
Otter
Creek

PARK
LOOP
RD.

Otter Cliff

Otter Point

Seal Harbor

Stanley
Brook
Entrance

Way

A T L A N T I C

O C E A N

*Little Cranberry
Island*

*Baker
Island*

2 mi
2 km
N

often suffers from traffic congestion and crowded parking lots along the shore section called **Ocean Drive.**

Nonetheless, here's the secret of beating the crowds: "People forget that there are really beautiful views and interesting things to do at night between sunset and sunrise," says Sonya Berger, park interpreter. "One of my favorite places to go after the sun sets is to one of the busiest places during the day, which is Ocean Drive. You can find your own private piece of rock and sit down and watch the stars come out.

"On a clear night along the coast you'll have an uninterrupted view of the swath of stars dipping down into the ocean. It's a fantastic view." It helps that in 2008, Bar Harbor initiated light-control rules to help protect the island's night skies.

3 **Jordan Pond** Despite the crowds, Jordan Pond is a must for all park visitors, for two main reasons: the view of the twin hills called **The Bubbles** and the popovers at the **Jordan Pond House** restaurant. These baked delights make a nice reward for a completed hike or bike ride.

Deer encounter

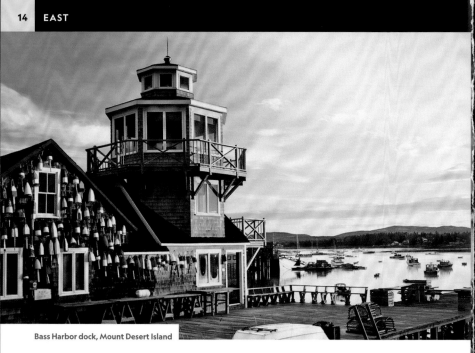

Bass Harbor dock, Mount Desert Island

A favorite walk for some park interpreters is the easy **Jordan Stream Trail,** which heads south along the outlet creek of Jordan Pond. It ranks among the park's prettiest locations, and as a bonus, after 0.6 mile you reach the first, and perhaps most famous, of the carriage road bridges. This bridge is the only one faced with cobblestones instead of cut rock.

Wherever you walk in Acadia, check the possibility of using the free **Island Explorer** buses (summer only) to do one-way hikes and avoid full trailhead parking lots.

❹ **Cadillac Mountain** The 3.5-mile Cadillac Summit Road, part of the Park Loop, leads to the top of 1,530-foot Cadillac Mountain. Heading south along the Atlantic shore trail, you'll find no higher mountain spot until Rio de Janeiro.

Watching the sunrise from the pastel pink granite summit has become a Mount Desert Island rite, attracting big crowds. For a less congested alternative, head along **Ocean Drive** or to the **Ship Harbor Trail.**

Alternatively, drive up the mountain well before dusk and find a seat near the **Blue Hill Overlook,** less than 0.25 mile back down the road from the summit parking lot. If the clouds and the light align properly, you'll be treated to one of the best sunset views of your life.

CARRIAGE ROADS

Acadia is justly famed for its carriage roads: wide, broken-stone lanes on which motor vehicles are banned and walkers, bicyclists, horseback riders, skiers, and, yes, carriages rule.

Forty-five miles of these roads wind through the national park, with another few located on private land outside the park. (Bicycles are prohibited on carriage roads outside the park.) The 17 bridges, each with its own design and faced in native stone, decorate the park routes.

The busiest carriage roads are those between Bar Harbor and Jordan Pond, such as the loop around **Eagle Lake.**

For a less congested (and more strenuous) hike or ride, use the unmarked parking lot along Maine 3 north of **Upper Hadlock Pond** and travel the route climbing northwest of **Sargent Mountain.** It's steep in places, but offers some fine western vistas. (Think of the popovers waiting.)

For a real workout, you can continue to make the full **Around Mountain Loop** of 11.1 miles. Otherwise, retrace your path back to Maine 3.

❺ Parkman Mountain Though no carriage road goes all the way to the summit, while you're in this area consider a hike to the top of 941-foot Parkman Mountain.

Even if it's not one of the park's most famous summits, this peak's rocky top provides views westward over glacier-carved **Somes Sound.**

❻ Amphitheater Loop To see two of the famed stone bridges in a little more than 5 miles, park at the Brown Mountain

NOT TO BE MISSED: *Travel to Bar Island by canoe or by foot during low tide.* ▸ *Skip the crowds at sunrise and take in a spectacular sunset view near the Blue Hill Overlook.* ▸ *Watch the people disappear and the stars come out along Ocean Drive after sunset.* ▸ *Bike, hike, or ride along 45 miles of unpaved carriage roads.* ▸ *Try the strenuous Perpendicular Trail up Mansell Mountain for views of Long Pond.*

Gatehouse on the way to Northeast Harbor and follow the carriage-road route called Amphitheater Loop, which hugs hillsides between two ridges to form a natural amphitheater.

THE QUIET SIDE

The area of Acadia west of Somes Sound is often called the park's "quiet side"—though **Bass Harbor Head Light Station**

LOCAL INTELLIGENCE

A different sort of wildlife can be found along the rocky shore of Mount Desert Island—a type that many visitors overlook. The Ship Harbor Trail, a 1.3-mile loop just east of the **Bass Harbor Head Light Station** provides easy access at low tide to the island's intertidal zone, a fascinating ecosystem with a surprising number of species including fish, reptiles, amphibians, and invertebrates.

Find a tide pool and a place to sit amid the pink granite ledges, and spend some time just looking down into the clear water. Creatures such as barnacles and mussels will be obvious, but by watching closely you'll likely spot crabs, periwinkles, whelks, limpets, sea stars, sea urchins, and many other animals. (Please do not disturb.) Sure, it's fun to see large wildlife such as white-tailed deer or Bald Eagles elsewhere, but the teeming life of a tide pool is in its own way just as rewarding to observe—not to mention a solitary escape from the island's crowded roads and towns.

Morning fog above an autumn forest

and **Echo Lake** certainly get their share of visitors.

Nonetheless, this section is generally calmer than the hubs of Jordan Pond and Cadillac Mountain.

❼ Echo Lake Moderately challenging trails (leading from the parking lot for the swimming area) ascend to fine views of Echo Lake and surrounding areas of the island as well as of the **Cranberry Isles** off the southern coast.

❽ Beech Cliffs Trail This route is among many built here by the Civilian Conservation Corps in the 1930s. Beech Cliffs Trail includes some very steep sections where ladders are used; the **Canada Cliffs Trail** is less precipitous. For an enjoyable round-trip hike of about 2 miles, ascend the Beech Cliffs Trail and then head home by descending the Canada Cliffs Trail back to the Echo Lake parking lot.

❾ Perpendicular Trail If the steepness of the Beech Cliffs Trail doesn't faze you, consider climbing the Perpendicular Trail, a strenuous ascent of **Mansell Mountain** that begins at the southern end of **Long Pond.** The climb is short, leading to rewarding views of Long Pond.

Another CCC project of the 1930s, the trail "was beautifully constructed. You won't find a prettier set of stonework and steps," says Gail Gladstone, cultural resources program manager for the park. "Once you get up the trail you've got three or four options to come down, depending on how far you want to walk: Mansell Mountain, **Razorback, Great Notch, Sluiceway,** even the **Bernard Mountain Trail,** which goes all the way around what's called **Western Mountain.** You can make the trek as long or as short as you want it. This area is mostly forested, with occasional rock outcrops with views, and it's not very traveled."

❿ West Ledge Trail The 3-mile West Ledge Trail, a spur off the **Bernard Mountain Trail** leading to Bald Mountain, offers views of the western coast of Mount Desert Island. It can also be reached from the unpaved road to **Seal Cove Pond,** a site for canoeists and kayakers looking for relaxing paddling. With its mixture of wooded shoreline and marsh, Seal Cove Pond often offers the chance to spot birds and other wildlife.

ISLE AU HAUT

High Island was the name given to this 12-square-mile island by Frenchman Samuel Champlain in 1604. Lying southwest of Mount Desert Island, Isle au Haut offers scenery and solitude to those who make advance arrangements to visit. The only access is by private ferry, operating from the mainland town of **Stonington** and providing space on a first-come, first-served basis.

About half the island is under National Park Service administration; a small campground is available (reservations needed). Even on a day visit, you're likely to find yourself alone on the 18-mile trail system, enjoying forest, bogs, rocky shoreline, and a freshwater lake.

A hike along portions of the **Goat, Cliff,** and **Western Head trails** is an ideal way to experience the island's highlights: listening to bird songs, smelling the ferns and conifers, and watching the fishermen on lobster boats checking their traps.

SCHOODIC PENINSULA

The only part of Acadia National Park located on the mainland, Schoodic Peninsula encompasses 2,266 acres of strikingly rugged granite landscape across **Frenchman Bay** from Bar Harbor.

A mainly one-way scenic drive leads to **Schoodic Point,** which, as one park guidebook accurately states, "provides an outstanding vantage point for witnessing the power of the sea."

Take the ferry (summer only) from Bar Harbor to Winter Harbor before hopping on an Island Explorer bus to make the Schoodic Loop. "You could see osprey for sure, and maybe an eagle or some harbor porpoises" enthuses park ranger Bill Weidner.

Many visitors walk to the top of 440-foot **Schoodic Head** for a sweeping view of the coastline. You can walk up the dirt road and down one of several hiking trails. "What you don't want to miss is Schoodic Point," Weidner says. "If there's any wind driving the surf, the wave action is spectacular." At any time, the granite shore with its "dikes" of solidified magma provides endless opportunities for photos or contemplation. Plan ahead to snag a coveted spot at the Schoodic Woods Campground, managed by the park.

Sunset from the Schoodic Peninsula

Red mangrove, Boca Chita Key

BISCAYNE

Getting off the beaten path at Biscayne may seem a bit more difficult than at most other national parks: You can't just lace up your boots, sling on a daypack, and head down a hiking trail. That's because 95 percent of the park's surface area is composed of the sparkling blue waters of Biscayne Bay and the Atlantic Ocean off Florida's southeastern coast—and most of the dry land is made up of islands accessible only by boat.

Don't be discouraged, though: The park offers many ways to experience its fascinating ecosystems and human history. A nonprofit partner, the Biscayne National Park Institute (BNPI), conducts a variety of guided tours ranging from the physically active—such as snorkeling and paddle boarding—to the very relaxing, including sailing and powerboat cruises that focus on scenic beauty and intriguing tales of pioneers, rumrunners, and millionaires.

Year-Round Visitor Center

■ Dante Fascell Visitor Center
*At Convoy Point,
9700 SW 328 Street, Homestead*

305-230-7275, nps.gov/bisc

of the Florida Keys, and the world's third largest coral reef system.

A memorable wildlife experience can start right away at Convoy Point, as park staffer Dani Cessna explains: "Manatees come through almost daily in our harbor, and sometimes we see crocodiles. We have parrotfish that poke along the rocks, and lots of frigatebirds, anhingas, and cormorants."

THE KEYS

❷ **Jones Lagoon** Along with everyone connected to the park, BNPI's Jordan Manges raves about the guided paddleboard tours of Jones Lagoon, a shallow site among the Keys in the southern part of the park, reached via boat from the visitor center.

"To experience Jones Lagoon is magical," she says. "It's a hidden gem in the park, where you completely forget that you're an hour south of Miami. The water is very clear and you get to see *Cassiopea,* the upside-down jellyfish, which are super-cool."

"The Jones Lagoon experience is wonderful," agrees Cessna. "It's so immersive. I've had nurse sharks swim under my paddleboard, and you see jellies and sponges and all kinds of birds." (Those wondering about getting so close to sharks should know that the small nurse sharks in this area are generally docile, ignoring human visitors to their undersea home.)

CONVOY POINT

❶ **Dante Fascell Visitor Center** Except for those using private boats, most activities begin at the Dante Fascell Visitor Center, located on the mainland south of Miami at a site called Convoy Point.

Some visitors walk out to the jetty here and, in the words of BNPI guide Hans Bockelman, "wonder why it's a national park," since there's almost nothing in sight except water.

Exhibits at the visitor center clearly explain the ecological basis for Biscayne's national park status: the wildlife of the coastal mangrove habitat, islands that make up the northernmost

3 Boca Chita Key For visitors with limited time, Manges likes the three-hour trip to Boca Chita Key. "If you're coming to the park for the first time and looking for a quick overview, I would definitely go to Boca Chita. That's where the lighthouse is, and that's the most iconic structure for the park. On that tour you can hear all about the history of the park, and you'll learn about the ecosystems we protect."

Boca Chita is home to one particularly quirky bit of park history: The 65-foot-high lighthouse was never intended to assist navigation. It was built in the 1930s purely for decoration by wealthy industrialist Mark Honeywell, who then owned the island.

The lighthouse observation deck is open occasionally to visitors, providing a spectacular panorama of Biscayne Bay and the skyline of Miami, 15 miles north.

4 Elliott Key There's a hiking trail on Boca Chita, and a much longer one on Elliott Key—one with its own unusual story. In the 1950s and '60s, when southern Florida was growing quickly, developers planned a new city (to be called Islandia) in Biscayne Bay, as well as an industrial port and a deep, dredged channel through the bay.

Conservationists protested the destruction these activities would bring to the pristine environment of Biscayne Bay, and a coalition of anglers, environmentalists, writers, and politicians began promoting a plan to create a national park that would protect a long stretch of undeveloped shoreline, part of the bay, several keys, and sections of coral reef. A bitter battle ensued, culminating in the creation in 1968 of Biscayne National Monument, later designated a national park.

In the meantime, though, angry would-be developers bulldozed a wide roadway down the length of Elliott Key, trying to make the environment less appealing for protection. This "Spite

Coral reef

SOUTH MIAMI

1

CUTLER RIDGE

BISCAYNE NATIONAL PARK

N 5 mi
5 km

Key Biscayne

Cape Florida
Lighthouse

BILL BAGGS
CAPE FLORIDA
STATE PARK

Stiltsville

Safety Valve

Arratoon Apcar
wreck □

Soldier Key

*Brewster
Reef*

Black Point

*Featherbed
Bank*

Ragged Keys

3 Boca Chita Key

Lewis Cut

*Star
Reef*

Fender Point

*Bowles
Bank*

5 Sands Key

BISCAYNE BAY

**1 Dante Fascell Visitor Center
and Park Headquarters**

□ Convoy Point
Homestead Bayfront
Park and Marina

*Pelican
Bank*

Turkey Point

Billys Point

4

E L L I O T T   K E Y

"Spite Highway"

H A W K   C H A N N E L

□ Lugano wreck
□ Mandalay wreck

*Long
Reef*

Erl King wreck □

Alicia wreck □

Adams Key

Caesar Creek

□ 19th-century
wooden sailing
vessel wreck

FLORIDA KEYS NATIONAL MARINE SANCTUARY

*Long
Arsenicker
Key*

**Totten
Key**

Old Rhodes Key

*Jones
Lagoon*

2

*CARD
SOUND*

Broad Creek

Angelfish Creek

JOHN PENNEKAMP
CORAL REEF
STATE PARK

Key Largo

FLORIDA KEYS
NATIONAL MARINE
SANCTUARY

*ATLANTIC
OCEAN*

Highway" has now recovered somewhat and serves as a trail allowing hikers to explore the tropical hardwood forest of the key, full of birds, butterflies, and distinctive plants. One of those butterflies is the extremely rare Schaus swallowtail, subject of intensive recovery efforts.

The park's only two campgrounds are located on Boca Chita and Elliott

Roseate spoonbills

Key; campers and hikers should bear in mind that winter is by far the best season for these activities. Mosquitoes, heat, and humidity can make hotter months unpleasant unless you're zipping across the bay in a boat.

As of 2019, there is no park-sponsored transportation to Elliott Key, but staffers are at work on offering public boat access, and tours should be back on the schedule soon. In the meantime, only

those with private craft can visit the park's largest island.

Among other available guided tours of the park are an evening cruise of Biscayne Bay, a boat trip focusing on local lighthouses, and a visit to Stiltsville, a historic offshore community that was once a controversial center of nightlife and gambling.

5 Sands Key Longtime park ranger Gary Bremen has one more off-the-beaten-path suggestion for those with their own boats. "There's a little hole in the middle of Sands Key, which is an area that most people don't visit. It almost became a marina in the 1960s when the whole area was threatened with development. Boaters who know where it is can sneak up in there and have this private lagoon in the mangroves all to themselves."

Visitors who take private boats into the park should read and be aware of regulations applying to both personal safety and protection of the environment. It's imperative to have nautical charts and to know tide schedules. Coral reefs and other areas of the seafloor are easily damaged by anchors and boat hulls.

MARITIME HERITAGE TRAIL

"People know about the reef, but they often forget about our shipwrecks,"

Exposed mangrove prop roots

says Bremen. "There are six sites on our Maritime Heritage Trail. I would focus on *Mandalay,* which ran aground on Long Reef on New Year's Day, 1966. The wreck has been there long enough that there's fire coral and other things growing on it, and there are lots of fish associated with the site. It usually has very clear water."

"Nowhere else along the Florida Keys is there a wreck shallow enough to snorkel on," Bockelman adds. "Most of the shipwrecks are in 30 to 100 feet of water, and the *Mandalay* is in about 15 feet of water. It's a unique opportunity to be able to snorkel on a shipwreck, as opposed to having to scuba dive it."

Cessna affirms that recommendation. "Really, I would describe the *Mandalay* as life-changing snorkeling, it is so fabulous." She remembers her first days working at Biscayne: "As soon as I got out and snorkeled the *Mandalay* I thought, 'Oh, I could work here forever.'"

NOT TO BE MISSED: *Enjoy diverse wildlife from a paddleboard in Jones Lagoon.* ▶ *Hop on a guided cruise to historic Stiltsville, once a hotspot for illegal gambling and drinking.* ▶ *Snorkel among colorful tropical fish in Florida's northernmost coral reefs.* ▶ *Take in Biscayne Bay and the Miami skyline from Boca Chita Key.* ▶ *Go underwater exploring at the Mandalay, one of the few area shipwrecks shallow enough for snorkeling.*

For divers with their own boats, a park brochure describes the five other wrecks on the Maritime Heritage Trail, which include the *Alicia,* which sank in 1905, and the *Lugano,* which at the time of its grounding in 1913 was the largest vessel ever to founder in the Florida Keys.

Great egret near the Anhinga Trail

EVERGLADES

Beyond the theme parks and hotel-lined beaches of South Florida, beyond the golf courses and city skyscrapers, Everglades National Park protects more than 2,400 square miles of Florida's primeval past.

Comprising most of the southern tip of the state's peninsula, the park has as its heart a "river of grass" where water flows seasonally north to south across a flat sawgrass prairie, fueling an ecosystem known for abundant wildlife, from alligators to flocks of colorful wading birds.

Agriculture and urban development have seriously altered natural habitats in the Everglades ecosystem, yet this place endures as a must-see destination for environmentally minded travelers. Nothing like it exists anywhere else on the planet—reason enough for its designation as a World Heritage site, an international biosphere reserve, and a wetland of international importance. It's an otherworldly place of secrets.

Year-Round Visitor Centers

- **Ernest F. Coe Visitor Center**
  At 40001 Fla. 9336/SW 344 St.,
  Homestead
- **Flamingo Visitor Center**
  On Main Park Road, 38 miles south
  of the park entrance
- **Shark Valley Visitor Center**
  36000 SW 8th St., Miami, 25 miles
  west of Florida Turnpike
- **Gulf Coast Visitor Center**
  815 Oyster Bar Ln., 5 miles south of
  Tamiami Trail, Everglades City
  305-242-7700, nps.gov/ever

Most backcountry campsites are reached by boat, however, and a canoe or kayak along the 44-mile wilderness waterway or out into Florida Bay is often the best way to enjoy the park in solitude.

Visiting in the off season (the rainy summer, from May through November) cuts the crowds, but brings discouraging issues: heat, humidity, curtailed park activities, and often abundant mosquitoes. Wildlife is dispersed through sprawling wetlands and harder to observe. The ideal time to see Everglades is usually January through March.

The main park road runs 38 miles from the **Ernest F. Coe Visitor Center** on the eastern edge of the park to the Flamingo area on Florida Bay. Driving out and back along this route and stopping along the way to hike, bike, canoe, or take a boat tour are the park's most popular activities.

MAIN PARK ROAD

Getting off the tourist trail is a little more difficult at Everglades than in many parks. Around 86 percent of the park is federally designated wilderness (the largest east of the Rockies), composed of freshwater and coastal prairie, marsh, pine and cypress woods, mangroves, and the waters and islands of **Florida Bay.** But you can drive through the heart of the park, and airboat concession companies offer a new way to explore its beauty.

While much of the wet-prairie and slough area seems fairly inaccessible to the average hiker, several walking trails highlight the variety of park habitats.

❶ Gumbo Limbo Trail The 0.5-mile **Anhinga Trail** at the **Royal Palm** area is definitely on the tourist itinerary, but the chance to see and photograph gators, turtles, and birds is too good to pass up.

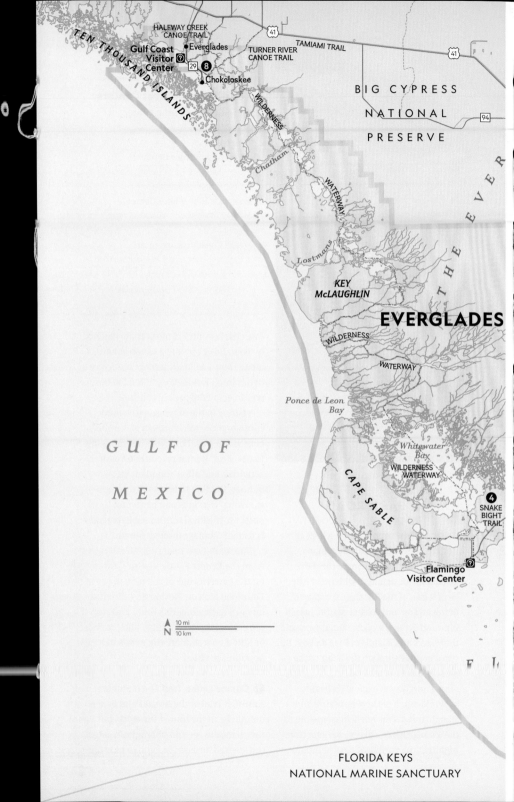

HALFWAY CREEK
CANOE TRAIL

Gulf Coast
Visitor
Center

• Everglades

29 **8**

TURNER RIVER
CANOE TRAIL

TAMIAMI TRAIL

41

41

▲ Chokoloskee

TEN THOUSAND ISLANDS

WILDERNESS

Chatham

WATERWAY

Lostmans

KEY
McLAUGHLIN

WILDERNESS

WATERWAY

BIG CYPRESS

NATIONAL

PRESERVE

94

THE EVER

EVERGLADES

Ponce de Leon
Bay

GULF OF

MEXICO

CAPE SABLE

Whitewater
Bay
WILDERNESS
WATERWAY

4
SNAKE
BIGHT
TRAIL

Flamingo
Visitor Center

▲ 10 mi
N 10 km

F I

FLORIDA KEYS
NATIONAL MARINE SANCTUARY

GLADES

27

821

Florida's Turnpike

Homestead Extension

95

41 TAMIAMI TRAIL 41

Shark Valley Visitor Center
7 ℗
6 BOBCAT BOARDWALK
OTTER CAVE HAMMOCK
TRAIL

TRAM TRAIL

997

826

836

MIAMI

1

Observation
Tower

SHARK RIVER SLOUGH

94

874

BISCAYNE
BAY

997 821

1

BISCAYNE

NATIONAL

PARK

NATIONAL PARK

Pa-hay-okee
Double Overlook
Dome
LONG PINE KEY TRAIL

3 PINELANDS
TRAIL

Homestead

Florida City

Ernest F. Coe
Visitor Center and
Park Headquarters
℗

RESEARCH RD.

MAIN PARK ROAD

Nike Missile Base **2**
Historic Area
Daniel Beard
Center

9336

1 Royal Palm
ANHINGA TRAIL
GUMBO LIMBO TRAIL

Mahogany
Hammock

TAYLOR SLOUGH

CARD SOUND

KEY LARGO

5 NINE MILE POND
CANOE TRAIL

Nine Mile
Pond

1

CROCODILE LAKE
NATIONAL
WILDLIFE REFUGE

BARNES 905
SOUND

JOHN PENNEKAMP CORAL REEF
STATE PARK

Snake
Bight

1

F L O R I D A   B A Y

Key Largo

OVERSEAS HIGHWAY

FLORIDA
KEYS
NATIONAL
MARINE
SANCTUARY

A T L A N T I C

O C E A N

Islamorada
Upper Matecumbe
Key

LIGNUMVITAE KEY
STATE AQUATIC
PRESERVE

1

Lower Matecumbe
Key

Palmetto plants, Pinelands area

The best advice: Be here just after dawn. Far fewer people take the time to walk the short Gumbo Limbo Trail nearby; if you do, you'll have a good chance to see songbirds and some of the park's fantastic array of butterflies.

2 Research Road Nearby Research Road is a place to experience what Lori Oberhofer, wildlife biologist, calls the Everglades soundscape. "I love the concert of peeps and croaks from frogs and toads after a late afternoon thunderstorm," she says. "There's an amazing chorus of green tree frogs, cricket frogs, chorus frogs, oak toads, and southern toads, among others. I'm impressed at how an area so quiet during the heat of the day comes alive with a symphony of sound after a cooling rainstorm."

3 Pinelands Trail The main park road passes through pine forest habitat (the short Pinelands Trail on the north side is a good introduction to this ecosystem), then reaches an area where bald cypresses are the dominant tree.

Note the circular stands of cypress locally called "domes." These are favorite destinations for naturalists who enjoy "slough-slogging," walking through shallow water that forms the "river of grass." Sturdy shoes and clothes you don't mind getting wet are essential, of course.

"I have gone into the slough since I was little, but each and every time it's a new adventure and I become like a child again, giddy about exploring," Yvette Cano, park ranger, says. "I love to discover the magic under the water. At first people are overwhelmed with fear and apprehension, but as soon as they set foot in the slough it transforms them, and they see the beauty and mystery."

Double Dome, near the Pa-hay-okee overlook, is a favorite destination for slough sloggers. If you're unsure of your abilities, check with a ranger for advice. Ranger-guided slough walks are offered during the dry season.

4 Snake Bight Trail All the interpretive trails along the park road, such as **Mahogany Hammock,** are worth trying,

but for a bit of solitude, Nicholas Aumen of the park's science staff recommends this 1.8-mile (one way) hike from the road to a "bight" (small bay) on Florida Bay. "Walk to the platform at the end of the trail," he says. "Take along binoculars for bird-watching and be prepared for mosquitoes at any time of year."

However vegetation can block views and the birds can be quite far away at low tide. For a different perspective on the same scene, Aumen says visitors should continue to the ranger station and marina at **Flamingo,** rent a kayak, and paddle out: "You'll have possible viewings of roseate spoonbills, eagles, reddish egrets, sharks, crocodiles, porpoises, and a wide variety of wading birds, especially on exposed mudflats at low tide—and the occasional flamingo."

You don't have to paddle all the way to Snake Bight to enjoy park bird life. "I like watching birds silhouetted across the setting sun as they fly by off Flamingo," Oberhofer says. "You can sit out there in a boat or kayak and watch flocks of ibises, egrets, herons, and

NOT TO BE MISSED: *Greet the dawn with birdsong and butterflies on the Gumbo Limbo Trail.* ▸ *Discover slough-slogging to cypress domes.* ▸ *Rent a kayak from the marina at Flamingo and paddle out for views of roseate spoonbills, eagles, crocodiles, porpoises, and more.* ▸ *Learn about the local ecosystem on a ranger-guided tram tour.* ▸ *Explore the mangrove tunnels of Ten Thousand Islands by tour or on your own.*

pelicans flying from the mainland to their night roosts on the islands in the bay. It's a beautiful and peaceful experience, and it reminds me of how diverse the wildlife is in this park and how accessible it is if you simply take a moment to really look and listen."

❺ Nine Mile Pond Consider taking a canoe trip on one of the trails near

Flamingo. The best for beginners is probably the 5-mile loop at Nine Mile Pond, which has numbered markers for guidance. (An optional shortcut makes the loop 3.5 miles.)

You'll likely see alligators and a wide variety of birds. Rangers tell paddlers not to be discouraged if the beginning of the trip, across the open water of Nine Mile Pond, is made strenuous by wind. Paddling gets easier once you're in the marsh. The trip takes four to five hours.

(Free guided canoe trips are offered during the December to March season, but you must make reservations well in advance. This can be done on the park's helpful website.)

SHARK VALLEY

Another option is to travel to Shark Valley in the northern part of the park, reached off US 41 (Tamiami Trail) west of Miami.

❻ Tram Tour There's one main attraction here: an old oil exploration route now a 15-mile scenic loop, which offers a look at the freshwater slough that makes up the heart of the park. The ranger-guided tram tour illuminates this ecosystem.

To get really close to the slough, rent a bicycle and use pedal power to travel the loop. The trip takes two or three hours, and, of course, the landscape is as flat as the proverbial pancake.

In the midst of this vast scene of seasonally flooded sawgrass, you'll appreciate the uniqueness of the water-powered natural world of the Everglades. Stop at the observation tower at the southern end of the loop for an elevated panorama of the terrain. (Bring plenty of water from home or the visitor center, as there are no facilities on the route.)

❼ Shark Valley Walks At the beginning of the loop (if you bike it in the recommended counterclockwise direction) are two short walks designed to showcase specialized Everglades habitats. The Bobcat Boardwalk passes through a bayhead, an isolated hardwood grove with a specialized group of species including red bay. The 0.25-mile Otter Cave Hammock Trail winds through a hammock, a dense stand of hardwoods growing just slightly higher than a bayhead,

Aerial view of the Ten Thousand Islands

with trees such as live oak, maple, mahogany, gumbo limbo, and cocoplum.

Anywhere along the loop, watch for the snail kite, a tropical raptor found in the United States only in southern Florida. As its name implies, it feeds mostly on large freshwater snails. Seeing one of these rare birds is a unique Everglades thrill.

GULF COAST

Continuing west from Shark Valley on the Tamiami Trail brings you to the turn south for **Everglades City** and the **Gulf Coast Visitor Center** in the Ten Thousand Islands.

8 Ten Thousand Islands Accurately described as a maze, this coastal region comprises mangrove islands separated by narrow channels, and stretches southeast more than 60 miles to Flamingo. The issue here, as Charles Wright, commercial tour guide, says, is that "the only access to it is by water."

The road reaches a dead end at **Chokoloskee,** and hiking trails here are almost nonexistent. Luckily, options are available for exploring the area. A park concessionaire offers cruises through both saltwater and brackish water areas. Others operate tours that take visitors to various destinations, such as a barrier island, by motorboat, then switch to kayaks for access to small channels and close-up looks at the environment.

"The big critters folks would normally see would be manatees, dolphins, various types of sea turtles, various raptors including eagles and hawks, lots of shorebirds, and wading birds," Wright says. But on the Tunnel Tour more inland creatures are seen—alligators, river otters, turtles.

Travelers who want to explore the park's Gulf Coast area on their own can bring or rent canoes or kayaks for routes ranging from a few hours to several days (the latter only for well-prepared and experienced paddlers).

The **Halfway Creek and Turner River Loop,** for example, takes about four hours and passes through tunnels of mangroves for much of the way.

Talk to rangers about where to go, and take maps, a compass, proper clothing, sun protection, and water.

Dawn from Clingmans Dome

GREAT SMOKY MOUNTAINS

Its location, within a day's drive for tens of millions of Americans, helps make Great Smoky Mountains the most popular national park in the United States. The 800-square-mile international biosphere reserve is split about evenly between Tennessee and North Carolina, and it protects some of the oldest mountains on Earth. More than 1,500 species of flowering plants and 60 species of native mammals, including deer, black bears, and elk, live within these often mist-shrouded mountains. The 384 miles of park roads and more than 800 miles of hiking trails make it easy to stroll along a rushing stream without straying far from your car. Or join a ranger-led program to discover, among other things, a few of the park's 30 species of salamanders, the world's most diverse population for an area this size.

Year-Round Visitor Centers

■ **Cades Cove Visitor Center**
On Cades Cove Loop Road, near the midpoint

■ **Oconaluftee Visitor Center**
On US 441, north of Cherokee, N.C.

■ **Sugarlands Visitor Center**
On US 441, 2 miles south of Gatlinburg, Tenn.

Seasonal Visitor Center

■ **Clingmans Dome Visitor Contact Station**
At the Clingmans Dome trailhead, 7 miles off US 441

Visitor Centers Outside the Park

■ **Gatlinburg Welcome Center**
Off US 441, Gatlinburg, Tenn.

■ **Bryson City Visitor Center**
255 Main St., Bryson City, N.C.

■ **Townsend Visitor Center**
On US 321, Townsend, Tenn.

865-436-1200, nps.gov/grsm

CADES COVE

The paved, 11-mile, one-way driving loop through Cades Cove, in the park's southwest corner, offers a glimpse of pre-park Smokies life. Farm families who sold their land to create the park left behind homes, churches, and barns. These open-air museums—plus wildflowers and wildlife—make this an extremely popular tourist route. Pick up an auto tour pamphlet (donation suggested) at the orientation shelter for descriptions of the 18 numbered stops.

Traffic is heaviest on warm-weather weekends, and traffic jams occur any time a bear is spotted. Avoid the noise and congestion by walking or biking the loop when it opens at sunrise, on a weekday, or when it's closed to motorized vehicles Wednesday and Saturday mornings (sunrise until 10 a.m.), early May to late September.

❶ **Rich Mountain Loop Trail** Driving through Cades Cove can take two to three hours when traffic is heavy, providing even more incentive to park and walk. Motorists rarely notice the Rich Mountain Loop trailhead because it's on the right near the start of the one-way loop where horses typically graze on the left-hand side of the road. Follow the trail through the lowland

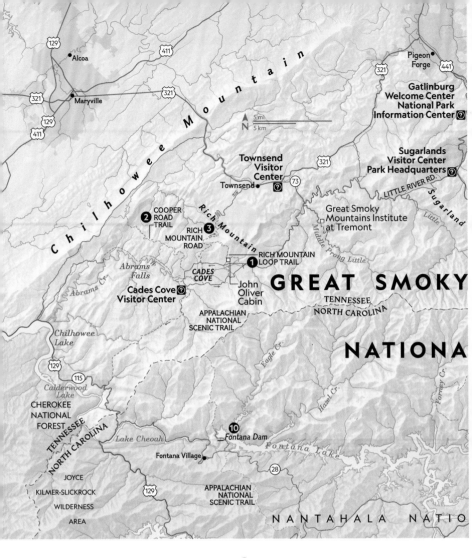

woods about 1.3 miles to the early 19th-century **John Oliver Cabin,** the cove's oldest log home.

"It's an easy, pleasant path meandering up and down along the base of Rich Mountain," says Liz Domingue, local naturalist, guide, and tour operator. "You are in the forest but you are walking along the edge of the cleared fields so it's a great way to see wild turkeys, as well as deer in the fields, in the woods, and sharing the path with you." The trail is closed in winter.

❷ Cooper Road Trail The route to **Abrams Falls** (trailhead between stops 10 and 11 on the auto tour) is the most popular hike in Cades Cove and one of the most heavily traveled trails in the park. Nearby Cooper Road (stop 9) isn't as dramatic (no roaring water flowing over a bluff), but it's guaranteed to be less crowded.

The former Native American trail once was the main wagon route connecting the cove to the city of **Maryville.** Named for Joe Cooper, who widened the

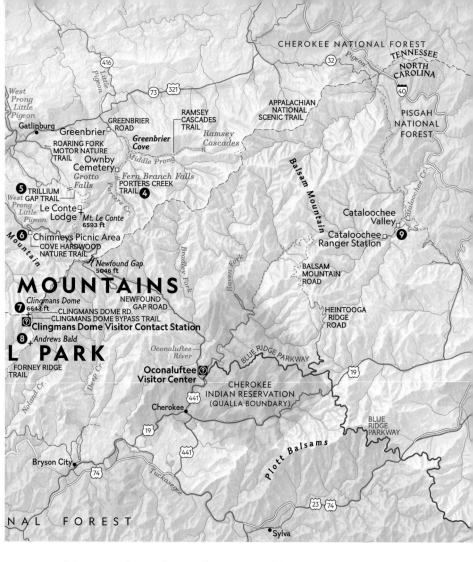

path for wagons, it extends 10.5 miles, so walk as far as you'd like across several creeks and small ridges.

❸ Rich Mountain Road The brown sign at the base of Rich Mountain Road is enough to make most motorists pass by: "Unimproved, primitive access, one way (no re-entry)."

That's true, and it's also what makes the narrow, gravel route up and over Rich Mountain worth taking. Before you do, however, make sure you've seen everything you want to see in Cades Cove. It's 12 miles and about 90 minutes to Townsend (and civilization) from where the road begins, and there's no turning back.

Except for the occasional hikers and hard-core mountain bikers, you are likely to have the potholed route to yourself. With solitude comes several perks, including better odds of seeing black bears (from the safety of your car), and of hearing the distinctive trilling sound of the Eastern screech-owl.

As with everywhere in the Smokies, the views through the red maples, chestnut and scarlet oaks, magnolias, and black gums change with the seasons. In spring, trailing arbutus, galax, and dogwoods bloom pink and white. Come fall, the crest of the road is the best place to pull off and take in the blazing red and soft yellow Cades Cove foliage panorama below.

GREENBRIER COVE

Off the beaten tourist path, yet easily accessible from the main road, the Greenbrier Cove section of the park is a local favorite.

The single brown sign marking the park border is easy to miss. From Gatlinburg, head out 6 miles on US 321 and turn right onto Greenbrier Road at the Little Pigeon River Bridge.

The transition from highway to deep woods is immediate: big trees, bountiful wildflowers, and (spring through early fall) dozens of butterflies leading the way through one of the park's prettiest and most discreet side entrances.

Purple phacelia

The narrow, partially paved road hugs the rushing **Middle Prong Little Pigeon River,** and there are plenty of pull offs to park and picnic, or (carefully) climb on to the boulders to view the cascades.

4 **Porters Creek Trail** Greenbrier's biggest draw is the **Ramsey Cascades Trail,** a strenuous 8-mile round-trip hike leading to the park's tallest (100-foot) waterfall.

The views from Porters Creek aren't as dramatic, but it's an easy trail through eastern hemlocks and Frasier magnolias with roaring cascades, 30 to 40 species of wildflowers, and remnants of the thriving farming community that once stood here (stone walls, homesites, and the Ownby Cemetery)—most visible within the first mile.

Park at the one-way traffic loop at mile 4.1 and walk to the gate at the end of the lot to start the hike. It's 3.6 miles from here to 40-foot **Fern Branch Falls** and back, yet you don't have to venture that far to safely get "lost" in the woods.

ROARING FORK MOTOR NATURE TRAIL

Meandering at 10 miles per hour along this 6-mile, one-way motor loop is like hiking in your car. For people with limited mobility, driving the winding trail is the best way to get up-close views of rushing mountain streams, historic log cabins, and old-growth forest.

If mobility isn't an issue, Roaring Fork also puts some of the park's prettiest waterfalls and premier destinations (including **Mount Le Conte**) within somewhat easier reach.

5 **Trillium Gap Trail** A moderate 2.6-mile round-trip hike on the Trillium Gap

Those students and tourists you see throughout the park catching, tagging, and releasing monarch butterflies in a meadow or mapping fungi locations with a handheld GPS likely are "citizen scientists." With a little advance planning, you can be one, too.

"Citizen scientists are nonscientists who help with seasonal research projects in the Smokies," says Ken Voorhis, executive director of the Great Smoky Mountains Institute at Tremont (GSMIT). "Check out our website (gsmit.org) to see if there is a program—like bird-banding or monitoring the streams for salamander populations—that you can participate in during your visit."

Data you collect could become part of the All-Taxa Biodiversity Inventory (ATBI), the long-term effort to identify and map all of the park's 50,000 to 100,000 estimated species.

Trail brings you to **Grotto Falls,** the only waterfall in the park that you can walk behind. Note black bears are sometimes seen along this trail.

Even if you don't want to hike, the Trillium Gap trailhead is worth a visit on Monday, Wednesday, or Friday mornings mid-March through mid-November, when the llama train arrives to gear up for the climb to Le Conte Lodge. No roads lead to the lodge (which, sitting near the summit at 6,360 feet, is the highest resort east of the Mississippi), so pack llamas are used to carry in supplies. Of all the trails to Le Conte, the 6.5-mile route up Trillium Gap is the easiest for the llamas to navigate. The llamas usually hit the trail by 8 a.m., so if you're planning a hike, walk ahead of the pack part of the way (behind, or downwind, is less pleasant).

NEWFOUND GAP ROAD (US 441)

If you only have a day in the park, this 30-mile (one way) scenic drive is the one to take. Connecting the park's major visitor centers **Sugarlands** (near Gatlinburg, Tennessee) and **Oconaluftee** (near Cherokee, North Carolina), the road climbs to 5,046 feet at its midpoint, Newfound Gap.

A wooden sign in the middle of the parking lot here marks the border between the states. If you see any hitchhikers with serious backcountry gear up here, chances are they are Appalachian Trail (AT) through-hikers looking for rides down to **Gatlinburg** to restock supplies and get a hot meal and shower. The Appalachian Trail diagonally crosses the Newfound Gap parking lot. Walk past the restrooms (just beyond the stone **Rockefeller Memorial** where President Franklin Roosevelt dedicated the park on September 2, 1940) to meander along the AT for a bit yourself.

It's frequently misty and foggy up here, so don't count on seeing much from the overlook. Your best bets for scenic views are on the drive back down to Gatlinburg. All the bends and switchbacks on Newfound Gap Road make it easier to spot the cascades and overlooks heading south to north.

6 Cove Hardwood Nature Trail The **Chimneys Picnic** area is extremely popular in summer, and for good reason: picnic tables tucked under the trees, big river rocks that tempt some to walk on in the clear stream (although the park discourages it), and lots of shade. What's less obvious—and often overlooked—is the Cove Hardwood Nature Trail located up the wood planks on the right side of the parking area.

"One of the great features of this short walk (0.75 mile) is it goes through our most diverse forest community, one of the few remaining stands of old growth in the park," says Domingue.

Pick up a pamphlet at the trailhead to follow the self-guided trail. There are sugar maple and yellow buckeye trees here more than 100 feet tall and at least 150 years old.

Signpost 15 marks the logging line. Above this point, spared from the sawmill, are the largest cove hardwoods. The white basswood, yellow birch, beech, and silverbell trees stretch so high in the sky that it's tough to see the leaves, but the colors during spring wildflower season and fall leaf turning rival other spots in the park.

CLINGMANS DOME

Reaching the highest point in the park, 6,643-foot Clingmans Dome, is fairly easy since it's only a 0.5-mile climb from the parking area to the summit. The path is steep, but it's paved and there are benches along the way.

The real challenge is in seeing anything from the observation platform up top. On the Smokies' rare, brilliant blue sky days, the mountain, forest, and foothill views can extend nearly 100 miles north into Tennessee and south into North Carolina. When clouds or the

NOT TO BE MISSED: *Explore the forest in solitude in Greenbrier Cove.* ▸ *Meet the llama train at Trillium Gap.* ▸ *Meander the Roaring Fork nature trail.* ▸ *Hike to the summit of Clingmans Dome into the park's signature smoky blue haze.* ▸ *Take a picnic into the Cataloochee Valley (and watch out for elk).* ▸ *Carefully traverse the AT over the top of the Fontana Dam holding the pristine waters of Fontana Lake.*

park's smoky blue haze hangs over the ridgeline, however, it can be tough to see beyond your own outstretched arms.

If possible, choose a sunny day to make the 7-mile drive up Clingmans Dome Road (closed in winter) from Newfound Gap.

7 **Clingmans Dome Bypass Trail** Grab a pair of trekking poles to hike this less traveled trail to the top, suggests Vesna Plakanis, an experienced Smokies guide and tour operator.

Reach the bypass by turning left at the **Forney Ridge Trail** sign (just before the paved path) and then right on the AT. This short, twisting route leads past exposed metamorphosed sandstone rocks more than 570 million years old.

"While these rocks were forming, there was almost no multicelled life on Earth, and the rocks are devoid of fossils. You are truly walking across the spine of time," says Plakanis.

8 **Andrews Bald** Unobstructed views and colorful shrubbery make the Smokies' treeless, grassy "balds" some of the best places to hike in the park. One of the easiest to reach is Andrews Bald, a 3.6-mile round-trip hike from the Clingmans Dome parking lot via the Forney Ridge Trail. The trailhead is located at the far end of the parking lot.

"A bald is a natural clearing. This means great visibility when the sun goes down and turns those rolling hills into purple mountain majesty," says Paul Hassell, local adventure photographer and guide. "Remember to bring a couple flashlights. The walk home is much easier if you can see."

EASTERN SIDE

The park's more than half million acres are divided pretty evenly between western North Carolina and eastern Tennessee, yet most day visitors gravitate toward the Tennessee side. Some of the North Carolina sections are more remote, but there are plenty within easy driving distance where you won't have much company.

⑨ Cataloochee Valley Neither route into this former farming community is easy. The 45-minute curvy crawl along Route 32 from North Carolina to Cosby, Tennessee, is legendary for inducing motion sickness.

The other option is a serpentine mountain road from I-40 (NC exit 20, Cove Creek Road) that doesn't have guardrails.

On a clear day with a picnic and a full tank of gas, however, there's no better place in the park to view elk and wild turkeys, and walk a trail with few other people in sight. The remote location also is popular with local equestrians (there's a horse camp here).

This isn't a drive you want to make in the dark, so arrive early in the day. (As a plus, the elk tend to congregate in the meadows early in the morning, so your crack-of-dawn wakeup will be wonderfully rewarded.)

⑩ Fontana Dam Fontana Lake forms the park's southwestern border, and 480-foot Fontana Dam formed the lake. It's the tallest concrete dam east of the Rocky Mountains, and one of two Tennessee Valley Authority (TVA) dams with Appalachian Trail crossings on top (the other is Watauga Dam near Elizabethton, Tennessee).

Take the short AT walk over the top to look down (very carefully) at the powerhouse on one side and across pristine Fontana Lake on the other. The view offers a rare peek into the park's remote southwestern reaches.

Clear day atop Clingmans Dome

Shenandoah's fall landscape

SHENANDOAH

Protecting some of the most beautiful landscapes of the ancient Appalachian Mountains, Shenandoah National Park covers more than 300 square miles of ridgeline between the Piedmont and the Shenandoah River Valley in Northern Virginia. The park's most notable attraction, 105-mile-long Skyline Drive, runs from US 340 at Front Royal, Virginia, south to Rockfish Gap at Interstate 64. Mileposts set on the west side of the road are numbered beginning at zero in the north, making it easy to give directions and find locations. Skyline Drive is justifiably famous for its nearly 70 scenic overlooks with ever changing vistas of the Appalachian region known as the Blue Ridge Mountains. Even with its speed limit of 35 miles an hour, Skyline Drive can be traversed in four hours—but those who see the park only from vehicle windows and overlooks are missing a vast diversity of plants, animals, geological features, and human history.

Seasonal Visitor Centers
■ Dickey Ridge Visitor Center
At milepost 4.6 on Skyline Drive
■ Harry F. Byrd, Sr. Visitor Center
At milepost 51 on Skyline Drive

540-999-3500, nps.gov/shen

acquiring land belonging to more than 400 families.

"Hikers are sometimes surprised when they're in the backcountry and there's a standing chimney from some of the residents who were here before the park was established," says park staffer Claire Comer. "Relocation and eminent domain were used to condemn the land, and that story can be a shock to some. We want people to understand that the park came at a cost, and not just a monetary cost."

❶ **Fox Hollow Trail** This easy 1.2-mile loop trail, beginning across Skyline Drive from the Dickey Ridge Visitor Center, leads hikers past evocative stone walls as well as an old family homesite and cemetery—reminders of those who gave up their property for today's park.

❷ **Compton Peak** One of the most interesting geological features of Shenandoah can be found at Compton Peak (mile 10.4). This is one of several places in the park where hikers can access the famed long-distance **Appalachian Trail** (AT), which runs through the park for 101 miles.

Take the trail south for less than a mile and turn on the side path to the eastern Compton Peak viewpoint. Continue down the steep path, following the blue blazes, to see a fine example of columnar jointing: multisided columns of volcanic greenstone formed

NORTH DISTRICT:
SKYLINE DRIVE FROM FRONT ROYAL TO BYRD VISITOR CENTER

Just 5 miles south of Front Royal, the **Dickey Ridge Visitor Center** provides a chance to pick up information about the park, talk to rangers, and enjoy one of many wonderful views of the Shenandoah Valley to the west. Don't be in a hurry to continue the drive, though. Across the road is a glimpse into an important aspect of park history.

Unlike national parks in the West, which often were created in vast areas of unpopulated terrain, the creation of Shenandoah in the 1920s and '30s meant

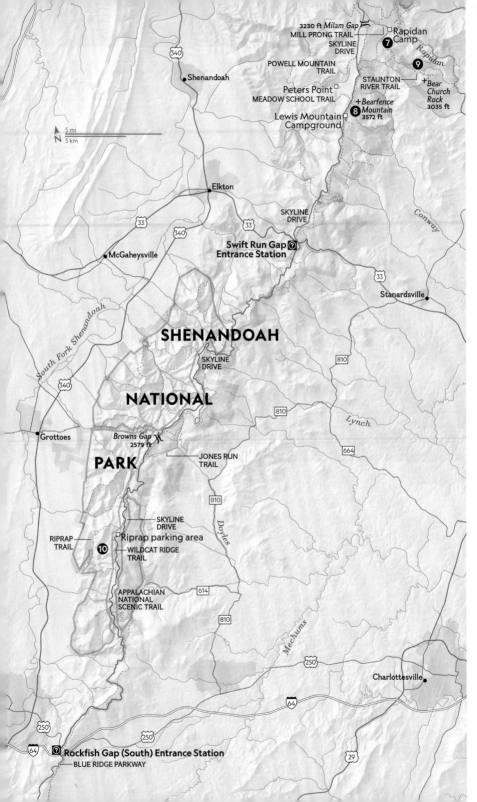

3230 ft *Milam Gap*
MILL PRONG TRAIL
SKYLINE DRIVE
7 □ Rapidan Camp

Rapidan

9

POWELL MOUNTAIN TRAIL

STAUNTON RIVER TRAIL
+ *Bear Church Rock* 3035 ft

Peters Point □
MEADOW SCHOOL TRAIL

+ *Bearfence Mountain* 3572 ft
8

Lewis Mountain Campground □

□ Shenandoah

340

Conway

Elkton

340

33

SKYLINE DRIVE

33

33

Swift Run Gap Entrance Station ⊘

Stanardsville ●

McGaheysville ●

810

Lynch

SHENANDOAH

SKYLINE DRIVE

340

810

664

Grottoes ●

Browns Gap 2579 ft ✕

NATIONAL

Doyles

JONES RUN TRAIL

810

PARK

SKYLINE DRIVE

RIPRAP TRAIL

□ Riprap parking area
10
— WILDCAT RIDGE TRAIL

614

APPALACHIAN NATIONAL SCENIC TRAIL

810

Mechums

250

Charlottesville ●

64

250

29

64

250

⊘ Rockfish Gap (South) Entrance Station
— BLUE RIDGE PARKWAY

5 mi
5 km
N

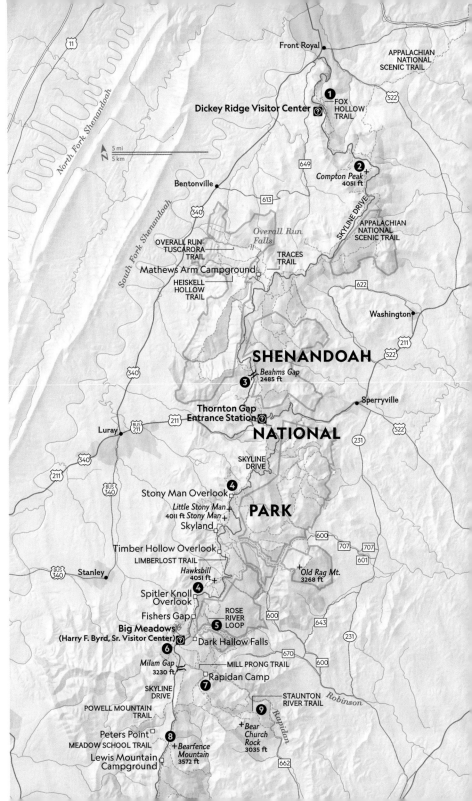

by the cooling of magma hundreds of millions of years ago.

③ Beahms Gap The Appalachian Trail also crosses Skyline Drive at Beahms Gap (mile 28), which ranks as one of the best places to sample Shenandoah's diversity of birdlife. "More than 200 species of birds are found in the park," says local naturalist and author Ann Simpson.

"In summer, look for scarlet tanagers, indigo buntings, and rose-breasted grosbeaks. In fall, eastern towhees, sparrows, and migrating warblers love the scrubby, insect-filled cover here."

CENTRAL DISTRICT:
THORNTON GAP TO SWIFT RUN GAP

Of all Shenandoah's attractions, the tradition of watching sunsets from west-facing viewpoints may be the most popular.

④ Stony Man to Spitler Knoll Overlooks Many spots offer scenic vistas, and Stony Man Mountain (mile 41.7) offers one of the most magnificent panoramas of the Shenandoah Valley, reached by a

Eastern tiger swallowtail

NOT TO BE MISSED: *Watch the sunset from Stony Man Mountain or Spitler Knoll.* ▸ *Hike to Dark Hollow Falls or another of the park's graceful waterfalls.* ▸ *Walk or take a van tour to Rapidan Camp, President Herbert Hoover's "Brown House" fishing retreat.* ▸ *Visit the Harry F. Byrd, Sr. Visitor Center to learn the true stories of families displaced from their land for the park's creation.* ▸ *Stand in Big Meadow at night.*

1.6-mile round-trip hike. For a different experience, more than one local recommends the view from the popular restaurant at **Skyland** (mile 41.7), glass of wine in hand.

Park botanist Wendy Cass has a great suggestion for sunset-watchers, whether at famed Stony Man or other splendid viewpoints such as **Timber Hollow** (mile 43) or Spitler Knoll (mile 48): "When everyone is staring at a sunset from one of the overlooks, turn around and look in the other direction so that you can enjoy the golden glow of the sunset light on the trees behind you," she says. "The beauty of that often rivals that being provided by the sunset."

⑤ Rose River Loop One of park staffer Comer's most recommended hikes begins at the **Fishers Gap** parking area (mile 49.4). The moderately strenuous 4-mile Rose River Loop past cascades and waterfalls is "a less traveled trail and one of my favorites," she says, "especially on a rainy day." For a small additional effort, enjoy another location where water cascades down a series of

Red hues on the fall fields in Big Meadows

rock ledges by taking a side trip to **Dark Hollow Falls,** about halfway around the Rose River Loop.

❻ Big Meadows Located at mile 51, the **Harry F. Byrd, Sr. Visitor Center** is the best place to learn about park history, including the relocation of early residents and the work of the Depression-era Civilian Conservation Corps, which built much of the park infrastructure from 1933 to 1942.

Just across Skyline Drive lies one of the park's most iconic landscapes: the expansive open area called Big Meadows, an ecosystem beloved of botanist Cass.

"I would recommend that people resist the urge to just look at the meadow from the visitor center, and instead get out there and follow one of the paths down into the middle," she says. "As you walk you can see a variety of meadow wildflowers, insects, and birds. Try standing still and listening very carefully for the sound of the wind and insects around you."

Night can be a magical time for many visitors to Big Meadows as well. "When you're from the city and you've never seen a non-polluted night sky, it's absolutely incredible," Claire Comer says. "Just to go out and lie on your back in the meadow and contemplate the universe is an experience all its own." Check the calendar on the park's website for occasional ranger-led night sky–viewing programs offered here.

❼ Rapidan Camp Too often overlooked, Rapidan Camp offers a fascinating view into American presidential history. This rustic complex was built in 1929 by President Herbert Hoover as a place where he could enjoy what he called "the simpler life of the frontier": fishing for trout and escaping the pressure of dealing with the Great Depression. Hoover's "Brown House" cabin has been restored to its period appearance, with exhibits inside on American life in the 1930s.

Rapidan Camp can be reached via a 4-mile round-trip hike beginning at the Milam Gap parking area (mile 52.4) or on a ranger-led van trip (reservations required) from late spring through fall.

⑧ Bearfence Mountain A parking lot at mile 56.4 marks the start of the short hike to Bearfence Mountain, with a fabulous 360-degree view of forested ridges stretching to the horizon. Although it is less than a mile from the trailhead, Bearfence involves scrambling over and around boulders, requiring a certain degree of agility and fitness—and the reward definitely justifies the effort.

A side road off Skyline Drive near milepost 59, leads to an area that demonstrates especially well how migratory birds follow Appalachian ridgetops in their twice-yearly journeys. "The most famous spot in the park among birders

is **Pocosin Cabin Trail**," says local bird watcher Vic Laubach. "It's a real magnet for neotropical birds in spring and fall. I make special trips to go up there—it's definitely a little gem."

Lewis Mountain (mile 57.5), the park's smallest campground, provides a sobering history lesson as well as a pleasant overnight stop. In the 1940s, when African Americans were often forced to use so-called "separate but equal" facilities, this site was officially designated "for the exclusive use of negroes." Debate about segregation at Shenandoah continued through the decade (and led to several National Park Service staff shake-ups), until fully integrated facilities were established in 1950.

⑨ Staunton River Trail Although plenty of trails begin on or near Skyline Drive, local hikers often start their treks from trailheads on the borders of Shenandoah, reached from secondary

Sunrise view from Bearfence Mountain

Although not technically in Shenandoah National Park, the Rockfish Gap hawk watch, held in a parking lot adjacent to the southern entrance of Skyline Drive, is well worth a visit for any nature lover. "We have 14 or 15 different species that we have recorded at Rockfish Gap," says birder Vic Laubach. "The second and third weeks of September are the busiest, with broad-winged hawks seen in the highest number. We've recorded more than 10,000 in a single day in mid-September. Bald eagles used to be rare, but now we get them every single day."

Watchers are happy to point out passing raptors—including northern goshawks and red-tailed hawks—to novices, and "our hawk watch is always open for people to visit," Laubach says. Volunteers scan the sky here from mid-August through November.

roads outside the park. One example is the Staunton River Trail, reached by taking Va. 662 north from the community of Wolftown 6.6 miles to a small parking area. There's a great view rewarding those who make the 7.4-mile round-trip ascent to **Bear Church Rock,** but for those who want a shorter hike, the first part of the walk along the Staunton River offers lovely scenery and beautiful mature forest.

SOUTH DISTRICT:
ROCKFISH GAP & NORTH

Generally speaking, the section of Shenandoah National Park south of US 33 sees fewer visitors than the northern and central areas. Much of the park's 79,000 acres of wilderness is found here as well.

Of course, Skyline Drive from Swift Run Gap to Rockfish Gap boasts many fine overlooks, including **Brown Mountain** (mile 77), **Rockytop** (mile 78.1), and **Blackrock Summit** (mile 84.4).

At Blackrock, an easy half-mile hike leads to an extensive talus slope: a jumble of boulders formed of quartzite, hard material created when heat and pressure acted on sand of an ancient beach. The view here is truly spectacular and is a particular sunset favorite of photographers both professional and amateur.

⑩ Riprap-Wildcat Ridge Loop For physically fit hikers who want a terrific experience in the Shenandoah wilderness, the 9.8-mile Riprap-Wildcat Ridge Loop provides a lot of beauty for a strenuous day of trekking.

Start at the Riprap parking area (mile 90), following the Appalachian Trail south for about 2 miles, descending steeply on the **Wildcat Ridge Trail** to the **Riprap Trail,** then following it north and east back to the Appalachian Trail and the parking area. Local hikers recommend doing this loop clockwise, but no matter which direction you take, there's a tiring uphill walk at the end.

"This is a really nice circuit hike," Claire Comer says. "There are streams and a lush little valley and some very interesting geological formations." On a hot day, swimming holes in Riprap Hollow make for a refreshing midday break. Heading back uphill from the hollow, hikers enjoy great views from the Chimney Rocks and Calvary Rocks areas.

MORE PARK SECRETS

CONGAREE

BOTTOMLAND HARDWOOD I 803-776-4396 I *nps.gov/cong*

Located just 20 miles from South Carolina's capital, Congaree National Park encompasses 27,000 acres of old-growth bottomland hardwood forest, the largest such expanse remaining in the southeastern United States. With an average canopy height of over 100 feet, the trees form one of the tallest temperate deciduous forests in the world.

Hiking trails are concentrated in the western section of the park, leaving access to the central part mostly by canoe or kayak. "Paddling among the cypress and tupelo allows visitors a unique perspective," says park ranger Jonathan Manchester. Entering at the Cedar Creek canoe access, committed paddlers can take a two-day trek following the creek through the center of the park to the **Congaree River,** which forms the southern boundary. Trees overhang the narrow, black-water creek, while alligators bask in the sunshine on the broad river.

"Very little logging took place here," explains Manchester. "So people today see what the conservationists who helped preserve this land saw—one of the best examples of a bottomland hardwood forest left in the country."

DRY TORTUGAS

CORAL REEFS I 305-242-7700 I *nps.gov/drto*

Some of North America's most pristine coral reefs cluster around the low-lying islands of the Dry Tortugas. Ships, carrying everything from Spanish explorers to coffee and tobacco, used to get tangled in the seven sand and coral islands about 70 nautical miles from Key West, Florida, so it's no surprise that this park is both naturally beautiful and historically significant. Visits often start at **Fort Jefferson,** one of the Americas' largest masonry-built forts.

Snorkelers at Dry Tortugas, which is only accessible by boat or seaplane (look for the namesake sea turtles on the journey there), need only wade into the water to see purple sea fans and brain coral along with bluehead wrasse and rainbow parrotfish. Less known is that this is also one of the country's best places to see wild conch. The giant-shelled mollusk's populations have shrunk, but here they still crawl among the sea grasses.

Late March and the month of April bring thousands of migrating thrushes, warblers, buntings, orioles, and other species, as well as avid bird-watchers who flock here to enjoy the spectacle. Birds migrating north across the Caribbean Sea or the Gulf of Mexico spot Garden Key and drop in for a rest.

MAMMOTH CAVE

CAVE MAZE | 270-758-2180 | *nps.gov/maca*

Under the hills of Kentucky, the world's longest known cave system twists and turns for more than 410 miles. "The cave was extensively explored by Native Americans between 4,000 to 5,000 years ago using nothing more than simple reed torches to light their way," marvels Molly Schroer, one of the park staff.

In more modern times, curious tourists have wandered Mammoth Cave's tunnels for about 200 years, but spelunkers still discover and chart new limestone caverns and passageways today.

The only way to descend into the labyrinth is on a ranger-led tour, which typically follows electrically lit passageways. For a different perspective, take this relatively secret excursion: Grab a kerosene lamp as tourists did two centuries ago for the Violet City Lantern Tour.

The soft light casts monster-size shadows, and without the usual illumination to see, your other senses heighten as you listen for water cascading through the caverns, feel the ancient cave walls, and smell the fresh cave air.

VIRGIN ISLANDS

ANCIENT PETROGLYPHS | 340-776-6201 | *nps.gov/viis*

Protecting over 7,000 acres, Virgin Islands National Park comprises almost two-thirds of the island of St. John, the smallest of the United States Virgin Islands. Within the park, archaeological sites dating from as early as 840 B.C. to Columbus's arrival in 1493 can be found on almost every beach and bay.

Discover ancient petroglyphs—rock carvings—on the **Reef Bay Trail.** Located on an old Danish West Indies cart road, the trail descends steep slopes through a moist tropical forest to the coast. About 2 miles along the trail, an offshoot leads to petroglyphs that are "a well-kept secret and a special experience for folks," says Superintendent Mark Hardgrove.

The island's early inhabitants, the Taino Indians, carved the geometric symbols into a 70-foot-tall rock face. A quiet waterfall usually flows over the carvings into a large pool at the base of the cliff. It sometimes dries up in winter—splash water from the pool onto the carvings to make them pop for photos.

"The park also manages more than 18,000 acres of adjacent submerged land to protect the underwater habitat," notes park ranger Laurel Brannick. For a different experience, get trained to monitor the local hawksbill turtle nests.

2 | MIDWEST

Gateway Arch National Park, St. Louis, Missouri

"From views of Theodore Roosevelt National Park that inspired a President's conservation efforts to pioneer history at the Gateway Arch, the Midwest's national parks hold hidden gems and wonders just waiting to be explored."

—DARLEY NEWMAN
HOST AND PRODUCER,
TRAVELS WITH DARLEY AND *EQUITREKKING*

Eroded mud buttes off Badlands Loop Road

BADLANDS

Reports from early explorers crossing the Great Plains led many to call the region the "Great American Desert." Ironically, parts of it now make up one of the world's most productive agricultural areas. In much the same way, places once dismissed as "bad" lands often rank with our most spectacular and fascinating natural areas. One good example: Badlands National Park in southwestern South Dakota—a forbidding place of secrets.

Shaped by erosion into countless bluffs, spires, and other striking formations, the landscape here presented difficult barriers to travelers, from the Arikara and Lakota tribes to French trappers to 19th-century pioneers. Today, visitors are awed by the infinite variations of this colorful terrain, as well as the rolling expanse of one of the largest remaining tracts of mixed-grass prairie in the United States. Diverse wildlife and abundant fossils provide additional good reasons to spend time here.

Year-Round Visitor Center
Ben Reifel Visitor Center
*Cedar Pass off S. Dak. 240,
Badlands Loop Road*

Seasonal Visitor Center
White River Visitor Center
Junction of BIA 2 and 27

605-433-5361, nps.gov/badl

road in an hour," says Paul Ogren, a park volunteer. "And unfortunately, that's what the majority of visitors do."

A far more satisfying experience awaits those who take the time to explore places such as the Cliff Shelf Trail, a 0.5-mile loop passing through an area where part of the Wall has "slumped" downward, creating a forested environment good for wildlife-watching, especially birding.

❷ **Ben Reifel Visitor Center** Stop at the visitor center to watch a fine introductory video and to get advice from park rangers on enjoying Badlands. For an easy, off-the-map hike follow the recommendation of Julie Johndreau, a former park education specialist, and look for a prairie wash just across the road from the visitor center.

Head cross-country along this natural path (be sure to seek advice from a staff member if you are unsure where to go). On the unmarked walk, "you can find lots of things like animal tracks, interesting rocks, and blooming flowers," Johndreau reports. "It's a really great walk to do with kids. Our Junior Ranger book has a scavenger hunt; you can bring it along and look for things on the bingo card. The walk is very open, through the grasslands. It's maybe 0.75 mile if you want to go all the way to the Badlands Wall.

| NORTH UNIT

Most development is found in the eastern (**Cedar Pass**) part of the park, reached from the Cactus Flats exit off I-90. Stop at the **Big Badlands Overlook** to see this region's most famous geological feature: **The Wall.** This eroded cliff separates the higher-elevation prairie to the north from the lower prairie of the White River drainage to the south. A half million years of sculpting by water created the bizarre formations. A 30-mile paved loop road (S. Dak. 240) follows the Wall through the park.

❶ **Cliff Shell Trail** "If you don't stop for anything, you can drive the whole loop

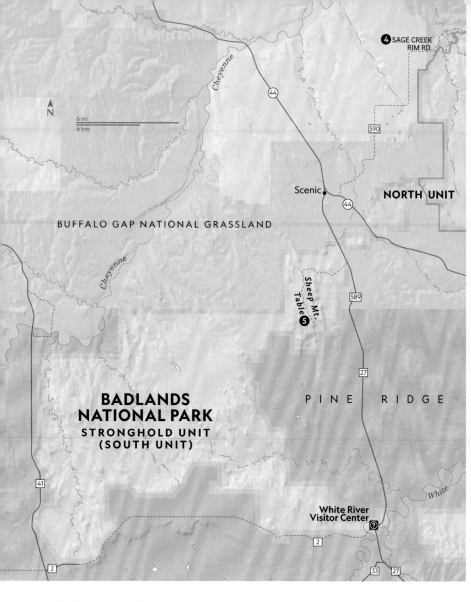

"Badlands National Park is very accessible by car, but if you park and do that short hike, it's even more like you feel you're in the middle of nowhere. It's a lovely area, and you get a different perspective."

③ Deer Haven Continuing west on the loop road, the **Fossil Exhibit Trail** is a must-see. You'll have learned about the park's abundant fossils at the visitor center, and on this 0.25-mile trail you'll see some reproductions of several now-extinct animals.

Just west of the **Yellow Mounds Overlook** near Dillon Pass, turn south on Conata Road to reach a relatively little-used trail that Aaron Kaye, park ranger, calls a personal favorite. Drive through the Conata picnic area to a

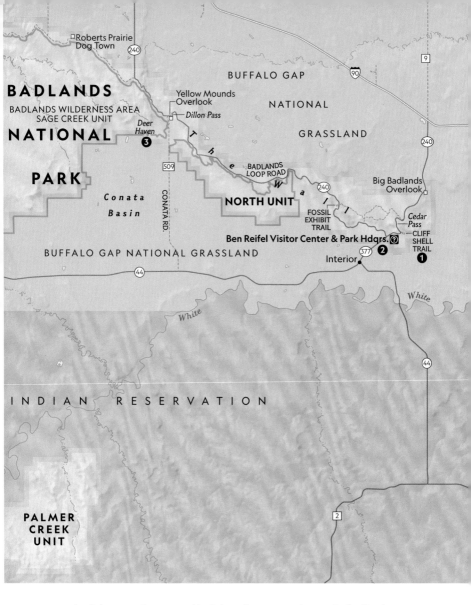

gravel cul-de-sac at the rear, and look for the backcountry trail register. From here, it's a 3-mile round-trip to explore Deer Haven.

"The hike combines walking in the prairie, along the edge of the Badlands Wall, and then a scramble up onto a timbered shelf, which is actually a slump covered with juniper trees," Kaye says. "The timbered area is a unique perch

because you've got the badlands surrounding you like a cirque [a hollow on a mountainside]."

Kaye says that the hike "is not too challenging, because most of it is on relatively flat ground," but recommends the usual preparations and precautions, such as proper footwear (most injuries at Badlands National Park result from falls on rugged terrain), plenty of water, a

Bighorn sheep

topographic map, and watching for bad weather or the occasional rattlesnake.

"It's a trip that's a little bit off the beaten path," Kaye says. "You're getting the best of both worlds that the park has to offer."

❹ Sage Creek Rim Road When travelers reach the point where **Badlands Loop Road** (S. Dak. 240) turns north toward the town of Wall, most visitors follow the paved road out of the park. In so doing, they miss a beautifully scenic drive along the unpaved Sage Creek Rim Road on the northern edge of the park's 64,250-acre wilderness area.

The road passes by the large **Roberts Prairie Dog Town** (watch for the burrowing owls that share the tunnels with the rodents), and a side road reaches a primitive campground that is Ogren's favorite park location. "I encourage properly prepared people to walk away from the campground and find a canyon in the backcountry and just wander through it," Ogren says. "You never know what you might see. There's a lot of wildlife around there: coyotes and bobcats, golden eagles and ferruginous hawks.

"The wilderness area is also where we have our herd of 700 to 800 bison. Many times people wake up in the morning and there are anywhere from 10 to 200 bison right in the campground, which is pretty exciting for people who haven't seen them before." Ogren also points out that visitors should keep a safe distance from these huge animals, which can run far faster than people.

SOUTH UNIT

The South Unit of Badlands lies within the **Pine Ridge Reservation** of the Oglala Lakota Nation, and much of it comprises private land with limited access. Travelers are encouraged to stop at the **White River Visitor Center** (summer only) for information.

❺ Sheep Mountain Table One site on the South Unit that's always open for public access is Sheep Mountain Table, reached by an unpaved road heading west from BIA 27, a few miles south of the town of Scenic.

Christine Czazasty, the park's chief of interpretation and resource education, elaborates on how best to visit this area. "The 5-mile dirt road climbs to the top of Sheep Mountain Table, ending at an overlook. There are amazing views of the White River Badlands formations. On a clear day, you can see all the way to the Black Hills.

"From the overlook, it is a 2-mile hike to the south end of the table. You will come to an area with lots of junipers and ponderosa pines. The view shows badlands formations more steeply eroded and spired than in other areas of the park. Sheep Mountain Table is sacred to the Oglala. We ask visitors to be respectful and not disturb any offerings."

NOT TO BE MISSED: *Marvel at the bizarre formations along The Wall.* ▸ *Encounter (reproductions of) long-extinct animals on the Fossil Exhibit Trail.* ▸ *Experience both prairie and forest on a hike to Deer Haven.* ▸ *Drive scenic Sage Creek Rim Road.* ▸ *Safely view the park's enormous bison herd.* ▸ *Hike Sheep Mountain Table, sacred to the Oglala Lakota.*

Storm clouds over Sheep Mountain Table, South Unit

River Bend Overlook, North Unit

THEODORE ROOSEVELT

Few other national parks besides Theodore Roosevelt in North Dakota offer such a combination of epic scenery, wildlife, and history yet remain so secret to the average American. Only some 750,000 people experienced this park in 2018 (in contrast to the more than 11 million who visited Great Smoky Mountains National Park that year), and the numbers would be even lower if it weren't for the interstate highway running through it. (You can exit I-94 and be at the visitor center in less than five minutes.) An easily accessible scenic drive lets visitors cruise through, stop at a couple of overlooks, and be on their way again. That's a nice attribute for people in a hurry, but why rush? Take time to see the complete park—and to explore a landscape that inspired the nation's greatest conservationist president.

SOUTH UNIT

Theodore Roosevelt National Park is composed of three units; the great majority of visitors see only the South Unit, located just north of the town of **Medora.** Here you'll find a 36-mile scenic loop road, an assortment of trails, several miles of the Little Missouri River, and outstanding views of the North Dakota badlands.

The park is named for the 26th U.S. president, who arrived in this region in 1883 to hunt bison and experience the West. He was so fond of the landscape that he became a partner in a cattle ranch and bought another on his own, living here sporadically for many years.

Year-Round Visitor Center
■ South Unit Visitor Center
In Medora, off Pacific Avenue

Seasonal Visitor Center
■ North Unit Contact Station
Entrance to North Unit
■ Painted Canyon Visitor Center
South Unit, off I-94

701-623-4466, nps.gov/thro

"I enjoyed the life to the full," he later wrote of his ranching career. Near the visitor center you can see the **Maltese Cross Cabin,** where he lived for a time. It was moved here from the original site 7 miles south.

❶ **Wind Canyon Trail** Take the quarter-mile loop road to enjoy fine panoramas of the badlands landscape, a rugged terrain created by stream deposition of sediments, volcanic action, and erosion.

Roosevelt described the cliffs and buttes as "so fantastically broken in form and so bizarre in color as to seem hardly properly to belong to this earth."

Don't miss following the Wind Canyon Trail to an overlook of the **Little Missouri River.** It's a favorite of local resident Dylan Edwards, who observes: "It's a beautiful overlook with great scenery and interesting geological features that you can't see from the road."

Park rangers recommend the spot for superb sunset viewing.

❷ **Jones Creek-Lower Talkington-Lower Paddock Creek Trail Loop** For those who want a moderately strenuous hike, Edwards suggests the Jones Creek–Lower Talkington–Lower Paddock Creek

Trail Loop, an 11-mile route that makes a circle mostly within the loop road.

"You can see a good variety of the terrain in the park," he says. "There's just a little bit of up and down. You pass through prairie-dog towns, and I've seen groups of bison, elk, and feral horses."

Indeed, Theodore Roosevelt National Park is known for wildlife, including bison, elk, wild horses, mule and white-tailed deer, pronghorn, bighorn sheep, badgers, coyotes, and porcupines, as well as abundant bird life. Many people, though, don't get much chance to enjoy this diversity.

Timing a visit is important. Park Superintendent Valerie Naylor notes, "The bison are usually cooperative, and the prairie dogs, but beyond that you don't see animals. People need to go out in the early morning or late in the evening. It's hard to make yourself get up, but once you do there's definitely a reward."

"The badlands hold a fantastic array of native plants in four distinct habitats," says Laura Thomas, park ranger. "The diversity of life here is rivaled only by the diversity of a rain forest. To experience these wonders firsthand, visitors can borrow a free family fun pack that

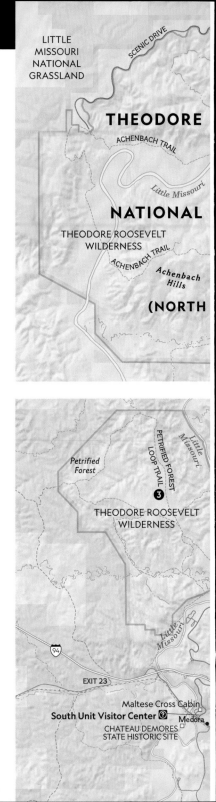

Adult bison and calves graze on grasslands

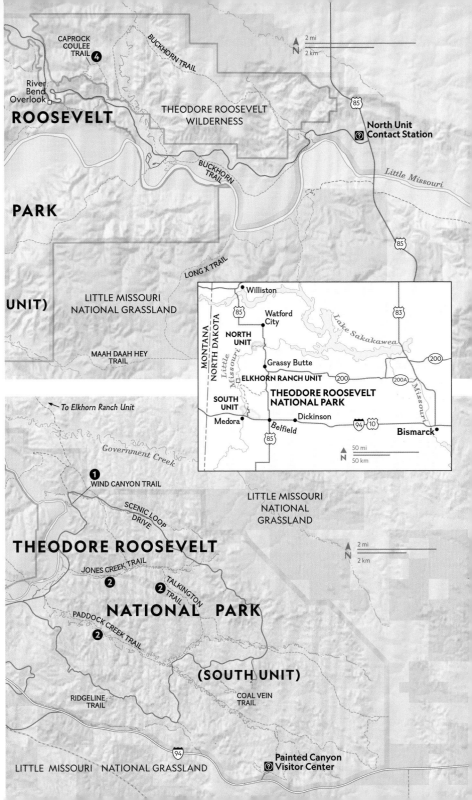

ROOSEVELT

CAPROCK COULEE TRAIL ❹

River Bend Overlook

BUCKHORN TRAIL

THEODORE ROOSEVELT WILDERNESS

2 mi
2 km
N

US 85

North Unit Contact Station

Little Missouri

BUCKHORN TRAIL

PARK

US 85

LONG X TRAIL

(UNIT)

LITTLE MISSOURI NATIONAL GRASSLAND

MAAH DAAH HEY TRAIL

Williston

US 85
Watford City

MONTANA NORTH DAKOTA Little Missouri

NORTH UNIT

Lake Sakakawea

US 83

Grassy Butte

200

200

200A

Missouri

■ **ELKHORN RANCH UNIT**

SOUTH UNIT

THEODORE ROOSEVELT NATIONAL PARK

Medora

Belfield

Dickinson

I-94 US 10

US 85

Bismarck ●

50 mi
50 km
N

To Elkhorn Ranch Unit

Government Creek

❶ WIND CANYON TRAIL

SCENIC LOOP DRIVE

LITTLE MISSOURI NATIONAL GRASSLAND

2 mi
2 km
N

THEODORE ROOSEVELT

JONES CREEK TRAIL

❷ ❷ TALKINGTON TRAIL

NATIONAL PARK

PADDOCK CREEK TRAIL ❷

(SOUTH UNIT)

RIDGELINE TRAIL

COAL VEIN TRAIL

I-94

LITTLE MISSOURI NATIONAL GRASSLAND

Painted Canyon Visitor Center

includes field guides to plants and birds of the badlands, hand lenses, and binoculars. In a given day, one can find easily 30 species of plants and as many, if not more, birds."

❸ Petrified Forest Loop Trail A significant portion of the park is designated wilderness, and in the South Unit that wilderness contains the third highest concentration of petrified wood in North America. "The Petrified Forest Loop is a great hike for anyone looking for a foray into the wilderness," says park ranger Lincoln Eddy, "including those who might be new to hiking in more remote landscapes."

The reward for leaving the beaten path on this 10-mile hike includes traversing large areas of prairie while also descending dramatically into the petrified forest. Stumps have eroded out of

---

NOT TO BE MISSED: *Watch for wildlife at dawn or dusk.* ▸ *Hike into ancient times on the Petrified Forest Loop.* ▸ *Take in the vistas that inspired TR himself.*

---

colorful hillsides here, allowing visitors to imagine ancient times when this was a swampy plain where forests of magnolia, sequoia, and bald cypress grew.

It's not necessary to do the entire 10-mile loop to see petrified trees, however. Take the West River Road exit off I-94 and follow dirt roads to the western edge of the park. From here, it's just a 1.5-mile (3 miles round-trip) hike to some petrified trees.

Get a map and directions at the visitor center, pack plenty of water, and check the weather forecast before setting out. Note that a high-clearance vehicle may be needed.

NORTH UNIT

With its access from I-94, the South Unit attracts far more visitors than the North Unit, though the latter can be reached by an easy drive 52 miles north of the interstate on US 85.

"Many people prefer the North unit because it's quieter than the South Unit," says Eileen Andes, the park's chief of interpretation. "The scenery is more dramatic and the pace is more relaxed. It's definitely worth the trip."

Cannonball concretions, North Unit

A 14-mile scenic road here (out and back) passes trailheads for both easy walks near the **Little Missouri River** and longer hikes into the backcountry. Watch for longhorn steers; this is a herd maintained to commemorate the historic Long X Trail, a 19th-century cattle-drive route.

❹ **Caprock Coulee Trail** For a bit of everything the North Unit has to offer, Andes suggests that visitors hike the Caprock Coulee Trail, a 5.7-mile loop.

"It's a moderately strenuous trail that climbs up for incredible views of the bad lands," she says. "It goes through dry washes, prairie, and woodlands. There are opportunities to see a variety of habitats and wildlife."

The first 0.7 mile of the route, the **Caprock Coulee Nature Trail,** is only mildly strenuous and the park provides a trail guide to make this an enjoyable hike. The rest of the longer trail is steeper and more rugged in places. "No matter where they hike in the park, visitors should check at the visitor center for trail information," Andes advises.

As you walk this or any trail in the park, keep in mind this advice from Thomas: "If you do a thorough job of seeing, you can find more in one small area than you'll be able to see in 10 miles of strenuous walking. So slow down. Distance does not equal discovery. Discovery is a matter of seeing, not seeking."

ELKHORN RANCH UNIT

Later in his life, Roosevelt famously wrote, "I never would have been President if it had not been for my experiences in North Dakota." It was at his Elkhorn Ranch on the Little Missouri that he developed much of the appreciation of nature that led him to establish the U.S. Forest Service and create important nature preserves, national parks, and national monuments.

The Elkhorn Ranch Unit is the site of Theodore Roosevelt's "home ranch." Although the ranch buildings no longer exist, the landscape remains largely unchanged from Roosevelt's time.

A 1.5-mile round-trip hike takes visitors to the ranch house site, where only the foundation's stones remain. Exhibits explain the history. Here you can see what Roosevelt described as the "sheer cliffs and grassy plateaus" and "weird-looking buttes" that he gazed upon from the veranda of his ranch house.

"The Elkhorn Ranch site is the most culturally significant part of the park," says Andes. "It was here that Roosevelt's thoughts about conservation began to solidify. It preserves the solitude and beauty of the Badlands that he so valued."

For visitors who take the time to travel here, absorbing these same vistas serves as a secret link to the president who arguably did more for conservation than any other American.

Sunset on giant thundercloud over Wind Cave's open prairie

WIND CAVE

Rangers at Wind Cave National Park in southwestern South Dakota encourage visitors to experience the "two worlds" of the park—that is, secrets above and below. One realm lies beneath the surface, while a far different, yet equally rewarding, environment awaits those who explore the national park's aboveground 44 square miles of prairie and pine forest. See only one of these two worlds and you will have missed half of this park.

Wind Cave is famed among geologists and serious cavers as the world's seventh-longest cave system, and it is known for formations rare in other underground locations, especially the gratelike structure called "box-work." Above its picturesque passageways lies a diverse terrain that's among the country's most underrated natural areas. As Mike Laycock, park ranger, explains, "This is a great wildlife park. I've been in only two areas that are comparable—one's Yellowstone and one's Alaska."

Year-Round Visitor Center

◼ Wind Cave Visitor Center

Off US 385, 11 miles north of Hot Springs

605-745-4600, nps.gov/wica

WIND CAVE

There's no getting off the tourist trail while experiencing the underground world of the park, because all visits are made on ranger-guided tours.

These outings range from the easy **Garden of Eden Tour** to the strenuous, crawling-required **Wild Cave Tour.** Advance reservations are needed for the latter, and strongly recommended for the **Candlelight Tour,** on which participants see the cave without electric lights, the way tourists did when it was a commercial attraction in the late 19th century. (For other tours, reservations are not accepted.)

Nevertheless, park staff members have a few hints for more enjoyable cave visits. In summer vacation season, the busiest days are not weekends but Tuesday through Thursday. This means that, if you arrive at midday on one of those days, the chances are good you'll have to wait a while for an open spot on a cave tour.

You'll increase the odds of getting in quickly if you arrive early in the morning or on weekends. If you do find tours booked when you get to the visitor center, simply purchase tickets for a tour later the same day and enjoy the park via a hike or scenic drive.

Ranger Laycock's favorite cave tour is the 0.5-mile, moderately strenuous **Natural Entrance Tour,** which gives visitors a chance to see the park's largest natural cave opening. (You'll actually start the tour by entering through a nearby man-made entrance.)

Wind Cave got its name because a difference in air pressure between the surface and cave causes strong air currents in the natural entry.

"You see great examples of boxwork, which is the main decoration that Wind Cave is known for," Laycock says. "This tour has 300 stairs, but 289 of them go down. Then you get on an elevator to come out."

Bear in mind that the temperature in the cave is 53 degrees year-round, so a jacket or sweater will feel good.

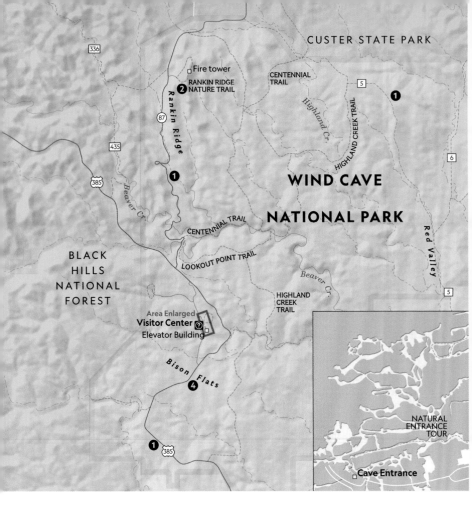

THE PARK ABOVE GROUND

With its combination of grassland (a blend of tallgrass and short-grass prairie), ponderosa pine forest, and riparian habitat, Wind Cave National Park supports a wide array of animals. The generally open, rolling landscape means wildlife can often be seen well from roads, including US 385 and S. Dak. 87, both of which wind through the western part of the park.

① Park Loop Staff members highly recommend an early morning or late afternoon drive on a 35-mile loop that comprises both paved and gravel roads.

From the park visitor center, drive north on US 385 a short distance and turn right on S. Dak. 87. Continue north about 6 miles and turn right onto unpaved Park Road 5. Follow this route east and south about 10 miles to 7-11 Road, also known as County Road 101. Turn west here and return to US 385. If you have time, a detour north on Park Road 6, which intersects Park Road 5, is often productive for animal watching.

"I've seen people in the visitor center who have just driven the loop, and they come in and their eyes are really big,"

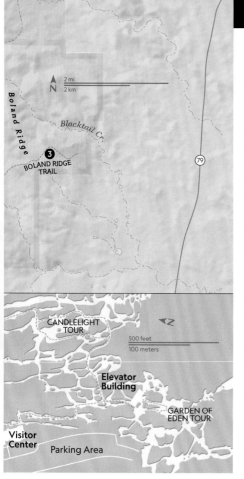

Vidal Davila, park superintendent, says. "They say, 'Hey, I just saw my first bison.' It's really a great wildlife-viewing road."

In addition to bison (also known as buffalo), Wind Cave's loop road can bring sightings of pronghorn, prairie dogs, mule and white-tailed deer, and coyotes. Elk are seen less commonly, most often at dawn and dusk.

❷ Rankin Ridge Nature Trail Seeing the park's environment on more intimate terms is made easy by a variety of hiking trails, including fairly easy nature trails. The 1-mile Rankin Ridge Nature Trail in the park's northern portion is a favorite of Laycock's, and one he often recommends.

"The loop goes up to our fire tower, through ponderosa pine forest," he explains. "It's one of the highest places in our park, so the view is excellent. And it's also pretty much above the prairie areas, so people usually don't have to worry about encountering bison."

The park features a relatively large herd of bison. Though these beasts often look sluggish, they can run much faster

Coyote with summer coat

Rolling prairies of Wind Cave

than humans. Eschew the temptation to get close for photos. Park policy requires people stay at least 25 yards away from wildlife, but common sense should tell you to keep even farther away from these dangerous animals. The bison in the park are descendants of 14 animals reintroduced to the park in 1913 by the New York Zoological Society.

Wind Cave offers other trails, including a doable 4.5-mile loop that combines parts of the **Centennial, Highland Creek,** and **Lookout Point Trails** off S. Dak. 87.

❸ Boland Ridge Trail On the east side of the park, the Boland Ridge Trail, a strenuous 2.6-mile (one way) hike, provides an opportunity to experience the solitude and panoramic vistas that greeted the pioneers crossing the American prairies. The Boland Ridge trailhead is located on Park Road 6 about a mile north of the junction with Park Road 5. This challenging trail climbs the ridge to panoramic views of Wind Cave National Park, the Black Hills, Red Valley, and Battle Mountain.

LOCAL INTELLIGENCE

Before or after a visit to Wind Cave, take a tour through **Custer State Park,** encompassing 71,000 acres in the Black Hills just to the north. A drive along the 18-mile **Wildlife Loop Road** brings almost certain sightings of bison, as well as the chance of spotting deer, pronghorn, bighorn sheep, and feral burros. Fine hiking trails abound in the park, and some are open to mountain biking.

Boland Ridge also gives hikers one of the best chances to catch sight of elk.

❹ **Bison Flats** Travelers can go for a walk anywhere, as off-trail hiking is allowed here. "That's good for people to be aware of," Laycock says. "They can hike out a hundred yards, or half a mile—whatever they desire. And that's a little bit easier in Wind Cave than in most parks, because the terrain usually isn't bad. There are a lot of rolling hills."

A favorite site for cross-country exploration is Bison Flats, stretching across US 385 just south of the road to the visitor center.

"I've gone out there and seen burrowing owls and badgers, and ventured a little farther and seen elk, all in the same easy stroll," Laycock says. "And I wasn't 300 yards from my car."

From this area there are panoramic views of the park, Buffalo Gap, and the Black Hills. Hike west across Bison Flats less than a mile from the highway for a superb sunset-viewing opportunity.

NOT TO BE MISSED: *Tour the caves the way tourists did centuries ago—by candlelight.*
▸ *Marvel at intricate cobwebs of boxwork on the Natural Entrance Tour.* ▸ *Drive the Park Loop for prime wildlife viewing in early morning or late afternoon.*
▸ *Climb the fire tower on Rankin Ridge.* ▸ *View (from a safe distance) the park's herd of enormous bison.* ▸ *Trek cross-country across Bison Flats.*

MORE PARK SECRETS

CUYAHOGA VALLEY
SUSTAINABLE FARMS | 330-657-2752 | *nps.gov/cuva*

Named for an American Indian word meaning "crooked river," the water that flows between Cleveland and Akron in Ohio forms the core of one of America's most eclectic national parks. Here you can hike through a rocky gorge, but also attend a concert; ride a scenic railroad, then refine your golf swing; or explore beaver habitat in the morning, then admire art at an old, repurposed gas station in the afternoon. For a lesser known experience, tour the dozen or so farms affiliated with Cuyahoga Valley. These aren't historical sites focused on blacksmith demonstrations and old-fashioned agriculture (though you'll find that too, at the independently operated **Hale Farm and Village** inside the park). Instead, they're small, privately run sustainable farms dedicated to preserving the Midwest's agricultural landscape and lifestyle. If visiting on a summer Saturday, be sure to stop by the farmers market at Howe Meadow.

GATEWAY ARCH
LOOKING WEST | 314-655-1600 | *nps.gov/jeff*

The St. Louis park formerly known as Jefferson National Expansion Memorial received a new designation and a new name in 2018, as well as a comprehensive renovation to better help it tell the story of America's westward growth. Gateway Arch National Park now serves as a green and inviting link between the legendary Mississippi River and downtown St. Louis, with year-round activities throughout its 91 acres.

The focal point remains the dazzling **Gateway Arch,** the 630-foot-high structure designed by Eero Saarinen that has since its 1965 opening become one of the most recognizable icons in North America. The tram ride to the top provides far-reaching views of eastern Missouri and across the Mississippi into Illinois. Especially in summer, visitors are advised to reserve tickets and even plan their itinerary in advance, either through the park's website or by downloading the free interactive Gateway Arch smartphone app.

Below the Arch, the park's museum has been expanded and upgraded and is now "sleek, high-tech, and engaging," in the words of writer Ellen Lampe. A new west-facing entrance features a glass wall looking toward the beautiful 19th-century **Old Courthouse,** also part of the park. Here, visitors can learn of the famous Dred Scott trials, vital to the eventual abolition of slavery in the United States, and the Virginia Minor case, involving women's right to vote.

INDIANA DUNES

BEACHES, BIRDS & BOGS I 219-395-1882 I *nps.gov/indu*

Beginning in the late 19th century, conservationists and commercial interests battled for decades over the fate of this biologically diverse area at the southern end of Lake Michigan. Following the creation of a state park in the 1920s and a larger national lakeshore in 1966, Indiana Dunes received full national park status in 2019. Today's park protects 15,000 acres of dunes, woods, grasslands, and wetlands between Gary and Michigan City, Indiana.

For many in nearby urban areas (including Chicago, about an hour away), the park's major attraction is its 15 miles of beautiful sandy beaches, inviting swimmers and sunbathers. On summer weekends parking lots can fill by mid-morning, so consider taking one of the two free shuttle buses, which access beaches from spots along US 12 including Miller train station and Dunewood campground.

There's much more to Indiana Dunes than sun and sand, though. Surprisingly, this area so near steel mills and skyscrapers boasts an astounding array of flora and fauna, with 50 miles of trails providing access. "What most people don't realize is that despite being just an hour from Chicago, Indiana Dunes has the fourth highest biodiversity of all the national parks," says ranger Rafi Wilkinson.

The park's more than 1,100 plant species range from colorful prairie wildflowers to the endangered black oak savanna habitat, which can be explored on the **Paul H. Douglas Trail** though Miller Woods. "This area gets overlooked by many locals and tourists, but is spectacular," Wilkinson says. "The savanna is dotted with small interdunal ponds and teems with wildflowers in spring and summer."

The park's education specialist, Christine Gerlach, recommends the dune area at West Beach. "You can walk the **Dune Succession Trail**—be warned, there are 500 steps to climb—and explore a northern jack pine forest." Gerlach adds, "Be sure to hike through the ravines just north of the historic Chellberg Farm and enjoy the sugar maples' explosion of color in October."

With a park list of more than 350 species, "Indiana Dunes offers spectacular birding year-round," says local birder Matt Beatty. "In spring, migrant songbirds bunch up against Lake Michigan before continuing their journey. The **Cowles Bog Trail** is a great location to look for migrant warblers, where the high dunes meet the Great Marsh." So diverse is the habitat at Cowles Bog that it has been designated a National Natural Landmark.

Pinhook Bog is a favorite spot for supervisory park ranger Bruce Rowe. "When you walk through the bog, you feel like you're in an almost alien place. Thanks to a floating mat of sphagnum moss, you are literally walking on top of an ancient kettle lake. Growing out of the mat are carnivorous plants such as sundew and pitcher plant that survive by eating insects. Because it's such a fragile habitat, you can enter only on a ranger-led hike or open house. But it's worth the wait."

The national park also protects several significant historic buildings, most open only via guided tour. Check the park website to plan your visit.

ISLE ROYALE

PASSAGE ISLAND I 906-482-0984 I *nps.gov/isro*

Located in the northwestern portion of Lake Superior 56 miles from Michigan's Upper Peninsula, Isle Royale National Park preserves the largest island in the world's largest freshwater lake, as well as more than 450 surrounding islands. For more than 60 years, Isle Royale's isolation has made it the perfect place for scientists to study its wolves and their predator-prey relationship with moose—and a secret spot for you to explore.

Experience the farthest boundaries of the park on **Passage Island,** located about 3.5 miles off the northeast end of the main island. Visitors can reach this special place via their own boats or the excursion boat M.V. *Sandy,* operated by the Rock Harbor Lodge. "Most people only know about Passage Island because there is a lighthouse there, but it is so much more," says Liz Valencia, the national park's chief of interpretation and cultural resources. "There are no moose there, so the vegetation is different than on the main island. In the summer, it has an almost jungle-like quality."

Note that Isle Royale and its surrounding islands are inaccessible to visitors annually from November through mid-April, although the Lake Superior waters are open to boaters. The visitor center in Houghton, MI, is open weekdays year-round.

VOYAGEURS

CHAIN OF LAKES I 218-283-6600 I *nps.gov/voya*

Named for the French-Canadian adventurers who transported furs in birch-bark canoes, Voyageurs National Park protects more than 200,000 acres along Minnesota's Canadian border. Moose, timber wolves, black bears, and white-tailed deer roam the park's boreal forest and exposed Precambrian rocks that are more than two billion years old.

Avoid the crowds on the larger waterways and take the 2-mile **Locator Lake Trail** to the **Chain of Lakes,** a set of four inland bodies of water on the Kabetogama Peninsula. Canoes stored at the head of Locator Lake can be rented for a day, and campsites at each lake allow for longer explorations.

"I liked the anticipation of wondering what the next lake might look like, and looking for bear or moose," says Kathleen Przybylski, a former park staffer who paddled the length of the chain. "It's a more wilderness type of experience, feeling like you're the only ones out there. There's a good chance you will be the only people on the lake." Voyageurs rewards those who plan ahead, and its website is a great way to grab such opportunities as renting a boat, reserving a ranger-led tour, and even booking a campsite on your own private island.

Kabetogama Lake, Voyageurs National Park

3 | SOUTHWEST

First light at White Sands National Park, New Mexico

"The Southwest's national parks showcase our breathtaking scenery, our deep and complex history, and our unique cultures. They offer endless opportunities for adventure and inspire a lifelong connection to conservation."

—Senator Martin Heinrich, New Mexico
National Park Trust 2018 recipient,
Bruce F. Vento Public Service Award

North Window and Turret Arches

ARCHES

The 119 square miles of Arches National Park hold the world's greatest collection of natural stone arches—more than 2,300 of them—along with a supporting cast of fins, spires, hoodoos, domes, and towers.

This is the real Jurassic Park, a 300-million-year-old story written in stone of a time when coastal dunes and a primeval inland sea deposited sediments that have since been uplifted, carved, eroded, and scoured by the forces of nature.

A single 18-mile paved road with two short spurs threads it all together, offering easy access to the iconic arches and rock formations for which this park is famous. In fact, visitors can see a lot without leaving their cars, but doing so would mean missing the park's many secrets. "Arches may be a small and famous park," explains Karen Garthwait, the park's lead interpreter, "but it still has a lot of hidden corners waiting for folks to explore."

Year-Round Visitor Center
◼ Arches Visitor Center
On US 191, north of Moab

435-719-2299, nps.gov/arch

miss this impressive mile-long hike down a corridor of sandstone skyscrapers with such names as **Nefertiti Rock** (instantly recognizable).

While strolling though the gently descending sandy wash, listen for the warble of canyon wrens and keep an eye out for white-throated swifts flitting around the cliffs. The trail ends back on the main road at **The Organ.** Unless you arrange a ride, it's a slightly more aerobic hike back to the trailhead.

❷ Courthouse Wash Experienced hikers may want to try this route through dense and sometimes thorny vegetation—and possibly quicksand. Beaver dams can mean multiple water crossings. Come prepared with a compass or GPS for route finding.

From the parking lot by the bridge, head upstream via the dry wash bed, or go downstream into a narrowing canyon shaded by tall cottonwood trees. Look out for birds, including spotted towhees, dippers, and great blue herons.

At the numerous stream crossings, scan for animal prints in the sand—mule deer, beaver, coyote, bighorn sheep, and if you're lucky, the pad marks of a rare mountain lion.

Plan on four hours to meander down **Lower Courthouse Wash,** which comes out a mile southeast of the park entrance, on US 191. (Leave a vehicle at the parking lot here beforehand for a ride back.)

⏐ ARCHES SCENIC DRIVE

From the visitor center, the main road into the park makes a pulse-pounding entrance as it switchbacks up steep cliffs of white Navajo sandstone and into the salmon-hued Entrada slickrock. Every curve in the road reveals new and surreal vistas of monolithic formations, arches, and sweeping panoramas—**Balanced Rock,** the **Windows,** and **Fiery Furnace,** for example—before the road ends in a giant roundabout at **Devils Garden.**

❶ Park Avenue Those who want to see the park's famous arches are likely to

Don't depart before checking out the haunting 3,000-year-old **Archaic-era rock paintings** of life-size spectral figures at trail's end—a sign will point you in the right direction.

Ute petroglyphs at Wolfe Ranch

❸ Windows Primitive Trail You can escape the crowds viewing the park's most visited arches in the Windows Section while enjoying a better view of them by taking this short trail at the base of **South Window Arch.**

The narrow 1-mile path bends around the backside of these towering spans, revealing not only a dramatic panorama overlooking **Salt Wash,** but, from this perspective, showing that the two separate **North** and **South Windows** are actually cut from the same Entrada sandstone fin. They combine into a single feature resembling a pair of sky blue eyes with a big rock nose in the middle, what locals traditionally call **"The Spectacles."** (It's a favorite early morning photo op.)

❹ Wolfe Ranch & Ute Petroglyphs
Going to Arches without visiting **Delicate Arch** is like going to the Louvre

Eagle Park

Klondike Bluffs

❼ Tower Arch

Marching Men

Courthouse Wash

191

313

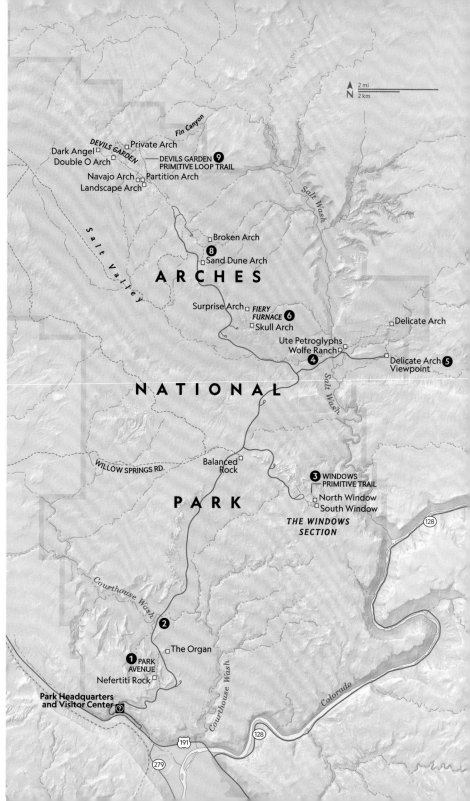

N
2 mi
2 km

Fin Canyon

Private Arch
DEVILS GARDEN
Dark Angel
Double O Arch
DEVILS GARDEN **9**
PRIMITIVE LOOP TRAIL
Navajo Arch Partition Arch
Landscape Arch

Broken Arch

8
Sand Dune Arch

Salt Valley

A R C H E S

Surprise Arch *FIERY*
FURNACE **6**
Skull Arch

Salt Wash

Ute Petroglyphs
Wolfe Ranch
4

Delicate Arch

Delicate Arch **5**
Viewpoint

N A T I O N A L

Salt Wash

WILLOW SPRINGS RD.

Balanced
Rock

3 WINDOWS
PRIMITIVE TRAIL

North Window
South Window

P A R K

THE WINDOWS
SECTION

128

Courthouse Wash

2

The Organ

1 PARK
AVENUE
Nefertiti Rock

**Park Headquarters
and Visitor Center** 📍

Courthouse Wash

Colorado

128

191

279

128

Delicate Arch landscape

without seeing the "Mona Lisa." But don't get caught up in the daily "march to the arch" without taking the time to view **Wolfe Ranch,** a roughshod cabin in which Civil War veteran John Wesley Wolfe and his family lived at the turn of the 20th century. It's the park's only evidence of permanent habitation, a stark reminder of how unaccommodating this land is to humans.

The native Fremont, ancestral Puebloan, and Ute knew better than to actually live here, though they left evidence of their passing. Walk up 600 feet from the cabin to ponder a Ute petroglyph panel, one of the few to depict horses (and dogs), which dates them to after the mid-1700s Spanish incursion.

⑤ Delicate Arch Viewpoint If the day is a scorcher, or if hiking 3 miles over steep slickrock is beyond your ability, you can still see the state's iconic arch on something other than Utah's license plates.

NOT TO BE MISSED: *Skip the crowds and view The Spectacles from the Windows Primitive Trail.* ▸ *Wake up early, avoid the heat, and see Delicate Arch from a trail accessible to all.* ▸ *Channel your inner Spider-Man and squeeze along the sandstone fins of the rugged Fiery Furnace.* ▸ *Find solitude at Tower Arch.* ▸ *Gaze at Landscape Arch, the world's longest. If you're fit, keep hiking on to the largest concentration of natural arches in the world.*

Drive 1 mile past the Delicate Arch trailhead to where the road ends. The 300-foot-long handicapped-accessible "lower" trail and the 0.5-mile-long "upper" trail will not get you as close to the arch (it's still 0.5 mile away), but you'll see the big picture that people hiking to the arch miss—the arch itself is actually perched on the precipitous edge of a monumental cliff. (While Delicate Arch glows in the sunset, from here the best viewing is in the early morning light.)

6 Fiery Furnace This confusing maze of sandstone fins makes up the park's most rugged terrain. Topological maps and GPS coordinates are useless, and leaving behind cairns or trail markers to find your way out is forbidden.

"This is pure wilderness in a little pocket in the park. It's all about exploration, with no destination other than what you find," says Henker.

The only safe way to navigate this labyrinth is by joining a scheduled three-hour tour led by park rangers (you can reserve up to six months in advance at *recreation.gov*).

How tough a hike is it? "You'll definitely have a chance to channel your own inner Spiderman," says Henker. "There are some fun little moves."

Resourceful hikers are allowed in unescorted after paying for a permit and watching a mandatory video explaining the rules of environmental protection—stay on slickrock, walk in washes, and don't build cairns, for example.

The reward? **Skull** and **Surprise Arches,** the possibility of stumbling upon **Abbey Arch** (discovered by Edward Abbey himself), potholes teeming with micro-life, and an up close look at the Arches biscuitroot, a plant that only grows in sandy soil between fins of Entrada sandstone.

With not a lot of room to navigate between the fins—in some places you may squeeze through sideways—this is a good place to keep an eye out for the

Prickly pear cactus

Tower Arch, Klondike Bluffs

trees, claret cup cactus (one of the few cacti found at these higher elevations), and leafless clumps of Mormon tea. Three pinnacles, called the **Marching Men**, point you in the right direction.

The 2.5-mile-long trail ends at the park's fifth largest arch, backed by a minaret-like tower, which inspired the inscription carved into its northern base by its purported discoverer: MINARET BRIDGE H.S. BELL 1927.

The name never stuck, as the park's founding father, Alex Ringhoffer, had actually discovered the arch five years earlier. (His name—mysteriously misspelled—is inscribed on the arch's southern base.) In fact, this grand arch motivated Ringhoffer to lobby for help making Arches a national monument in 1929, and, in that sense, Tower Arch can be considered the park's founding arch.

❽ **Sand Dune & Broken Arches** A short trail connects kid-friendly Sand Dune Arch, tucked up in a sandbox fin marking the northern boundary of Fiery Furnace, with Broken Arch on the southern edge of **Devils Garden** via a wide grassy meadow bright with wildflowers and tweeting birds. (Listen for the melodious call of the western meadowlark.)

"It's not a very popular hike, and every time I do it, I'm grateful for that fact, because I never run into anybody. It is a nice easy loop, under a mile round-trip, and it explores in between the fins," says Henker. "It doesn't have famous arches, but a lot of them are hiding in here."

The level open terrain makes this trail especially appealing for a full moon hike, though Henker warns: "A lot of the desert's wildlife is out at night, including scorpions and our one-and-only rattlesnake species, the midget faded. So folks

park's only venomous snake, the midget faded rattlesnake.

Don't let the name Fiery Furnace scare you. Come summer, this is one of the shadier spots in the park.

❼ **Tower Arch** To experience a truly monumental arch in sublime solitude, this is your best bet, thanks to the 8.3 miles of dirt-pack washboard that keeps the general public at bay.

"It's my favorite arch, and you just might have it to yourself," says park ranger Kathryn Burke. "It's the first place I heard my own heartbeat."

It may take a little heart-thumping to scramble over the rocky ridge marked by cairns before descending on a sandy single track through a valley full of juniper who want to take night hikes should wear close-toed shoes and keep their fingers and toes out of little dark holes, because that's where the dangerous stuff is hanging out."

9 Devils Garden Primitive Loop Trail

The paved road ends at Devils Garden trailhead, which is filled with cars and RVs in season, but the crowd thins once you trek beyond the trail's first attraction, **Landscape Arch,** the world's longest arch.

There's a reason for this. "Past Landscape, the primitive trail takes it up the next notch as far as the height of exposure and difficulty of scrambling. You definitely need to have flexible hips and good observation skills to see the trail markers," says Henker. "Since this is the longest trail in the park—7.2 miles round-trip—you should plan on spending at least half a day."

The payoff? The largest concentration of natural arches in the world, including **Partition, Navajo, Private,** and **Double O.**

Before returning along the backside of the primitive loop, which offers jaw-dropping views of **Fin Canyon,** take a 0.5-mile side trip out to **Dark Angel** (to the northwest from Double O Arch). This brooding 150-foot-high sandstone spire was used as a historic landmark by ancient travelers, and you might stumble across petroglyphs and the signatures of ancient Puebloan or early sheepherders who used this area as a natural campsite. (Denis Julien, a French-American trapper, was the first white man to record his presence in the park in 1844.)

Beyond Dark Angel lies the most remote part of Arches, the trailless **Eagle Park district,** where the sandstone fins of Devils Garden open to empty wide-open spaces.

Wandering atop Devils Garden

Rio Grande near Hot Springs

BIG BEND

Set in remote southwestern Texas, far from major cities and interstate highways, Big Bend National Park isn't a place travelers visit on a whim. It lies just across the Rio Grande from Mexico, at the end of a long road that doesn't go much of anyplace else. Most of the park is Chihuahuan Desert; in the center, the Chisos Mountains rise to 7,832 feet.

There are those who simply cruise the park's paved roads by car, ascending to the stunning Basin and descending to Santa Elena Canyon, and then move on. Perhaps they're a little intimidated by Big Bend's jagged terrain and immense distances; by plants armed with spines and points; by the black bears, mountain lions, and rattlesnakes that find homes here. That's a shame, because the park offers a great many relatively easy ways to experience its secrets, including striking rock formations, spectacular vistas, and awesome river canyons.

Year-Round Visitor Centers

- **Panther Junction Visitor Center & Park Headquarters**
  3 miles east of Chisos Mountain Basin Junction, 26 miles south of North Entrance
- **Chisos Basin Visitor Center**
  On Chisos Basin Road, 6 miles south of main park road

Seasonal Visitor Centers

- **Castolon Visitor Center**
  On Ross Maxwell Scenic Drive, 22 miles south of Santa Elena Junction
- **Persimmon Gap Visitor Center**
  On US 385, at North Entrance
- **Rio Grande Village Visitor Center**
  20 miles east of Panther Junction

  432-477-2251, nps.gov/bibe

at a saddle where the vista is almost as good, taking in Casa Grande, **Juniper Canyon,** and a long-distance view south into Mexico.

2 Boot Canyon Chisos Basin Road continues to the Basin itself, with its campground, ranger station, and Chisos Mountains Lodge (the only noncamping accommodations in the park). A variety of hikes are possible here, from strenuous multiday backpacking trips around the Chisos Mountains to the 0.3-mile, accessible **Window View Trail** loop.

The latter should not be confused with the longer (5.2-mile round-trip) **Window Trail,** leading from near the lodge to a low place in the Basin wall where all the rainfall in the area drains via Oak Creek, known as **The Window.**

Trails in the Basin area are well traveled, so it's difficult to get off the beaten path. Nonetheless, if you're going to do

| THE BASIN

Heading up Green Gulch on Chisos Basin Road, a first-time visitor will likely be amazed by the mountain scenery at the Basin, where the massive rock formation called **Casa Grande** looms enticingly ahead.

1 Lost Mine Trail At 5.1 miles from Basin Junction is the trailhead for one of the most popular moderate hikes in the park. The Lost Mine Trail is a 2.4-mile out-and-back hike, ending in a wonderful panoramic view after an elevation gain of more than 1,000 feet. An alternative is to walk just the first mile, stopping

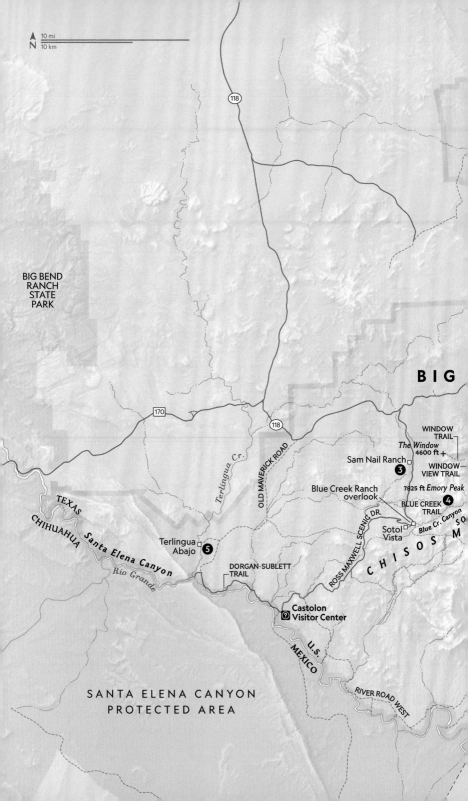

N
10 mi
10 km

118

BIG BEND
RANCH
STATE
PARK

170

118

Terlingua Cr.

OLD MAVERICK ROAD

BIG

WINDOW
TRAIL
The Window
4600 ft
WINDOW-
VIEW TRAIL

Sam Nail Ranch
3

7825 ft Emory Peak

Blue Creek Ranch
overlook
BLUE CREEK
TRAIL
4

Sotol
Vista

Blue Cr. Canyon

CHISOS M

SO

TEXAS

CHIHUAHUA

Santa Elena Canyon

Terlingua
Abajo
5

Rio Grande

DORGAN-SUBLETT
TRAIL

Castolon
Visitor Center

U.S.

MEXICO

RIVER ROAD WEST

SANTA ELENA CANYON
PROTECTED AREA

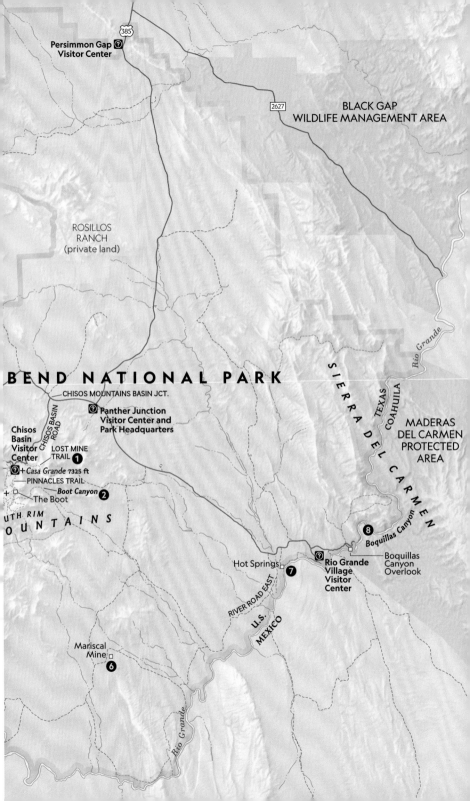

Persimmon Gap
Visitor Center ⑦ US 385

BLACK GAP
WILDLIFE MANAGEMENT AREA

2627

ROSILLOS
RANCH
(private land)

BEND NATIONAL PARK

CHISOS MOUNTAINS BASIN JCT.

Panther Junction
Visitor Center and
Park Headquarters ⑦

CHISOS BASIN ROAD

Chisos
Basin
Visitor
Center

LOST MINE
TRAIL ❶

⑦ +Casa Grande 7325 ft
PINNACLES TRAIL
+ □ *Boot Canyon* ❷
□ The Boot

UTH RIM
OUNTAINS

SIERRA DEL CARMEN

TEXAS
COAHUILA

MADERAS
DEL CARMEN
PROTECTED
AREA

Rio Grande

Boquillas Canyon

❽

Hot Springs □ ❼

⑦ **Rio Grande**
Village
Visitor
Center

Boquillas
Canyon
Overlook

RIVER ROAD EAST

U.S.
MEXICO

Mariscal
Mine □
❻

Rio Grande

only one hike here, consider the fairly strenuous 9-mile round-trip to Boot Canyon (bring plenty of water). It's a steep climb up switchbacks on the **Pinnacles Trail** (3.5 miles) to a pass with wonderful views of Big Bend country, where you're surrounded by spires of volcanic rhyolite. From there it's a comparatively easy walk to get a view of **The Boot**, an odd rock column that does look like an upside-down cowboy boot.

ROSS MAXWELL SCENIC DRIVE

This 30-mile (one way) paved road leads from the main east-west park highway southwest to Santa Elena Canyon on the Rio Grande with views of the Chisos Mountains to the east. According to Tom VandenBerg, Chief of Interpretation at the park, "a visitor could spend an entire day, or more, exploring the trails and historic sights along this drive."

❸ **Sam Nail Ranch** A few miles along the route, stop at the Sam Nail ranch to see the remains of a homestead dating from 1916. "This is our favorite site on the west side of the park for a quiet, cool birding experience," say Ron and Jane Payne, park volunteers. "You can sit on a bench, beneath the pecan trees planted by Sam and Nena Nail in the early 20th century,

NOT TO BE MISSED: *Test your stamina on the strenuous trek into Boot Canyon.* ▸ *Birdwatch at Sam Nail Ranch.* ▸ *See the unusual rock formations of Blue Creek Canyon.* ▸ *Hike the Dorgan-Sublett Trail into Santa Elena Canyon.*

and enjoy a dozen or more bird species and perhaps even a javelina or gray fox that has come to water beneath the creaky cranking of the windmill."

❹ **Blue Creek Trail** Less than 5 miles farther, stop at the Blue Creek Ranch overlook, the start of a moderately strenuous hike with fine scenic rewards. Walk down to the buildings below the road, built for a ranching operation in the 1930s.

Then hike the first 2 miles or so of the Blue Creek Trail. This route was established to move sheep from the hot lowlands into the cooler Chisos in summer. It's a hard climb all the way to the top, but you don't have to go that far to enjoy the red rocks of **Blue Creek Canyon,** where you'll be surrounded by a variety of spires and "balanced" rocks in a multitude of delightful forms.

❺ **Terlingua Abajo** Past the historic community of **Castolon**, Ross Maxwell Scenic Drive parallels the Rio Grande to

LOCAL INTELLIGENCE

Along the Ross Maxwell Scenic Drive is one of the park's major attractions, **Sotol Vista,** named for an abundant plant with dagger-like leaves and a tall flowering spike. But for a special experience, visit in the evening. "I chose this spot for an evening program so I could enjoy magnificent sunsets and watch the craggy mountains and deep canyons disappear into the shadow of twilight," says Gail Abend, park interpreter. "The silence on Sotol Vista enhances the celestial display as the stars appear one by one, unaffected by any man-made light."

magnificent **Santa Elena Canyon,** where the river has cut a deep canyon with claustrophobia-inducing walls. A walk into the canyon is a must-do at Big Bend.

"A hundred years ago this was amazingly inhabited for the middle of nowhere," says local guide Greg Hennington, speaking of the time when Mexican farmers, Anglo ranchers, and mining companies were scattered across this harsh landscape. The **Dorgan-Sublett Trail** (0.8 mile round-trip), at mile 5 along the road to Santa Elena Canyon, is evocative of this era. VandenBerg calls it "a gem of a trail. It takes visitors to an array of historic homesites contemporary to the community of Terlingua Abajo—and the views are awesome."

WEST & EAST RIVER ROAD

Santa Elena Canyon

6 **Mariscal Mine** About halfway along River Road lies Mariscal Mine, significant as Texas' best preserved historic site from the era of mercury mining. The Big Bend country once produced one-third of the country's output of "quicksilver."

"The Mariscal Mine brings in the human occupation of Big Bend, which started with the Native Americans," Hennington says. "I like to walk up to the top of those ruins and just sit there and contemplate what life must have been like in the late 1800s and early 1900s, mining mercury by hand."

The site, a national historic district, includes houses, offices, kilns, furnaces, and a blacksmith shop.

THE EASTERN PARK

A visitor center, store, picnic area, and very popular campground make the **Rio Grande Village** area a primary destination for many park visitors. A walk on the nature trail accessible from the campground is a must for wildlife-watchers (especially birders).

7 **Hot Springs** Here you can see the ruins of a bathhouse constructed in the early 20th century. Possibly the first tourist attraction in the area, it offered "healing" water to visitors for decades. Only the foundation of the bathhouse remains, but you can still soak tired muscles in the 105°F water flowing from the ground.

8 **Boquillas Canyon** Also of note is Boquillas Canyon, at the end of a spur road 4 miles east of Rio Grande Village. A 1.4-mile round-trip walk here takes you to the top of a cliff overlooking the Rio Grande and then into the canyon itself.

View from Sunrise Point

BRYCE CANYON

Angka-ku-wass-a-wits ("red painted faces") is one of several names for Bryce Canyon attributed to the Paiute people, who believed the ruddy pillars of the area were their human ancestors turned to stone. From another storytelling tradition, it is said that pioneer Ebenezer Bryce, for whom the canyon is named, gazed down into the rocky maze and quipped that it was "one heck of a place to lose a cow."

The canyon's great secret may be that it's not a canyon at all; rather, it's a series of 14 limestone amphitheaters cut into the eastern edge of the Paunsaugunt Plateau in southern Utah. The domes and pillars (collectively called "hoodoos") were formed over millions of years by snow, frost, and rainwater weathering the weak Claron formation limestone. While red is the predominant hue, closer inspection reveals Bryce's palette features more than 60 distinct colors.

Year-Round Visitor Center

Bryce Canyon Visitor Center
*On Utah 63, 1.5 miles inside
North Entrance*

435-834-5322, nps.gov/brca

follow the Fairyland Loop to formations such as **Tower Bridge** and the **China Wall.**

❷ Dave's Hollow Meadow Another mile down the main road is **Bryce Canyon Visitor Center** with its displays on park natural and human history, an orientation film, and plenty of advice on where to go and what to do during your sojourn at the park.

Ask about the various interpretive programs and ranger-led activities that take place daily, especially during the summer season. These provide an excellent introduction to aspects of the park that may be missed by the casual visitor.

Directly west of the visitor center is Dave's Hollow Meadow, which flows down into **Dixie National Forest.** Sarah Haas, park biologist, says this is the "very best place in the park to see prairie dogs. If you look toward the west, there are a couple of colonies that are very easy to see from the parking lot or the road."

❸ Rim Trail East of the visitor center, Bryce Amphitheater's Rim Trail provides an opportunity to see the depression from above. Four spectacular overlooks along the edge can be reached by foot, private vehicle, or the free park shuttle.

Linking these viewpoints is the popular 5.5-mile (one way) Rim Trail, which gains height as it moves from north to south, peaking at 8,296-foot **Bryce Point.** Tom Hart, assistant general manager of

BRYCE AMPHITHEATER

This amphitheater is the largest and most popular one in the park, but it shouldn't be skipped, as the park's central features are located along it.

❶ Fairyland Point On their rush into the heart of Bryce Canyon, visitors often overlook a turnoff to the left just beyond the park entry sign.

One mile down a side road flanked by ponderosa pines is Fairyland Point, which looks out across chromatic **Boat Mesa** and **Fairyland Canyon,** just a hint of what's to come farther into the park. Those who can't wait to see hoodoos can

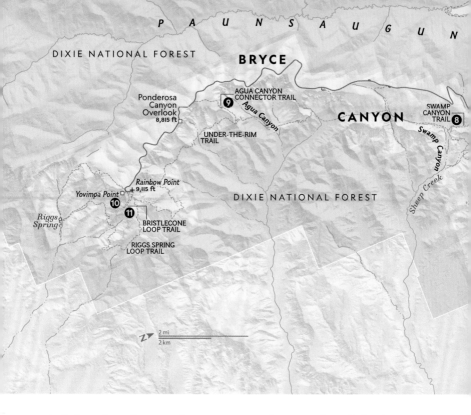

the Lodge at Bryce Canyon and a veteran Utah rock climber, recommends that visitors explore the same overlook or trail at three or four different times during a given day and to take special notice of how the landscape changes.

"The trails have a varied look and feel depending on the time of day," says Hart. "It's not just such a visually majestic park because of the nature of the formations and the sandstone cliffs, but also because it looks completely different at dusk, or at sunrise, or in the bright sunshine in the middle of the day as the reds, the oranges, and the browns pick up the sunlight."

❹ Peek-a-boo Loop Trail You can descend into the main amphitheater at six different points along the rim (one of them is reserved for equestrian tours).

Don't expect to have the hoodoos to yourself on popular trails such as the **Queens Garden** and **Navajo Loops.** But you can get long periods of solitude along some of the tougher walks.

From Bryce Point, the Peek-a-boo Loop circles the southern part of the amphitheater, passing the **Wall of Windows,** the **Three Wise Men,** and other remarkable geology. Given the steep grade coming back up, allocate three to four hours for this 5.5-mile (one way) hike.

❺ Tropic Trail The least-traveled route in the main amphitheater area is the Tropic Trail that runs across the middle of the park to **Bryce Canyon.** This can be done as a round-trip to the park boundary and back, or as a one-way (mostly downhill) walk to the pioneer town of

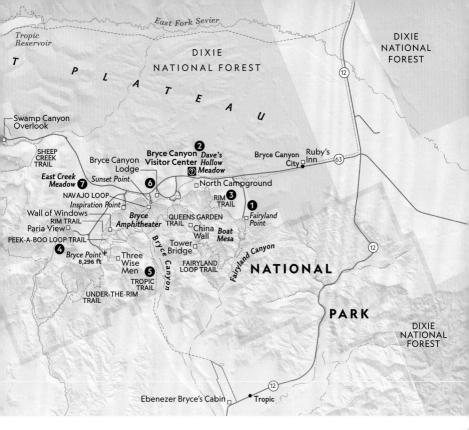

East Fork Sevier

Tropic
Reservoir

DIXIE
NATIONAL FOREST

DIXIE
NATIONAL
FOREST

PLATEAU

T

Swamp Canyon
Overlook

SHEEP
CREEK
TRAIL

East Creek
Meadow 7

Bryce Canyon
Lodge

Bryce Canyon *Dave's*
Visitor Center *Hollow*
2   *Meadow*

Bryce Canyon   Ruby's
City Inn   63

Sunset Point 6

North Campground

NAVAJO LOOP
Inspiration Point

Wall of Windows
RIM TRAIL
Paria View

PEEK-A-BOO LOOP TRAIL

RIM
TRAIL 3

1

Bryce
Amphitheater

QUEENS GARDEN
TRAIL   China
Wall

Fairyland
Point

Boat
Mesa

Bryce Point
8,296 ft 4

Three
Wise
Men

Tower
Bridge

FAIRYLAND
LOOP TRAIL

Fairyland Canyon

12

NATIONAL

TROPIC
TRAIL 5

UNDER-THE-RIM
TRAIL

PARK

DIXIE
NATIONAL
FOREST

12

Ebenezer Bryce's Cabin   Tropic

Tropic, which requires prearranged transport back into the park.

Be sure to look for **Ebenezer Bryce's log cabin** (built circa 1881) near the south end of Main Street in Tropic. "This is the trail I probably walk the most because I live in Tropic," says biologist Haas. "On most days when I walk it—even during the summer high season—I don't see anyone else. It still has wilderness character and it's a great birding area. As you descend, the landscape transitions from ponderosa pine into Gambel oak and a manzanita understory."

6 Bryce Canyon Lodge The Bryce Canyon Lodge is also worth a look. This masterpiece of American national park architecture was built in the 1920s and is now a national historic landmark. Although it's been renovated several

Prairie dog, a park favorite

Natural Bridge in winter

times since, the lodge retains its rustic ambience. It consists of a large main building with a distinctive green roof and log cabins set along the canyon edge. Constructed by the Union Pacific Railroad to lure visitors to Bryce, the lodge was designed by Gilbert Stanley Underwood, one of the mavens of the national park style.

"It's been modernized over the years, but it's also been kept to its historical grandeur," says Hart, who works in the main building. "This is the only lodge from that period [in Utah] that hasn't burned to the ground and been rebuilt. This is the only one in its original state. But these are very hard buildings to maintain. Eighty percent of the windows in the lodge are hand-blown glass and there's only one place left in the world that makes them anymore. So it's a big deal when we have to replace one. When I go to work, I feel like I'm a steward of a piece of history."

18-MILE SCENIC DRIVE & RAINBOW POINT

Beyond Bryce Amphitheater, the park thins into a narrow wedge atop part of the **Paunsaugunt Plateau**, a scenic tableland that runs roughly north-south at an altitude between 7,000 and 9,100 feet within the park. Meandering along the top of this ridge is an 18-mile scenic drive that ends at Rainbow Point in the deep south. Most people drive the route—flanked by red-rock chasms on one side, woodland, and meadows on the other—but a free shuttle also plies the ridge twice a day in summer season.

❼ **East Creek Meadow** One of the first things you come across on the scenic drive is East Creek Meadow, sprawling along the road just south of the turnoff to Bryce Point. Experience this from your own car, or take the free **Rainbow Point Tour** (reservations necessary).

"This is the park's largest meadow," says Haas, "and a good place to see wildlife. It's pretty rare if you don't spot a pronghorn, deer, wild turkey, or raptor. We're also trying to get prairie dogs back into the meadow. Stop in the Civilian Conservation Corps [CCC] picnic area."

❽ Swamp Canyon Trail While the overlooks can get crowded at times, the trails that descend into the canyons seldom do. Swamp Canyon Trail may be one of the park's most rewarding hikes, given its diverse habitats and terrain. It winds down through a maze of hoodoos to a lush canyon fed by creeks and springs. It's not a swamp per se, but there is enough moisture for willows, reeds, and the toxic western iris, which contains a poisonous chemical. Keep an eye out for tiger salamanders in the wetter areas.

"In the bottom of Swamp Canyon is a huge wetland meadow," says Haas. "It's the only place in the park like that. The willows are pretty thick. We have bears in that area and lots of deer. Some of our rare bird species will be down there too."

Swamp Canyon Trail eventually tumbles into the 22.9-mile **Under-the-Rim Trail**, the park's major backcountry route.

LOCAL INTELLIGENCE

While it may seem counterintuitive—given its iconic desertlike landscapes—Bryce Canyon transforms into a frozen wonderland between November and April, when the plateau is often shrouded in snow. "It's like *The Shining* in the wintertime," says lodge manager Tom Hart. "There are years where you can't see 8-foot-tall trees because they're covered with snow."

The park service plows the entire main road and also keeps the main parking lots near **Sunset Point** snow free so that visitors can access **Bryce Amphitheater.** "You can still get on some trails," says Hart. "So if you want to get on your boots and go down into the canyon itself, you can. When they're covered in snow, the hoodoos look like some crazy dessert or ice cream cone."

Snowshoers and cross-country skiers can follow the **Rim Trail** to **Inspiration Point,** or along the **Fairyland Point** or **Paria View Roads,** which are left unplowed for this purpose. Ranger-guided snowshoe hikes are held when snowpack levels permit—sign-up is at the visitor center. Note that traction devices and/or poles are strongly recommended for any winter hikes.

Both cross-country skiing and snowshoeing are prohibited on park trails below the rim, but right outside the entrance gate is a Nordic ski area with some 20 miles of groomed trails maintained under special permit by **Ruby's Inn** (1.4 miles north of the park entrance; *rubysinn.com/winter-activities*). Snowshoes and cross-country gear can be rented, and the lodge also offers sleigh rides, ice skating, and snowmobiling in the national forest.

Hart also recommends a winter visit for avid stargazers. "With the altitude, the coldness of the night air, and the lack of pollution, this is one of the best places in the United States to view the night sky. You can be amazed on no-moon nights, especially in the wintertime, looking up into the heavens and seeing the entire Milky Way."

Winter visitors may stay at the **North Campground,** and the Lodge at Bryce Canyon has begun to keep its **Sunset Motel** property open year-round.

Mule deer foraging in the woods

Hang a left and walk about a mile to the **Sheep Creek Trail,** which leads back up the wall to the **Swamp Canyon Overlook.**

"The whole loop is about 4.5 miles," says Haas. "It takes two or three hours depending on how fast you hike."

➒ Agua Canyon Connector Trail

Another good hike off the scenic road is the Agua Canyon connecting trail, which starts near the **Ponderosa Canyon Overlook** but travels immediately north, running through woodland before plunging into another hoodoo-filled chasm.

Rock formations called **The Hunter** and **The Rabbit** dominate the foreground, but

---

NOT TO BE MISSED: *Travel the Rim Trail for spectacular views.*
▸ *Count the hoodoos in Agua Canyon.* ▸ *Gaze at nature's colors from Rainbow Point.* ▸ *Leave the crowds behind on the Swamp Canyon Trail.* ▸ *Hike into the backcountry near Riggs Springs.*

---

your eyes soon migrate to that massive geological feature dominating the eastern horizon—the **Grand Staircase.**

Don't expect a lush oasis at Agua Canyon, though. "The name is a bit of a misnomer," explains Haas. "The area does have some springs, but there's no perennial water source."

➓ Yovimpa Point

At the bottom end of the road is the aptly named **Rainbow Point,** where nature's colors run a spectrum from sky blue and cloud white to pink, orange, beige, and vermilion stone and the dark green trees of the plateau top. Soaring to more than 9,100 feet, this is the park's highest point and one of its most dramatic.

A short trail leads to Yovimpa Point, with its panoramic views of the Grand Staircase. Squint your eyes and imagine you're standing at the prow of a great ship sailing southward toward Zion and the Grand Canyon. The view—sometimes approaching 200 miles—truly makes you feel you're the king of the world.

⓫ Bristlecone Loop Trail Also starting from the Rainbow Point parking lot is the short Bristlecone Loop Trail, which ambles through a mixed forest of spruce, firs, and bristlecone pines; some of the latter are more than 1,600 years old and without doubt the oldest living things in the Bryce Canyon area. If you haven't eaten lunch, chow down at the **Rainbow Point** picnic area within the trees, then head out for some expansive views.

Reenergized, have a jaunt down part of the **Riggs Spring** or **Under-the-Rim Trails.** The 8.8-mile Riggs Springs Loop dives into one of the park's most remote corners. It can be tackled as a long (and very rewarding) day hike or a two-day walk with overnight at one of four primitive campsites along the route.

You can look forward to soothing your walk-weary muscles at Riggs's namesake spring near the halfway point, an oasis-like patch of water, grass, wildflowers, and ponderosa pine.

The Under-the-Rim Trail features eight campsites. Both it and Riggs are considered backcountry hiking and suitable only for the experienced and physically fit; the air gets thinner as you climb through elevations ranging from 6,800 feet to 9,115 feet. Note that permits are required for overnight stays; these, along with maps and terrific advice, are available at the visitor center.

The park's signature hoodoo spires

View from Mesa Arch Overlook, Island in the Sky

CANYONLANDS

This is the Great American Outback, a vast park containing the rawest, most rugged land in the lower 48, an untrammeled wilderness that looks no different than when Maj. John Wesley Powell made his first trip through it on his Colorado River exploration of 1869. The 527-square-mile park has been neatly carved into three districts—Island in the Sky, The Maze, and The Needles—by its primary engineers, the Green and Colorado Rivers, which join forces at the Confluence, the park's arterial heart.

Each district is of distinct character. Motorists prefer Island in the Sky for its easily accessible yet far-reaching overlooks where views of 100 miles are not uncommon. The Needles district appeals to hikers seeking to lose themselves amid the secrets of its surreal spires and wandering canyons. The Maze tests the limits of the most intrepid adventurer, and requires compass, topographic maps, and nerve to explore.

Year-Round Visitor Centers

■ Island in the Sky Visitor Center
On Utah 313, 23 miles southwest of US 191

■ Hans Flat Ranger Station
46 miles west of Utah 24

Seasonal Visitor Center

■ Needles Visitor Center
35 miles west of US 191

435-719-2313, nps.gov/cany

spectacle than the more popular Grand View Point Overlook—and you're likely to have it all to yourself. (There are only four parking slots at the trailhead.)

"I call it the O. Henry trail for its sudden ending," says Kathryn Burke, a seasonal ranger. "You're walking though piñon-juniper scrubland and bam, the end hits you and you can hardly breathe. Your jaw just drops at the sudden appearance of the canyons below." (Watch your step, though; unlike at Grand View Point, there are *no* guardrails.)

The 300-degree views are of a geologic layer cake of chocolate-colored canyons frosted with White Rim sandstone, while the **La Sal** and **Abajo Mountains** ride on the horizon under a big western sky.

❷ **Murphy Point** This may be the best sunset-watching site in the whole Island in the Sky area (if not in the entire park), but ever since the dirt road was turned into a 1.8-mile-long foot trail, it gets far fewer visitors than the other overlooks.

From the promontory's ramparts, the far-reaching views of **Candlestick Tower, Turks Head, Soda Spring Basin,** and the distant Maze can occupy you for hours. This is also a prime place to pitch camp

ISLAND IN THE SKY

This high desert mesa (6,080 feet) towers 2,200 feet above the **Green** and **Colorado Rivers** below. It is crossed by 20 miles of paved road that winds through rice grass and juniper trees while stopping at the park's most popular sights: **Mesa Arch, Grand View Point,** and the **Green River Overlook.** It's perfect for a scenic drive, but if you're looking to steer clear of the car-bound crowds, a little sweat equity put into hiking pays huge dividends.

❶ **White Rim Overlook** This gentle trail leads a mile to the end of a narrow promontory offering an even wider panoramic

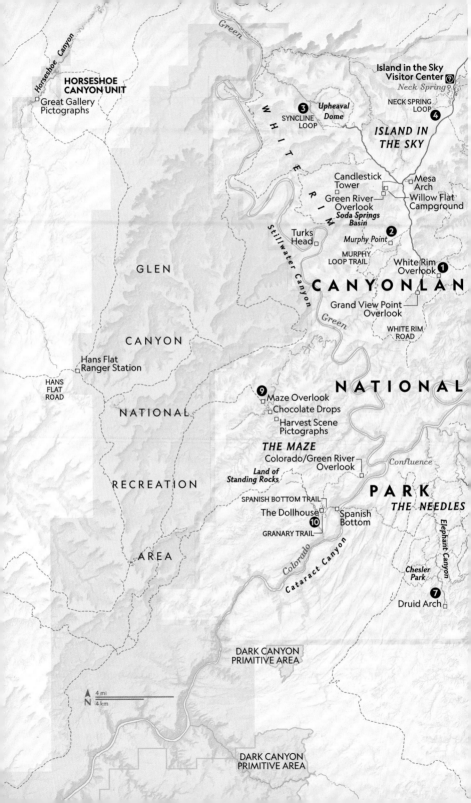

HORSESHOE CANYON UNIT
□ Great Gallery Pictographs

Horseshoe Canyon

Green

Island in the Sky
Visitor Center ⊚
Neck Spring

❸
SYNCLINE
LOOP

Upheaval Dome

NECK SPRING
LOOP ❹

ISLAND IN THE SKY

W
H
I
T
E
R
I
M

□ Candlestick Tower

□ Mesa Arch

□ Green River Overlook

Willow Flat Campground

Soda Springs Basin

Murphy Point ❷

□ White Rim Overlook ❶

□ Turks Head

MURPHY LOOP TRAIL

GLEN

Stillwater Canyon

CANYONLAN

Grand View Point Overlook

WHITE RIM ROAD

CANYON

Green

□ Hans Flat Ranger Station

HANS FLAT ROAD

NATIONAL

NATIONAL

❾ □ Maze Overlook
□ Chocolate Drops
□ Harvest Scene Pictographs

THE MAZE

Colorado/Green River Overlook

Confluence

Land of Standing Rocks

PARK
THE NEEDLES

RECREATION

SPANISH BOTTOM TRAIL

The Dollhouse ❿

□ Spanish Bottom

GRANARY TRAIL

AREA

Colorado

Cataract Canyon

Chesler Park

Elephant Canyon

❼ □ Druid Arch

DARK CANYON PRIMITIVE AREA

N 4 mi
4 km

DARK CANYON PRIMITIVE AREA

DEAD HORSE
POINT
STATE PARK

W H I T E   R I M

Colorado

D S

The Needles
Visitor Center (211)

5 — CAVE SPRING TRAIL

Cave Spring

Squaw Flat Campground

North
Sixshooter +
Peak
6374 ft

PEEKABOO
TRAIL

South +
Sixshooter
Peak
6132 ft

6

Squaw Canyon

Lost Canyon

Peekaboo
Spring

Salt Cr.

8

BEAR
EARS
NAT.
MON.

Cathedral Point
+*7120 ft*
—*Cathedral Butte*

atop the Island in the Sky mesa, although you'll need to snag a backcountry permit. (Since only one permit at a time is issued for Murphy Point, you'll have the place to yourself.) Or try the 12-site **Willow Flat** campground.

If you're feeling even more adventurous, take the nearby 10.8-mile **Murphy Loop Trail,** which descends 1,400 feet of switchbacks down cliffs of Wingate sandstone, then follows an exhilarating hogback all the way to the **White Rim Road** before looping back up.

3 Syncline Loop Those who complete the 8.3-mile trail around the rim of **Upheaval Dome** earn plenty of bragging rights, but hikers need to be prepared with map, compass, food, water, and a flashlight/headlamp. "It beats me up every time I do it," says Burke. "But I keep going back for more because it is so brutally beautiful. It's mostly cairned, and the terrain is rocky and varied, so you really have to keep an eye out. Most of our rescues take place here."

A resident lizard

Chesler Park in the Needles District

A 3-mile spur trail takes hikers into enigmatic Upheaval Dome, an inexplicable mile-wide bull's-eye of a crater. Scientists still argue whether it is a collapsed salt dome or the remains of an ancient meteor strike. "I think a good mystery makes every park better," says Burke. "This one is ours."

The six- to eight-hour trek gives plenty of time for hikers to puzzle over the green, purple, and brown geologic formations at the core of the crater.

❹ Neck Spring Loop Probably the most secret trail in the park, this 5.8-mile-long, three- to four-hour loop is the only moderate-length hike on the Island that doesn't mimic a StairMaster workout on the return leg. It also offers more of a chance to see wildlife than anywhere else, so bring binoculars.

The presence of year-round water attracts animals such as mule deer, coyotes, desert bighorns, and many smaller mammals. A sharp eye will also reveal flint-knapping chips from the Native American tribes, and weathered ranching gear left over from the park's cattle days. Just remember that collecting artifacts is prohibited.

"You aren't on top of the mesa, but underneath it," says Cindy Donaldson, park guide. "You follow in and out of these little drainages where you'll find some really neat things, like maidenhair ferns underneath the Navajo sandstone cap."

THE NEEDLES

Named after the red and buttery-white striped towers of Cedar Mesa sandstone that dominate the district, this is a backpackers paradise, offering more trails than either The Maze or Island in the Sky.

While most visitors will make a deserved beeline for the spire-fringed meadows of **Chesler Park**, those seeking a less traveled trail will love a more than 60-mile network of narrow interconnected routes that allow for plenty of improvisation when exploring the region's many canyons, joints (splits in the rock), graben valleys, and arches.

This area also has far more ruins, pictographs, and petroglyphs than elsewhere in the park, which adds a haunting human dimension to an already mind-bending landscape.

❺ Cave Spring Trail Often overlooked for being too short and easy, this 0.6-mile loop is a CliffsNotes version of the park, summing up all of its aspects in a quick 45-minute loop.

Due to the year-round springs, you'll come across a historic cowboy line camp in one alcove. Just beyond is evidence of an earlier occupation. "There are two sets of pictographs, one by the spring and the other one in the next alcove over on the ceiling. If you keep your eyes open you'll spot lots of archaeological stuff," says Donaldson.

More apparent to most visitors are the signs identifying many of the park's plants: Utah serviceberry, four-wing saltbush, and squawbush, for example. Two ladders are there to hoist you up to the slickrock, where, reports Donaldson, "you'll get amazing views of The Needles."

❻ Peekaboo Trail This 10-mile round-trip trail, which leaves the Needles campground and crosses both **Squaw** and **Lost Canyons,** is one of the few here that is mostly on slickrock, especially the last 2.5 miles to **Peekaboo Springs.**

"You walk on top of these headwalls that are pretty tall, which give you dramatic views of the **La Sal Mountains** and **Six-Shooter Peak,**" says Brad Donaldson, a backcountry ranger who counts this as his favorite hike. "There's some exposure. It's scary, but not risky," he adds.

Two well-placed ladders help with the scrambling as you navigate atop a labyrinth of mostly inaccessible canyons and drainages. The payoff?

"You come to a brilliant rock art site, with the oldest art at least 1,000 years old, with more recent—say 700-year-old—art painted right over it," says Brad.

❼ Druid Arch This trail shares the same path with popular Chesler Park for the first 2.1 miles. But as soon as it drops down into **Elephant Canyon,** it departs from the more trodden route and strikes up a scenic canyon for another 3.3 miles, passing narrow-leaf yucca, Mormon tea, Indian paintbrush, and seasonal pools of water. (Don't expect much shade on this hike.)

Island in the Sky is "home to the only native herd of desert bighorn sheep remaining in Utah, about 300 to 400 animals," says Chris Dyas, a seasonal park ranger. "Typically all the literature says that they stay below the White Rim, but we are getting more sightings of them atop the mesa. You'll have the best chance of spotting wildlife at places with water, such as **Upheaval Dome,** and close to the visitor center at **Neck Spring.**"

Look for their telltale white behinds on rocky slopes of 45 degrees. In hot summer, they stay close to water sources, and in late November, you might hear the resounding crack of the rams' head-butting contests. "They'll slam into each other about five times an hour," says Dyas, "which is when those big horns and double craniums come in handy."

NOT TO BE MISSED: *Survey the canyons in solitude from White Rim Overlook.* ▸ *Enjoy a spectacular sunset from Murphy Point.* ▸ *Watch for wildlife under the mesa along Neck Spring Loop.* ▸ *Head to the backcountry of The Needles.* ▸ *Strike out via four-wheel drive to the remote corners of The Maze.* ▸ *Spend the night at the Dollhouse.* ▸ *Drift along a river into the heart of the park.*

The same type of banded spires populating Chesler Park guard the canyon walls here. The last third of a mile is a scramble, helped with the aid of a ladder, before reaching the impressive Druid Arch, named after the creators of Stonehenge due to its angular look.

Photographers should get here early—locals say the morning light brings Druid Arch to life.

❽ **Salt Creek** Now that four-wheel-drive vehicles are banned here, prolific amounts of wildlife are returning to this riparian corridor. "You don't expect black bears in the desert, but there's a real possibility of running into one here," says Donaldson.

Obtain a backcountry permit, and take three or four days to hike this convoluted 23-mile-long cultural adventure, allowing time to explore the many cliff dwellings and granaries (a warning: Entry into these sensitive sites is against the law), viewing petroglyphs and pictographs, and other evidence of the Native American's centuries-long tenure. For example, the squash plants they introduced still grow wild in places.

Because backcountry permits are regulated, you won't run into many people. The northern trailhead begins near Cathedral Butte, outside the park. Don't forget to arrange for pick-up at the other end of the trail.

THE MAZE

The Maze can make parts of The Needles or Island in the Sky appear as civilized as Central Park. It's virtually trail-less, with routes usually marked by cairns—if at all. This is about as remote an area as there is in the American West, and any visit should entail a serious amount of planning, gear, and fortitude.

"People out here get in touch with their mortality sometimes," warns Joyce Evans, park ranger.

Just to reach most trailheads requires a high-clearance four-wheel-drive vehicle and three hours of rough-terrain driving from the **Hans Flat Ranger Station** (itself reached only after 46 miles of rough two-wheel-drive dirt road from Utah 24). Your reward? The same sense of satisfaction in self-reliant exploration shared with the early explorers to this region—only about 3,000 people a year make the trek.

❾ **Maze Overlook** The views across this curving labyrinth of interconnected canyons are worth every bump along the 30 miles of pretty rough four-wheel-drive road it takes to reach them (leaving from the Hans Flat Ranger Station).

From the overlook, you can see a frozen maelstrom of sandstone crested by the **Chocolate Drops**—350-million-year-old Organ Rock Shale formations. If the view isn't enough, take the cairned route that drops down into this maze, the portal for multiday backpacking adventures.

"It's not for the faint of heart or people who aren't comfortable scrambling over steep rocky areas," says Gary Cox, park ranger. "You have to lower yourself down to narrow ledges with steep drop-offs, worm yourself through very narrow cracks, and step down footholds carved into the rock."

If you don't have several days, a relatively short 2.3-mile, two-hour scramble down from the overlook brings you to the unforgettable 2,000- to 8,000-year-old **Harvest Scene pictographs.**

"They're very detailed and intricate," says Cox, "and best seen in the late afternoon light."

⑩ The Dollhouse One of the more remote, yet popular, campsites in The Maze (reached via 42 miles of tough four-wheel-drive road), the Dollhouse is named for the dreamlike rockscape.

"Hoodoos [rock formations] in variegated colors surround the campground. It looks like a procession of rock marching off into the desert," says Evans.

It also is the trailhead to three very different day hikes: the **Colorado/Green River Overlook** (9 miles), the **Granary Trail** (2 miles to ancestral Puebloan granaries), and the **Spanish Bottom Trail,** which drops 3 miles down to the Colorado River.

The mysterious ancient stonework along parts of the latter trail is historically significant. "The best information from oral history suggests the stone steps were built by French Basque sheepherders in the 1880s—they had lots of time on their hands—though there is romantic folklore that claims it's a branch of the Old Spanish Trail," says Cox.

The Dollhouse from Mineral Bottom

FLOATING THE GREEN & COLORADO RIVERS

While hiking has its rewards, take a page from Powell's journal and spend four or five days drifting 54 miles through the heart of the park, an option most visitors never consider—other than a few ripples, it's all flat water.

Start at **Mineral Bottom** on the Green River just north of the park, and glide through aptly named **Stillwater Canyon** to the confluence with the Colorado, then travel on another 4 miles to **Spanish Bottom.** (Don't go farther; that thundering is **Cataract Canyon,** home to some of North America's biggest rapids.)

Permits are available for a fee; fire pans and portable toilets are required. Choose any date; there are no daily launch limits. Rent rafts, inflatable kayaks, or canoes in Moab and schedule a pickup by jet boat.

Waterpocket Fold at Panorama Point

CAPITOL REEF

Until recently, Capitol Reef was one of the most underappreciated national parks in the country. But even though its visitor statistics are climbing, a real sense of discovery still awaits those who spend the time to get to know its landscapes. This 381-square-mile park in south-central Utah offers similar geologic wonders to Zion or Arches, but is larger than either, and it occupies an even more isolated and varied setting.

The park may stretch for 100 miles north to south, but like the "Reef" itself—a name given to impassable geologic barriers by the early explorers —it's quite narrow. Its defining feature is the Waterpocket Fold, a 100-mile-long monocline thrust up from the Earth's surface some 65 million years ago. Eroded from 6,800 feet to its current 1,500 feet, this ridge is a real wrinkle in time through which visitors seeking secrets can escape into untouched wilderness.

Year-Round Visitor Center

▦ Visitor Center

*Utah 24, Fruita District,
10 miles east of Torrey*

435-425-3791, nps.gov/care

Egg plums, or Red Astrachan apples. Beginning in mid-June (cherries) until mid-October (apples), visitors will usually find something fruiting. You can sample fruit for free on-site, or climb a ladder and harvest fruit to take home. Each orchard has a self-pay station with scales and a price list.

❶ **Cohab Canyon Trail** Next to the historic Fruita district, near the main campground, this one-way 1.75-mile-long trail is a more intimate alternative to often-crowded **Grand Wash**. You'll see far fewer people on this trail, underscoring its clandestine history. (According to local legend, Mormon polygamists or "cohabitationists" would hide up here to escape raids by the Feds intent on enforcing antipolygamy laws.)

"You're seeing the escarpment of the monocline here, a beautiful rock sequence," says Lori Rome, chief of interpretation. "You can explore three mini-slot canyons, then you go through a gorgeous water-pocketed canyon, and up to two really awesome viewpoints that put you right above Fruita, the orchards, and the river. It's visually stunning."

FRUITA HISTORIC DISTRICT

On the main road through the park, vestiges of a 200-acre settlement offer a taste of Mormon pioneer life in more ways than one. The pioneer remnants here include a one-room schoolhouse, a toolshed and blacksmith shop, a refurbished homestead, and rusting farm machinery. The standout feature is 19 orchards totaling some 3,000 trees, many still watered by the original gravity-fed ditches and pipes the pioneers used.

Some of the trees are antique varieties producing rare fruits you've never tasted: Flemish Beauty pears, Yellow

SCENIC DRIVE

The 8.3-mile Scenic Drive has a small charge per vehicle (payable at a self-pay station); it gives access to two of the park's most popular hiking trails.

Sunflowers and buttes

Tip: Ahead of your visit, download from the park website the excellent *Guide to the Scenic Drive,* a geological tutorial to the rock formations you will pass. Copies are also on sale at the visitor center.

❷ **Grand Wash** This easy 2.2-mile-long canyon trail is a proverbial walk in the park—unless there's a heavy rain, when flash floods can turn it into a death trap.

For 0.5 mile, the 300-foot-high sandstone walls narrow to within 16 feet of each other, an eerie sensation of being enveloped within the stony heart of the **Waterpocket Fold.**

Instead of following the crowd, break off on the side route, marked by signs, up to what looks to be one of the park's largest arches. This is **Cassidy Arch,** named after Butch, who allegedly used Grand Wash on his way back and forth from nearby **Robber's Roost.** As the trail comes out above Cassidy Arch, it's easy to overlook: You have to gaze below where you are standing to spot this span. While you are at it, keep an eye out for desert bighorn sheep, especially in the early morning or evening when they're active and easier to spot.

❸ **Capitol Gorge** Five miles beyond Grand Wash, this gorge was a historic thoroughfare, as seen by its two main attractions. You'll pass numerous but faint Fremont petroglyphs (A.D. 300 to 1300) carved into the north side of the wash.

Just 0.25 mile beyond that is the **Pioneer Register**, where those passing would stop to carve their names into the canyon wall, each trying to outdo the other. Some even tried to write their names with gunshot, but other inscriptions are a tad more elegant, like that of prospector, occasional outlaw, and former member of

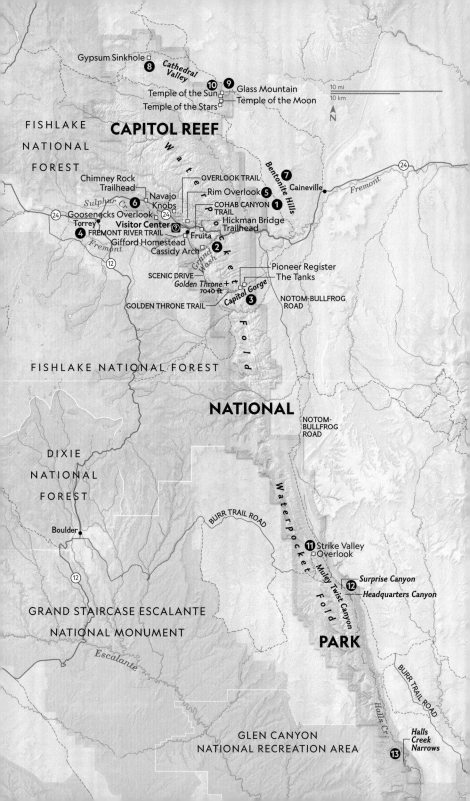

Quantrill's Civil War Raiders Cass Hite (for whom Hite Crossing at Glen Canyon National Recreation Area is named).

Today graffiti is illegal—and an increasing problem on public lands. Please be sure any children (and adults!) in your party do not deface the landscape.

Just beyond the Pioneer Register are **The Tanks**, another name for the many potholes prevalent in the fold, each teeming with its own mini-ecosystem of water striders, algae, and snails.

If you're looking for more exercise than scrambling up to the Tanks, or find the gorge views too confining, try climbing the 4-mile round-trip **Golden Throne Trail** (it begins at the parking lot), which puts you high up Capitol Reef at the base of monolithic **Golden Throne**, one of the prominent points in the park.

UTAH 24

The park, founded as a national monument in 1937, gained in visitation after Utah 24 was built in 1962 through the Fremont River Canyon to replace the old Capitol Gorge wagon road. It made parts of the park readily accessible to the passing public, yet despite the added pressure, it doesn't take much effort to shake the crowds and be immersed in nature's serenity.

❹ **Fremont River Trail** This footpath, just a mile long, begins with an easy stroll past an orchard (bring an apple for the climb), but after 0.5 mile, the crowd thins as the trail steeply ascends 480 feet for some great river views. On the way back, scan for prolific bird life along the river: warblers, Bullock's orioles, black-headed and evening grosbeaks, and the elusive yellow-breasted chat (it's heard at

NOT TO BE MISSED: *Travel the Scenic Drive to Grand Wash and Capitol Gorge.* ▸ *Bird-watch along the Fremont River.* ▸ *Gasp at the view from Rim Overlook.* ▸ *Stand in awe in Cathedral Valley.* ▸ *See the colors of Temple of the Sun.*

all hours, but rarely seen). Keep an eye out for rare golden eagles soaring high above (not to be confused with the more common turkey vulture, which has a V-shape).

❺ **Rim Overlook & the Navajo Knobs** Start from the **Hickman Bridge Trailhead**, where a popular self-guided 0.9-mile trek to a natural bridge begins. You'll pass vegetation such as four-wing saltbush, skunkbush, and dwarf yucca, known for its many uses (such as rope, needles, sandals, baskets, and even shampoo).

After 0.25 mile of switchbacks, break off on the **Overlook Trail**, leaving behind the tourist brigade, as you contour through the ledgelike Kayenta formation and past large black lava boulders to an overlook of **Hickman Bridge.**

Keep going to Rim Overlook (2.3 miles from the trailhead), which serves up another panorama of the visitor center and the Fremont River flowing through Fruita below. It's another 2.4 miles to the Navajo Knobs following cairns across the slickrock.

"I've worked in a lot of national parks in 15 years, and this has got to be one of the best hikes I've been on," says Rome. "You are on top of the world, you really feel the solitude, and there are stunning 360-degree views all the way across the fold to the mountains beyond."

⑥ Sulphur Creek Most visitors head to **Goosenecks Overlook** off Utah 24 for views of Sulphur Creek without realizing there's another, albeit more difficult way to experience this meandering stream. Although not an official, maintained trail, a 5.5-mile-long route follows Sulphur Creek on its way downstream from the trailhead 0.3 mile west of **Chimney Rock** on Utah 24. (Note, there are no park shuttles for this route— either arrange for a second vehicle to meet you or plan on an additional 3-mile hike along Utah 24 to return to your starting point.)

The trail passes through the **Goosenecks**, down three waterfalls, through various strata of rock (including Kaibab limestone, one of the park's oldest layers, as well as the youngest layer of the Grand Canyon), before emerging conveniently at the visitor center.

"It's a great route, and very pretty once you're in the canyon. There are stretches where you walk right in the water," says Rick Stinchfield, volunteer ranger and guidebook author. "And you've got a good light in there, even in the middle of the day, so it's great for photographers."

However, dangerous flash floods are a possibility on this route—check the weather before setting out and change your plans if there's any chance of rain.

CATHEDRAL VALLEY

Empty, desolate, and rich in looming silence, this northern reach of the park is certainly cathedral-like for the awe it evokes. (Even the monolithic towers are referred to as "temples.")

As in any good pilgrimage, to get here involves a bit of challenge in the form of a

Hickman Bridge spanning 133 feet

Temple of the Sun monolith

58-mile dirt road loop that demands high-clearance vehicles and the fording of a river 12 miles east of the visitor center.

"To do the full loop, you have to drive through the Fremont River. That's 10 to 18 inches of flowing water, something most people aren't used to doing," says Rome. Forget about it during spring run-off or during rains, she warns.

Access to Cathedral Valley is possible from the other end of the loop without crossing River Ford, 19 miles east of the visitor center, but you'll miss the **Bentonite Hills.** Plus you'll have to drive back the way you came or exit the park through Forest Service lands.

7 Bentonite Hills While not actually within the park, these barren badlands should be. The surreal, softly molded hills of Morrison formation shale are unique to the Southwest.

"The mounds are absolutely barren, denuded of vegetation," says Rick Stinchfield, "and there are a lot of colors besides gray at work: There are mauves and pinks and blues, and in a good light—

holy cow—it's just incredibly photogenic."

Some believe the Navajo name for the Capitol Reef region is Land of the Sleeping Rainbow, and nowhere is this better illustrated than here. The crinkly clay, which looks like a Berber carpet and is crunchy when dry, swells in the rain, turning into a sticky mud trap—not a good place to be mired. "Even during our busiest time, you might only see three or four vehicles during the entire day," says Stinchfield.

8 Gypsum Sinkhole As this big plug of gypsum (similar to Glass Mountain) dissolved underground, it created a true desert curiosity—a 200-foot-deep sinkhole. Visitors are advised to stay away from the edge for good reason: The area is quite unstable.

9 Glass Mountain This large 15-foot-high mound of selenite crystals glints like glass, and it looks like a sparkly geological platform for the nearby Temple of the Sun. Alas, this plug of gypsum is probably destined to end up someday as a sinkhole.

⑩ Temple of the Sun A monolithic sentinel of eroding Entrada sandstone rises 400 feet from the valley floor in a show of sheer physical prowess. If you're lucky enough to be here at sunset, the sight of its pink and reddish colors igniting in vibrant hues above the darkening valley floor is an unforgettable image, especially with **Temple of the Moon** brightening the background. If there is a secret icon of the American Southwest still to be discovered, this is it.

NOTOM-BULLFROG ROAD

This 45-mile-long road runs parallel to the Waterpocket Fold on its eastern side, connecting Utah 24 to the **Burr Trail Road** (5.3 miles within Capitol Reef) and the **Bullfrog Marina** on Lake Powell. This well-maintained road—it has both dirt and paved sections—dips into the southern half of the park, offering access to some of its rarely visited treasures.

⑪ Upper Muley Twist Canyon Considered by local experts to be the best day hike in the park, this 9-mile loop (15 miles if you lack the high-clearance vehicle needed to make it to the **Strike Valley Overlook** trailhead) serves up beautifully exposed Wingate and Navajo sandstone layers eroded into scenic shapes, including some big arches.

"Half of it is on a high skyline taking in the most stunning geologic scenery you've ever seen in your life, then you drop down in the Muleys, a narrow, winding, long canyon rimmed with water pockets," says Rome.

This is a route, not a maintained trail, so watch for cairns. While you're at it, keep an eye (and ear) out for the local bird life: ash-throated flycatchers, warblers, western kingbirds, and that feisty icon of the Colorado Plateau, the canyon wren.

⑫ Headquarters & Surprise Canyons These two family-friendly spots offer a taste of canyoneering in slotlike canyons (no equipment needed). Each is a moderate 2-mile round-trip hike, and the two are often combined into a half-day adventure.

Kids in particular like to scramble, squeeze, and scurry through the narrow clefts of the **Waterpocket Fold,** which allows visitors of any age to go as far as your canyoneering skills take you.

⑬ Halls Creek Narrows If Headquarters Canyon is for families, this remote narrows is for expert hikers only, as it requires a 22-mile, two-to-four-day trek to experience its 3-mile-long, tunnel-like slot. This often means wading in spots. Needless to say, thorough preparation and planning is necessary and well worth the time.

LOCAL INTELLIGENCE

The 1908 Gifford Homestead, in the heart of the Fruita valley, is a museum-like still-life of early Mormon pioneer days, but it's frequently overlooked by visitors, who miss out on the homemade pie sold in the old kitchen, not to mention the locally made scones, fresh ice cream, jellies, and dried fruit. But don't wait for the afternoon. "The best time for pie is 8 a.m.," advises Lori Rome, chief of interpretation. "That's when it arrives fresh and hot from the oven."

An ever changing play of light graces the canyon

GRAND CANYON

To understand the number of people who visit the Grand Canyon annually, picture all the passengers boarding airplanes for an entire year at a good-size airport—say, Kansas City International. In hard figures, that's close to five million yearly visitors.

The magnet for these journeys is what 19th-century explorer John Wesley Powell called the "most sublime spectacle on the earth"—the iconic mile-deep gorge that ranks among the world's most beautiful and most renowned geological features.

The Grand Canyon's climate and topography mean that the great majority of visitors arrive during a seven-month warmer weather period and gather at a limited number of sites. The crowding that often results can degrade what should be an inspirational experience. The secret is to find alternatives to the most popular roadside viewpoints.

Year-Round Visitor Centers

▪ Grand Canyon Visitor Center
*South Rim by Mather Point,
off South Entrance Road*

▪ Backcountry Information Center
*Village historic district,
east of Maswik Lodge*

▪ Verkamp's Visitor Center
*East of El Tovar Hotel and
Hopi House*

▪ Desert View Visitor Center &
Bookstore
*25 miles east of Grand Canyon
Village on South Rim*

Seasonal Visitor Center

▪ North Rim Visitor Center
*Grand Canyon Lodge, adjacent
to the parking lot on Bright
Angel Point*

928-638-7888, nps.gov/grca

| SOUTH RIM

It's simple to explain how to escape crowds at Grand Canyon: Descend into the canyon from the "rim"—the flattish plateau that surrounds the mammoth gorge—or travel to the North Rim.

The great majority of visitors enjoy the spectacular views down into the canyon without exploring its depths, and only about 10 percent of visitors leave the main tourist facilities on the South Rim to go to the north side of the park.

You shouldn't underestimate the physical effort and planning required to visit the inner canyon, however. Trails descend steeply, and in summer temperatures rise rapidly as elevation decreases. (The canyon floor at the Colorado River, at the bottom of the chasm, may be 25 degrees hotter than the rim.)

Every year park rangers have to rescue scores of people who hiked down a trail into the canyon without proper clothing or footwear, without enough food or (especially) water, or who didn't understand that it takes at least twice as much time and energy to ascend back to the rim as it takes to go down. The standard rule for a hike into the canyon is to turn around when you have drunk one-third of your water and/or spent one-third of the time you have available.

As for advice on visiting the North Rim: Although you can see it from the South Rim's Grand Canyon Village—it's an average of about 10 miles away—the

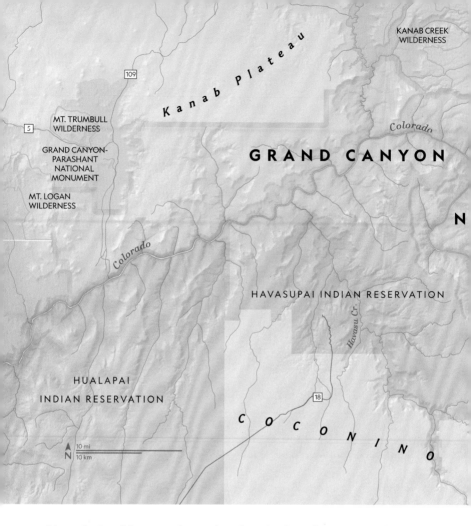

drive to the Grand Canyon Lodge area is 215 miles and requires at least five hours. Hiking from the South Rim to the North Rim is only for extremely fit people who have made advance arrangements to spend one or, preferably, two nights in the inner canyon. Park rangers say that hiking down to the **Colorado River** and back up in one day is more difficult than running a marathon.

❶ East to South Kaibab Trailhead
Grand Canyon experts do know a few ways, though, to avoid the most concentrated of the South Rim crowds, ranging from simple strolls to strenuous hikes. Take **Mather Point,** for example, the iconic spot where the **Grand Canyon Visitor Center** is located. Thousands of people enjoy the magnificent view here daily in summer; of those who walk part of the 13-mile **Rim Trail**, most head west toward the developments around Grand Canyon Village.

Instead, walk east along the easy paved trail toward the South Kaibab Trailhead. You won't be alone, but you'll have much less company along this path while you savor views into the canyon that are just as fine as elsewhere.

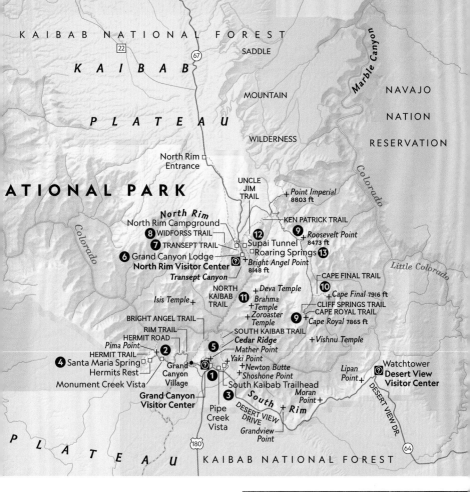

KAIBAB NATIONAL FOREST

KAIBAB

PLATEAU

[22]

[67]

SADDLE

MOUNTAIN

WILDERNESS

NATIONAL PARK

North Rim Entrance

UNCLE JIM TRAIL

+Point Imperial 8803 ft

Marble Canyon

NAVAJO

NATION

RESERVATION

North Rim

North Rim Campground

8 WIDFORSS TRAIL

7 TRANSEPT TRAIL

6 Grand Canyon Lodge
North Rim Visitor Center

Transept Canyon

KEN PATRICK TRAIL

12 □Supai Tunnel

□Roaring Springs **13**

9 *Roosevelt Point* 8473 ft

+*Bright Angel Point* 8148 ft

Colorado

Little Colorado

Isis Temple +

BRIGHT ANGEL TRAIL

RIM TRAIL

HERMIT ROAD

Pima Point

HERMIT TRAIL

4 Santa Maria Spring

Hermits Rest

Monument Creek Vista

NORTH KAIBAB TRAIL

11 +*Deva Temple*
+*Brahma*
+*Temple*
+*Zoroaster*
+*Temple*

CAPE FINAL TRAIL

10 +*Cape Final* 7916 ft

CLIFF SPRINGS TRAIL

CAPE ROYAL TRAIL

9 +*Cape Royal* 7865 ft

SOUTH KAIBAB TRAIL

Cedar Ridge

—*Mather Point*

+*Yaki Point*

2

5

+*Newton Butte*
+*Shoshone Point*

South Kaibab Trailhead

Grand Canyon Village

Grand Canyon Visitor Center

3

1

Pipe Creek Vista

South Rim

DESERT VIEW DRIVE

Grandview Point

+*Vishnu Temple*

Lipan Point+

Moran Point+

Watchtower **Desert View Visitor Center**

DESERT VIEW DR.

[180]

PLATEAU

KAIBAB NATIONAL FOREST

[64]

Options abound here: Walk 1.4 miles to the **Pipe Creek Vista** and catch the free shuttle back to Mather Point, or continue another 0.8 mile to the South Kaibab Trailhead and catch the bus there. Of course, you can walk back to appreciate the vistas from another direction.

2 Trail From Monument Creek Vista to Pima Point Andy Pearce, a park education specialist, recommends another less traveled section of the Rim Trail. It's reached via **Hermit Road**, which is closed to private vehicles March through November but is served by the shuttle.

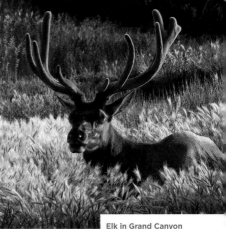

Elk in Grand Canyon

"Out near the end of the road there's a segment of the trail that's really nice, and that receives quite a bit less use than other parts of the Rim Trail," he says. "It's from Monument Creek Vista to Pima Point, and then on to **Hermits Rest**. If you do the whole thing it's about 2.8 miles, but Pima Point provides a midway shuttle-bus stop if you want to do half the hike."

Pearce points out that rising early is always a great way to avoid crowds and feel like you have the park to yourself. "The Hermits Rest shuttle bus starts running before sunrise," he says. "For anybody who's on it early in the morning, before 8:30 a.m. or so, it can be really quiet out there, even in the middle of the summer. Get up and take in the sunrise and have alone time on a trail that by ten or eleven o'clock is just packed."

❸ Desert View Drive The 25-mile road that runs east from Grand Canyon Village to the famed **Watchtower** is known for popular overlooks such as **Grandview**, **Moran**, and **Lipan Points**. One sure way to beat the crowds while enjoying the fantastic views from this part of the South Rim is to visit **Shoshone Point**, a highlight for former park staff member Richard Ullmann.

"This overlook is not shown on some maps of the Grand Canyon," he says. "The views are spectacular and panoramic. You can clearly see the Colorado River and glimpse the Desert View Watchtower along the rim some 20 miles away. There are rarely more than a few folks out there at any given time."

Via special permit, the national park makes Shoshone Point available for weddings and other celebrations (Ullmann's

own wedding took place there). When such events are taking place, other visitors should respect the privacy of those using the site.

The main reason for Shoshone Point's solitude, though, is access. To reach it, park along Desert View Drive at an unmarked side road with a locked gate 1.2 miles east of the Yaki Point Road. Then you must hike a mile along a dirt road to the point.

"The walk along the road is pleasant, winding through ponderosa pine forest," Ullmann says. "I often see deer and elk along the way." At the point, **Newton Butte** is prominent right below, while in the distance such formations as **Zoroaster, Brahma,** and **Vishnu Temples** are visible.

Educator Pearce adds a simple way to avoid the crowds along the rest of Desert View Drive's overlooks: Stop at some of the unnamed overlooks instead.

"It's funny," he says, "you put a sign with a name on it at a viewpoint and everybody thinks it's somehow going to be a lot more spectacular. In reality, a lot of those viewpoints without names are just as beautiful. Even in the busy part of the year, maybe a handful of other people stop there, and those places don't have the crowds of the marked viewpoints."

As you're traveling Desert View Drive, keep a watch for "roving rangers": These are park interpreters who station themselves at viewpoints. You won't regret stopping for informal chats with these helpful folks. It's a great chance to ask questions, learn about wildlife and geology, and generally get more out of your visit to this stunning national park.

Taking in the view along the Kaibab Trail

Grand Canyon Lodge at sunset

DOWN INTO THE CANYON

The most popular paths down into the canyon are the **Bright Angel** (24.8 miles) and **South Kaibab Trails** (7 miles). If you have the physical ability to descend into (and ascend out of) the canyon and would like a less crowded experience, consider the **Hermit Trail** (7 miles round-trip). The trailhead is reached by a brief walk from Hermits Rest at the end of Hermit Road.

If you're planning a longer hike and want to camp overnight in the canyon, you will need a permit from the park's backcountry office.

❹ **Santa Maria Spring** The Hermit Trail is not an easy walk. It descends steeply from the rim as it makes switchbacks down the canyon wall. Developed a century ago to serve a tourist camp, it has not been fully maintained and in places has eroded significantly.

Nonetheless, with proper gear and water, and by taking things slowly, moderately fit people can enjoy an inner-canyon day hike by walking to Santa Maria Spring, 2.2 miles one way. (Keep right at two trail intersections.)

There are notable views here, and sharp-eyed hikers may spot fossil reptile tracks in the rocks along the trail. Santa Maria Springs is 1,640 feet in elevation below the trailhead. The top portion of the Hermit Trail faces west, and so it is the first South Rim trail to be free of ice in springtime.

❺ **Cedar Ridge Hike** For many people, the best way to get a taste of the inner canyon is the ranger-led Cedar Ridge Hike, conducted daily from spring through fall. Beginning around 8 a.m. (check at visitor center for exact time) at

NOT TO BE MISSED: *Learn from the "roving rangers" along Desert View Drive.* ▸ *Stop at unmarked viewpoints for remarkable vistas without the crowds.* ▸ *Catch the early shuttle to Hermits Rest and enjoy a spectacular sunrise in solitude.* ▸ *Descend the canyon on the ranger-led Cedar Ridge hike from the North Rim.* ▸ *Take in the view from the Grand Canyon Lodge, then wander out to Bright Angel Point.* ▸ *Walk to Cape Final among the ponderosa pines.*

the South Kaibab Trailhead (take the free shuttle bus), this 3-mile round-trip hike takes three to four hours to descend and ascend 1,140 feet.

The ranger guide will check to make sure that all participants have proper footwear and at least two quarts of water. It goes without saying that the vistas along the trail are inspirational (one spot along the way is called **Ooh Aah Point**), and the guide will point out rock layers— Kaibab limestone, Toroweap formation, Coconino sandstone, and Hermit shale— on the descent.

Though more crowded than the Hermit Trail, this section is also an excellent day hike for prepared canyon newcomers to do on their own.

NORTH RIM

As noted above, simply by traveling to the North Rim of the Grand Canyon you're distancing yourself from 90 percent of the visitors to the national park. One thousand feet higher than the South Rim, the North Rim is closed to vehicles from around November to mid-May, depending on snowfall. (Intrepid hikers and cross-country skiers can enter in winter.) Lodging and other park facilities are also closed in winter.

Apart from less visitation, the North Rim offers other enticing aspects. It's cooler in summer than the South Rim and presents many more opportunities for relatively doable day hikes. Because of the general slant of the plateaus surrounding Grand Canyon and the resulting erosion, many of the park's most beautiful and iconic buttes (the "temples" of fanciful historical nomenclature) are closer to the North Rim than to the South.

❻ Grand Canyon Lodge A must first stop is the 1937 Grand Canyon Lodge, perched on the canyon edge and designed to offer visitors a "surprise view" through large windows in the Sun Room. Then, crowds or no crowds, it's time for the 0.25-mile walk on a paved trail to **Bright Angel Point.** Located on a narrow point between **Roaring Springs** and **Transept Canyon,** Bright Angel combines accessibility with one of the most awe-inspiring panoramas of the entire park.

Cactus in bloom

In 2011, Grand Canyon National Park experimented with the rental of bicycles. The effort went well enough that the park contracted with a concessionaire to continue the business on the South Rim. This offers visitors a new way to see the park, traveling, for example, along the paved **Greenway Trail,** which is the Rim Trail from Monument Creek Vista 2.8 miles west to Hermits Rest, as well as Hermit Road (7 miles), which is closed to private vehicles for most of the year. On a bike, you can cover more ground and see more sights than by hiking.

Don't hurry hiking to the point; there are views into both side canyons and visible fossils along the way. Although the Colorado River can't be seen from here, look for Brahma, **Deva,** and Zoroaster Temples, listen for the sound of Roaring Springs 3,000 feet below, and peer across the canyon to the distant **San Francisco Peaks,** including the highest point in Arizona.

❼ Transept Trail This trail provides a lot of scenery for little effort. Running just 1.5 miles between Grand Canyon Lodge and the main North Rim Campground, it looks down into the canyon for which it's named.

A similar but longer walk overlooking Roaring Springs Canyon is the 5-mile round-trip that begins on the **Ken Patrick Trail** and then branches off on the **Uncle Jim Trail** loop, leading to yet another canyon vista worth a few dozen photos.

❽ Widforss Trail For a longer hike and more solitude, drive north from the lodge area a little more than a mile and turn west on a side road to the trailhead for the Widforss Trail.

This is an out-and-back trail that makes for a 10-mile round-trip if you go all the way to a spot on the canyon rim about 2 miles west of Bright Angel Point.

There are nice views into **Transept Canyon** during the first couple of miles, so it's rewarding to hike even part of this path. In fall, the aspens can be colorful here.

❾ Roosevelt Point & Cape Royal Of course, if you've made the effort to reach the North Rim, you're going to want to drive to **Point Imperial** and Cape Royal, two famed viewpoints reached by road east of the lodge-campground area.

Point Imperial is the highest spot on either rim of the Grand Canyon (8,803 feet), and is renowned as a place at which to watch sunrise.

You probably won't be alone here even at dawn, but the experience is worth it. The **Roosevelt Point** and **Cape Royal Trails** are short, easy, popular, and inspiring.

❿ Cape Final Trail To escape the crowds at the major viewpoints, hike the 4-mile round-trip Cape Final Trail (an abandoned but easy-to-walk road).

"Cape Final is a really good example of what a ponderosa pine forest should look like," says one of Grand Canyon's interpretive rangers, Robin Tellis. "These days, with people keeping fires tamed, ponderosa forests have changed. A true ponderosa forest has a lot of space and few trees. Going down the Cape

Final Trail you can see big open areas with large ponderosas. And the views at **Cape Final** are truly some of the best."

Many longtime Grand Canyon travelers, in fact, consider this their favorite of the North Rim viewpoints.

⓫ North Kaibab Trail The only maintained trail down to the inner canyon from the North Rim is the North Kaibab Trail. As noted elsewhere, cautions apply concerning strenuousness and thorough preparation. The route starts out at a heady elevation of 8,250 feet. Use your common sense.

⓬ Supai Tunnel For a taste of the north side of the canyon below the rim, you can make the 1.5-mile round-trip hike to Coconino Overlook, which descends only 800 feet from the trailhead.

Tellis says that continuing to Supai Tunnel (4 miles round-trip, 650 feet in elevation change) takes you under trees, so it's shaded. Once you go through the tunnel, the scenery changes: The trees go away to reveal a great view. The Supai formation of red rock can be seen from the trail above or at this spot.

⓭ Roaring Springs Physically fit hikers who begin the trip very early in the morning might consider a trek to the cascades at Roaring Springs. Remember though, as a 9.4-mile round-trip with an elevation loss and gain of 3,050 feet, this is a journey only for the fit, prepared, and experienced.

Autumnal aspens on the North Rim

Cliff Palace with 150 rooms

MESA VERDE

Around the same time the Roman Empire was on its last legs and western Europe was sliding into the Dark Ages, an entirely different civilization was moving onto a broad, flat tableland that would later be called Mesa Verde. Soaring more than 8,500 feet above sea level, the sloping mesa *(cuesta)* provided an ideal perch for the ancestral Puebloan—a source of abundant food, shelter, and spiritual inspiration that would evolve into one of the richest archaeological caches of the American Southwest.

Mesa Verde National Park harbors nearly 5,000 ancient sites, including some of the nation's biggest and most impressive cliff dwellings—multi-story stone villages where hundreds of people once lived, worked, and worshipped in underground kivas. Residents left Mesa Verde by 1300. In 1906, President Theodore Roosevelt named the area the first national park protecting human, not just natural, treasures.

NORTH RIM

Although all visitors must pass through the park's northern escarpment to reach the renowned archaeological sites, the North Rim had long been overlooked and underused.

That changed in fall 2012 with the opening of the **Mesa Verde Visitor and Research Center,** just off US 160 near the entrance station. The complex is a must stop for park maps, brochures, and information. Along with the Chapin Museum and Durango Welcome Center, this is the place to sign up for popular ranger-guided tours of **Cliff Palace, Balcony House,** and **Long House.**

Year-Round Visitor Center

■ Visitor and Research Center
Off US 160, Park Entrance Station

970-529-4465, nps.gov/meve

Beyond the visitor center, the main road (built in 1914) crawls up the sheer face of the North Rim past the popular **Mancos Valley** and **Montezuma Valley** overlooks, as well as **Morefield Campground,** the only camping facility in the park.

But the rest of the North Rim remains refreshingly vacant. There are no major archaeological remains in the area, just sublime nature and the park's best animal viewing.

❶ **Point Lookout Trail** "Point Lookout provides great views of the surrounding landscape and the opportunity to see how modern cultures have shaped this long-inhabited area. It climbs to the top of that iconic formation seen from the park entrance," says Cristy Brown, the park's public information officer. The 2.2-mile path starts at the north end of the amphitheater parking area.

❷ **Prater Ridge Trail** Brown says the North Rim is also the best place for wildlife. "The area from the campground to the Montezuma Valley overlook provides the chance to see any of the park's large mammals. And in the fall, the shrubs and trees offer a patchwork mosaic of reds, yellows, oranges, and browns."

The chance of spotting critters is better away from the main road, especially along the 7.8-mile Prater Ridge Trail, which loops through the woodlands west of the campground.

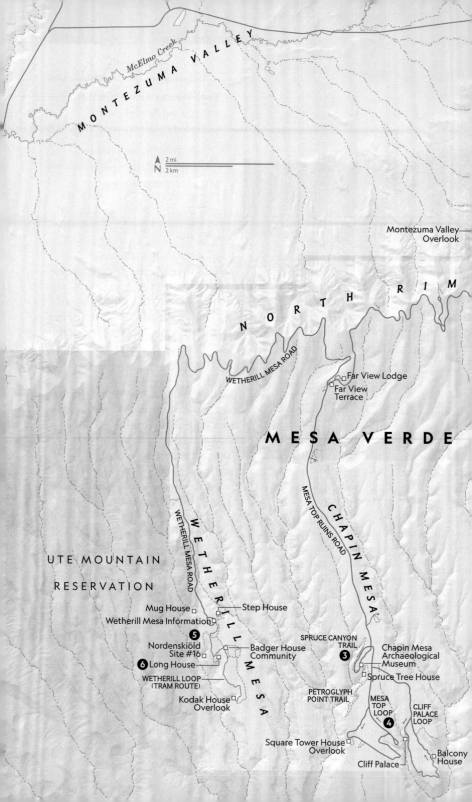

McElmo Creek

MONTEZUMA VALLEY

2 mi
N
2 km

Montezuma Valley
Overlook

NORTH RIM

WETHERILL MESA ROAD

Far View Lodge
Far View
Terrace

MESA VERDE

UTE MOUNTAIN

RESERVATION

WETHERILL MESA ROAD

WETHERILL MESA

MESA TOP RUINS ROAD

CHAPIN MESA

Mug House
Wetherill Mesa Information

Step House

5

Nordenskiöld
Site #16

6 Long House

WETHERILL LOOP
(TRAM ROUTE)

Badger House
Community

SPRUCE CANYON
TRAIL

3

Chapin Mesa
Archaeological
Museum

Spruce Tree House

PETROGLYPH
POINT TRAIL

MESA
TOP
LOOP

CLIFF
PALACE
LOOP

4

Kodak House
Overlook

Square Tower House
Overlook

Cliff Palace

Balcony
House

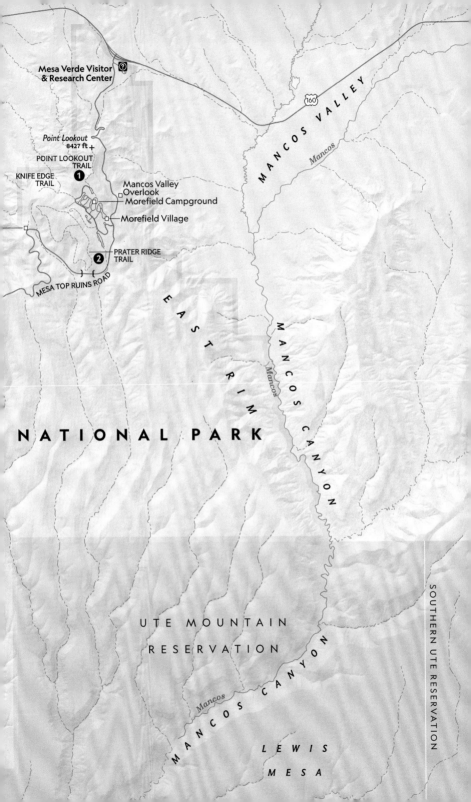

Mesa Verde Visitor
& Research Center

Point Lookout
8427 ft +
POINT LOOKOUT
TRAIL
❶

KNIFE EDGE
TRAIL

Mancos Valley
Overlook
Morefield Campground

Morefield Village

PRATER RIDGE
TRAIL
❷

MESA TOP RUINS ROAD

MANCOS VALLEY

160

Mancos

EAST RIM

MANCOS CANYON

Mancos

NATIONAL PARK

UTE MOUNTAIN

RESERVATION

Mancos

MANCOS CANYON

SOUTHERN UTE RESERVATION

LEWIS

MESA

FAR VIEW

At Far View, the main road through the park branches into forks that lead due south to **Chapin Mesa** and west toward **Wetherill Mesa**. Across the road is **Far View Lodge**, the park's only hotel. Even if you're not staying overnight, the lodge terrace is the place to check out the day-time view reaching four states or the star-studded night sky.

"There really isn't a bad time of day to sit on the patio here," muses Brown. "Sunsets are breathtaking, incoming thunderstorms are powerful, and the views are stunning with the changing light and shadows."

If you haven't eaten dinner, pop into the **Metate Room** for regional dishes that include ingredients that would have been used by the ancestral Puebloan.

CHAPIN MESA

Chapin Mesa has long been the park's focal point, both for its grand views of the **Four Corners** region and its renowned archaeological sites. Hundreds of artifacts from these sites are on display in the **Chapin Mesa Archaeological Museum**, built in 1924 and a historic structure in its own right. From just behind the museum, a 0.5-mile trail leads down to **Spruce Tree House**, one of the most notable cliff dwellings, tucked beneath a rock overhang.

3 Spruce Canyon Trail Most visitors head straight back up the cliff via the main trail. An alternative route back to the museum parking lot is the Spruce Canyon Trail, which can be combined with **Petroglyph Point Trail** into a nearly 6-mile jaunt through gorgeous mesa country.

4 Cliff Palace & Mesa Top Loops East of the museum are scenic roads that lead to more rewarding overlooks and ancient high-rise dwellings.

Both Cliff Palace and **Balcony House**—which can only be visited on pre-ticketed, ranger-guided tours—are situated along the 6-mile Cliff Palace Loop. Mesa Top Loop (6 miles) meanders through the piñon-juniper woodland to 12 pullouts with viewpoints of the landscape or archaeological sites.

LOCAL INTELLIGENCE

Mesa Verde's ancient inhabitants were part of a much larger cultural zone that now includes nearby sites in southwestern Colorado, such as **Hovenweep National Monument,** once home to more than 2,500 people; the **Canyon of the Ancients National Monument,** used or inhabited by humans for 10,000 years; and **Ute Mountain Tribal Park** on the Indian reservation of the same name. "All offer fantastic sites and exhibits to learn about the history of the ancestral Puebloan people," says Cristy Brown, public information officer.

Bordering Mesa Verde to the west and south, Ute Mountain Tribal Park is a rich store of ancient sites rarely visited because of their remoteness and rugged terrain. Starting from the visitor center in Towaoc, Colorado, tribal guides take visitors on half- and full-day tours to secluded cliff dwellings including **Eagle Nest House** in **Lion Canyon** as well as on once-a-year hikes to such almost-inaccessible cliff dwellings as **Casa Blanca** and **Casa Colorado.**

One of these looks down on **Square Tower House,** which "really demonstrates the craftsmanship capabilities of the ancestral Puebloan people," Brown marvels. "It's 27 feet tall—and built with stone tools!" It can be visited as part of the Park Service's summer "Backcountry Hikes" program launched to open a few of Mesa Verde's more fragile archaeological sites on a rotating basis to small, guided groups of ten people or fewer.

The trail, which descends 100 feet into the canyon, requires clambering over boulders, scaling three ladders, and slipping past steep drop-offs. The reward at the other end is a cliff dwelling that includes a four-story **Crow's Nest** and an original, intact kiva roof.

Another destination is **Mug House** on Wetherill Mesa. "It's tucked behind a corner in an alcove," Brown says. "So when visitors come around the corner, they really are 'discovering' it for the first time." Check the park's website for what ruins are open during your visit.

WETHERILL MESA

Open to the public as far back as 1973, the Wetherill Mesa area embraces some of the park's most impressive cliff dwellings, yet is visited by only about a quarter of the people who enter the park each year.

Spruce Tree House reconstructed kiva

Accessible from early May to late October, Wetherill Mesa Road rambles from Far View to the Wetherill Mesa information kiosk parking lot and picnic area. From there, visitors can walk or bicycle the **Wetherill Loop**—including a look down at secluded **Kodak House**—or strike off on several self-guided tours. The more popular of these options are the short hike to **Step House,** with its restored pithouse and cliff dwelling, and the wandering path to the **Badger House Community** mesa-top sites.

❺ Nordenskiold Site No. 16 It's the lesser used trails that reveal the richness of Wetherill. Named after a Swedish aristocrat turned archaeologist who undertook the first extensive survey of Mesa Verde in 1891, this one-mile round-trip leads to an elongated cliff dwelling with around 50 rooms.

❻ Long House The mesa's star attraction is Long House, the second largest and least visited of the park's five major cliff dwellings and accessible via pre-ticketed, ranger-led tours (summer only). It has more than 150 rooms spread across three levels.

NOT TO BE MISSED: *See four states at once from the patio of Far View Lodge.* ▸ *Expand your knowledge at the Chapin Mesa Archaeological Museum.* ▸ *Stop often along the Cliff Place and Mesa Top loop roads.* ▸ *Take a "backcountry hike" to a fragile site.*

Landscape littered with 225-million-year-old petrified trees

PETRIFIED FOREST

Of all our national parks, Petrified Forest surely ranks among the most susceptible to the dreaded drive-through visit. This situation results from the park's layout: A 28-mile road runs its length, with separate and convenient entrances and exits off busy I-40. It's easy for a visitor to cruise through, stopping to gaze over the Painted Desert and walk a short trail among the giant logs, before returning to the freeway. They are thus missing the secrets waiting in this 346-square-mile expanse of northern Arizona's Colorado Plateau region.

Instead, take time to explore. Start with a fascinating geological past (which created the colors that inspired the name Painted Desert as well as the petrified logs) then add fossilized prehistoric creatures, archaeological sites of ancient peoples, and diverse animals and plants.

PARK ROAD, NORTHERN SECTION

Just north of I-40, enter the **Painted Desert Visitor Center** to watch the film "More Spectacular Than Ever," shown every half-hour. After this overview of the park you're ready to start exploring—but first, take time for one more stop less than 2 miles north: the **Painted Desert Inn.** Built in 1924 on legendary Route 66, it was once home to the famed "Harvey Girls," waitresses who served travelers in the mid-20th century. The former inn, which features murals by Hopi artist Fred Kabotie, is now a museum with space for cultural demontrations.

Year-Round Visitor Center
Painted Desert Visitor Center
North Entrance, off I-40

928-524-6228, nps.gov/pefo

1 Black Forest Because of the nature of Petrified Forest's landscape and layout, getting off the tourist route often involves a bit of cross-country travel, and that means using basic backcountry equipment and skills. Wear good boots and a hat, take plenty of water and sunscreen, and carry a map and compass or GPS—and know how to use them. Even though some off-trail travel is fairly simple, it's always better to use too much caution than not enough. If in doubt, ask a park ranger for advice.

Your first chance to leave the beaten path begins at a trailhead behind the Painted Desert Inn. Seeing what Bill Parker, park paleontologist, calls "one of the most scenic places in the park" requires a 5-mile round-trip hike north into the Painted Desert—a small challenge with a big reward. It's about a mile to the usually dry **Lithodendron Wash,** and about 0.5 mile farther to the petrified logs of the **Angels Garden** area.

"The Black Forest is one of the largest accumulations of petrified wood in the park, but it's seen by only a small percentage of park visitors because of its remoteness," Parker says. This moderately strenuous route requires an awareness of the weather, as Lithodendron Wash should not be crossed if it's raining or threatening rain; consult a ranger if you're unsure of conditions.

You'll be glad you made this hike when you're standing amid massive petrified tree trunks, surrounded by the

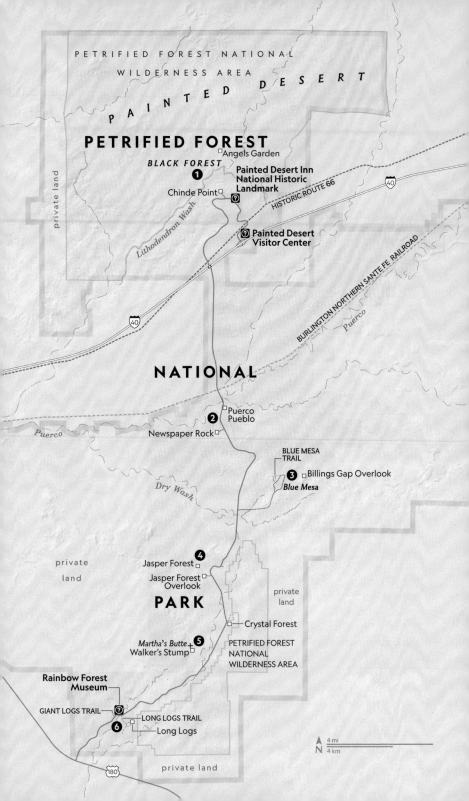

PETRIFIED FOREST NATIONAL

WILDERNESS AREA

PAINTED DESERT

PETRIFIED FOREST

Angels Garden

BLACK FOREST

1

Chinde Point

Painted Desert Inn
National Historic
Landmark

HISTORIC ROUTE 66

40

Painted Desert
Visitor Center

private land

Lithodendron Wash

BURLINGTON NORTHERN SANTE FE RAILROAD

Puerco

40

NATIONAL

Puerco
Pueblo

2

Newspaper Rock

Puerco

BLUE MESA
TRAIL

3 Billings Gap Overlook

Blue Mesa

Dry Wash

private
land

Jasper Forest **4**

Jasper Forest
Overlook

PARK

private
land

Crystal Forest

PETRIFIED FOREST
NATIONAL
WILDERNESS AREA

Martha's Butte **5**
Walker's Stump

Rainbow Forest
Museum

GIANT LOGS TRAIL

LONG LOGS TRAIL

6

Long Logs

N 4 mi
4 km

180

private land

deep reds and ochers of rugged land-forms. A free permit is required for over-night camping.

② Puerco Pueblo & Newspaper Rock
Back on the park road, continue across old Route 66, I-40, and the Sante Fe railroad line, stopping often to admire the Painted Desert scenery. Stop, too, at popular Puerco Pueblo to see the remains of a 100-room settlement of the ancestral Puebloan people, last occupied in the 14th century.

Another favorite is Newspaper Rock, with boulders covered in hundreds of petroglyphs. Resist the urge to add your mark—it's illegal. And remember to look, not touch. The oil from your hands can damage the petroglyphs.

③ Billings Gap Overlook Take the side road to the **Blue Mesa Trail**, about a mile loop into an otherworldly landscape of conical, multilayered hills formed of clay and sandstone. The moderately strenu-ous trail is well worth walking (the upper portion is flat and easy).

To see a less visited area, park at the fourth pullout on the loop road and strike out east along the northern edge of steep-sided **Blue Mesa**. A hike of less than a mile leads to the Billings Gap Overlook, which supervisory park ranger Sarah Herve notes offers "great opportu-nities to see the diverse landscape, from badlands to grasslands, petrified wood to wildflowers." (A gentle reminder: All petrified wood and artifacts should be left in place for future visitors.)

Striations on Blue Mesa

On your return, head southwest from the overlook about 0.4 mile for a view into the picturesque amphitheater, naturally created by the elements. This walk, though not difficult, is unmarked, so take normal backcountry precautions.

PARK ROAD, SOUTHERN SECTION

The Jasper Forest to Long Logs Trail section of the north-south park road contains the majority of the park's petrified wood. This ancient wood comes from trees that grew here more than 200 million years ago.

❹ Jasper Forest Back on the main road, it's about 3 miles south from the Blue Mesa Trail side road to the **Jasper Forest Overlook.** Most visitors simply stand and admire the view, but there's a new trail from this parking lot that gives a way to see what Parker calls "an incredible

NOT TO BE MISSED: *Enter the Painted Desert via the Black Forest.* ▸ *Puzzle over petroglyphs at Newspaper Rock.* ▸ *Take in badlands and grasslands from the Billings Gap Overlook.* ▸ *Marvel at the remains of trees some 200 million years old along the old Jasper Forest Road.*

garden of petrified wood" much more closely.

When facing the overlook from the parking lot, walk to your right (east) toward the main road. You'll see a path leading to what was once the Jasper Forest Road, which you can now hike into the forest. You will still see bits of asphalt along the way, as well as culverts.

Jasper Forest was once called First Forest, because it was the first group of petrified logs encountered by visitors

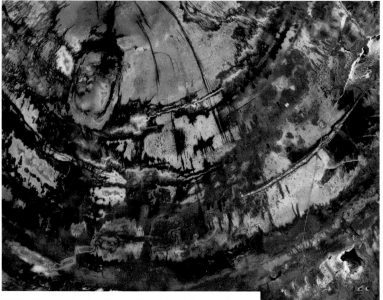

Petrified wood, cut and polished with intricate patterns and colors

Petrified logs along the Long Logs Trail

heading south by wagon from the rail station 6 miles away.

❺ Martha's Butte About 1.8 miles south of the **Crystal Forest** parking area is another opportunity for a solitary and rewarding walk. Park at the bridge over Dry Wash and look northwest for Martha's Butte, prominent on the horizon 0.8 mile away as the crow flies. To reach it, walk the bed of the wash north about 0.7 mile, then strike out northwest another 0.5 mile. You'll see petrified wood and, if you're lucky, fossils. You might spot artifacts from historic and prehistoric times, too.

Check about 100 yards southeast of Martha's Butte for **Walker's Stump**. It's not really a stump, but a petrified log that was buried upright by a flowing stream, then uncovered by erosion millions of years later.

❻ Giant Logs & Long Logs Trails South on the park road you'll find several must-see sites, including the **Rainbow Forest Museum**, with exhibits including a diorama of some of the extinct reptiles that lived in this region tens of millions of years ago, and examples of fossils found in the park. The museum sits in the **Rainbow Forest**, one of four major concentrations of petrified logs the park calls "forests."

Nearby are the Long Logs and Giant Logs Trails, both easy walks leading to some of the park's most impressive displays of large petrified trees. "**Old Faithful**," on the Giant Logs Trail, is nearly 10 feet in diameter. The great concentration of logs on the Long Logs Trail is thought to have resulted from a logjam in an ancient stream. Some of the logs seen here are more than 100 feet long.

The Virgin River flowing through sandstone walls in autumn

ZION

Although other great canyons awe with sheer size, Zion, a relatively small national park, wows in a much more subtle manner, with artistry rather than magnitude, rock canvases and stone sculptures that seem crafted by some ancient Michelangelo rather than the whim and fancy of nature.

The Mormon settlers who pioneered southern Utah from the 1850s to the 1860s thought the canyon was heaven sent. They named it after a biblical place of peace and endowed many of its natural features with spiritual appellations such as Great White Throne, Angels Landing, and Altar of Sacrifice.

The forces of nature—in particular floods—kept the canyon from being heavily settled and retained its atmosphere of secrecy. President William Howard Taft gave it federal protection as Mukuntuweap National Monument in 1909; ten years later it was renamed and elevated to national park status.

Year-Round Visitor Centers

- Zion Canyon Visitor Center & Backcountry Desk
  South Entrance, Zion–Mount Carmel Highway
- Kolob Canyons Visitor Center
  I-15, exit 40, East Kolob Canyon

435-772-3256, nps.gov/zion

landmarks, including **Emerald Pools, Zion Lodge,** and **The Grotto.**

At the first stop, the **Human History Museum,** a park film provides a good introduction to the area. The last stop lets visitors off at the start of the popular **Riverside Walk,** which snakes around the towering **Temple of Sinawava** to the lower end of **The Narrows.**

❶ **The Narrows (bottom-up)** Located at the upper (north) end of Zion Canyon, The Narrows remains the holy grail for hikers. The thrill is double-edged: walking, wading, and sometimes swimming in the **Virgin River** and peering up through a rock chasm that reaches 2,000 feet in height and that narrows down to 20 feet wide in some places.

"People are drawn there for the unique environment and the grandeur," says Amelia Gull, a native of southwestern Utah and one-time manager for a local tour operator in Springdale. "There really is no other place like it in the Southwest. It provides quite a few people with a sense of awe and solitude in a relatively quick and accessible way. You feel very big and very small at the same time. It's a humbling experience."

You can walk The Narrows "bottom-up" on your own or as part of a group tour offered by locally based private outfitters. (Ranger-guided hikes up the

ZION CANYON

Located in the town of Springdale, the **Zion Canyon Visitor Center** should be the first stop for anyone visiting the park. In addition to maps and brochures, the information desk has the latest weather reports and road conditions for anyone contemplating the main canyon hikes or a trip to the park's extensive wilderness. Watch out in particular for flash floods, a real danger here. No cell service means no way of reaching you with alarms. Use your common sense and be prepared.

Right outside the visitor center hop on the free shuttle that runs the length of Zion Canyon. It stops at various watercourse are no longer offered.) The lower part of The Narrows—up to **Orderville Canyon** and **Wall Street**—is fairly easy to negotiate, but often teeming with hikers during the summer season.

Avoid the rush by moving upstream from the Orderville junction into a part of The Narrows where few people tread. Time your hike out according to how long you want your total walk to be. It normally takes two hours to reach Orderville Canyon, so a total round-trip time of six hours should be enough to give you a few hours of sublime solitude.

Gull recommends setting off early in the morning—say 8 a.m. "If you go farther than about 2.5 miles in, you hardly see any people," she says. "You're really getting past the crowds, which you won't hit until your way back."

❷ **The Narrows (top-down)** Another option is a long day hike (permit required) all the way down The Narrows from Chamberlain Ranch, a route referred to as "top-down Narrows." Several local outfitters run one-way shuttles from Springdale to the ranch

Bighorn sheep

Kolob Reservoir

Blue Springs Reservoir

KOLB TERRACE RD.

Lava Point

Chamberlain Ranch **❷**

N. Fk. Virgin

Deep Creek

WEST RIM TRAIL

Wildcat Canyon Trailhead

❾

NORTHGATE PEAKS TRAIL

❽

viewpoint

ZION

N. Fk. Virgin

North Guardian Angel + 7395 ft

South Guardian Angel + 7140 ft

N A T I O N A L

Wall Street

Orderville Canyon

RIVERSIDE WALK

❶

Temple of Sinawava

Observation Point 6508 ft +

Weeping Rock 5785 ft *Angels Landing* +

Echo Canyon

Cable Mountain +

HIDDEN CANYON TRAIL

Emerald Pools

The Grotto

+ *Great White Throne* 6744 ft

Zion Lodge

EAST RIM TRAIL

❻

P A R K

SAND BENCH TRAIL

❹

Altar of Sacrifice + 7505 ft

Pine Cr.

ZION-MOUNT CARMEL HWY.

Many Pools

Checkerboard Mesa + 6670 ft

❼

Quilt Mesa

Zion Human History Museum Ⓟ

❸

Zion Canyon Visitor Center Ⓟ

CANYON OVERLOOK TRAIL

❺

WATCHMAN TRAIL

Watchman Campground

Springdale

North Fork Virgin

PARUNUWEAP CANYON

Coalpits Wash

Grafton (Ghost town)

9

Virgin

East Fork Virgin

trailhead. As the downstream hike takes 10 to 12 hours most people experience this as a two-day trip, with an overnight at a primitive campsite in the canyon.

No matter how you decide to tackle The Narrows here, a wilderness permit is required and special equipment is highly recommended—in particular waterproof boots or hiking shoes, neoprene socks, and a walking stick to aid balance on the slippery river rocks.

❸ **Watchman Trail** Don't expect peace and solitude along the canyon floor trails, especially during the summer months. But there are a few paths that don't attract crowds, in particular the Watchman Trail, a two-hour round-trip that commences at the campground of the same name near the canyon visitor center.

"It's got really nice views," says park ranger Adrienne Fitzgerald. "You hit a few different vegetation zones along the way, but you start out with the more low-desert stuff. There is a little spring that you come to. It's incredibly hot in summer, and you can only really hike it in the early morning because it does get baked. But in the spring you get some nice wildflowers. And it's a great winter hike. When a lot of the other trails are icy, this one can be in good shape."

❹ **Sand Bench Trail** Beginning at the Zion Lodge, the unpaved, 7.6-mile (round-trip) Sand Bench Trail can be explored by horseback via a tour with the park concessionaire (March–Oct.). Those traveling on their own feet can cut about 3 miles off the route by getting off at the Court of the Patriarchs shuttle stop and walking the rest of the loop.

"It's a sweet little trail with beautiful views of the Court of the Patriarchs,"

Hikers on Angels Landing

shares Erin Whittaker, park ranger. "It's probably our least trafficked route, but it can get quite hot in summertime, as it has very little shade."

EAST SIDE

Most visitors are content with staring up at the **Great White Throne** and the **Temple of Sinawava** formations on the park's east side. With a little effort, however, you can also get stunning horizontal views of Zion's geological icons. Blazed in the early 1920s, the trails to **Angels Landing** and **Observation Point** have long been popular day hikes from the canyon floor. But there are others much less trodden.

Less visited eastern Zion is also the best part of the park for wildlife viewing. In addition to mule deer and seldom seen mountain lions, desert bighorn sheep call this area home. "The sheep seem to like to pose for pictures on top of rocks and cause traffic jams along the Mount Carmel Highway," says Gull. "Look for them anywhere from the east entrance to the first tunnel. Early morning and later evening they'll be out a little more, especially during the summer."

⑤ Canyon Overlook Trail On the east side of the park, the Canyon Overlook Trail is short but sweet. It is a 1-mile walk from a small parking lot off the **Zion–Mount Carmel Highway.** The hike features some pretty steep drop-offs along the way, so be cautious. The view at the end is straight down **Pine Creek Canyon** to lower **Zion Canyon.**

"It's a wonderful view, a really cool little trail on slickrock," says Fitzgerald. "It's a fantastic short hike for a big view. The problem is that parking is really limited up there. So it's self-limiting in that sense—that is the reason you won't find a lot of people along that trail."

⑥ East Rim Trail Much more challenging (and rewarding) is the East Rim

Trail, which starts just inside the park's east entrance. The walk starts with a panoramic view of **Checkerboard Mesa** and ends with close-up views of **Echo Canyon, Cable Mountain,** and **Observation Point.**

Rockfalls in 2019 closed the Weeping Rock conglomerate of trails indefinitely, making this an out-and-back hike. Note that it is 10.6 miles, approximately six hours, to the canyon floor.

❼ Many Pools For a lesser known hike, drive the Zion–Mount Carmel Highway to the pull-off area just under a mile east past the smaller tunnel. Be aware of oncoming traffic as you carefully make your way along the road about 150 yards east to the beaten path leading down to the drainage. Follow this, keeping away from the culvert, into an open area known as Many Pools for the smooth-washed sandstone pockmarked by water-filled potholes reflecting the sky and surroundings. As Whittaker observes, "It's not on a trail, but a route on slickrock, so it feels more remote."

KOLOB TERRACE

The west rim is also less visited and ripe for exploration by those who want to experience a side of Zion that few visitors ever see. The best access is on **Kolob Terrace Road (KTR)** from Virgin, 15 miles west of Springdale on Utah 9. The paved route meanders 24 miles through the Zion wilderness to **Lava Point** and **Kolob Reservoir,** with trailheads and pullouts along the way.

"That road literally takes you on top of Zion National Park," says lead park ranger Mike Ball. "It's a steep mountain road with some steep grades, but it is

paved. It certainly is a great half-day or full-day adventure.

"You gain more than 4,000 feet until you're up at 8,000 feet above sea level. So you're in the high country."

❽ Northgate Peaks Trail Among half a dozen easy day hikes in the area, Ball recommends the Northgate Peaks Trail, which starts at the **Wildcat Canyon** pull-out and winds through ponderosa pine forest and ridgelines to a view of the white sandstone **Guardian Angel** summits.

"That's about a two-hour hike round trip. It's mostly level through the forest," Ball says. "You see parts of Zion that you wouldn't otherwise. For example, you look down on temples and towers that you would normally see from the canyon floor."

❾ West Rim Trail Farther up the road is a turnoff to **Lava Point** and the West Rim Trail, another special walk into the main canyon that can be accomplished in a single day.

Michael Plyler, Zion Canyon Field Institute director, highlights this as his favorite hike in the entire park: "The vistas off the trail are amazing in both directions. And if you start at the top it's downhill. It takes seven to nine hours—about 14 miles—and it's easily doable in a day if you're a relatively avid hiker."

KOLOB CANYONS

Spanish Franciscan monks Silvestre Vélez de Escalante and Francisco Atanasio Domínguez explored the Kolob Canyons in 1776 and in the process became the first Europeans to visit what is now Zion National Park.

After 19 years as a national monument, Kolob was added to the park in 1956, essentially doubling Zion's size. Despite its proximity to I-15, it remains the park's least used region.

"The Kolob Canyons area is a great hidden treasure of Zion," says Gull.

⑩ Timber Creek Overlook Trail Just off I-15 at East Kolob Canyon Road, exit 40, is the **Kolob Canyons Visitor Center.** A paved road leads about 5 miles to the splendid **Kolob Canyons Overlook** with its views across the park's wild west end.

Take the time to trek the short (1.2 miles one way) Timber Creek Overlook Trail to a bluff with a spectacular view across southwest Utah. "You see the whole region from up there," says Fitzgerald.

⑪ Middle Fork Taylor Creek For something a little more ambitious, hike up the Middle Fork Taylor Creek, a 5.4-mile round-trip that takes three to four hours.

A moderate day hike that's not going up a cliff, it takes you into a canyon drainage and up through an alcove with a double arch. In the spring there's often a waterfall coming off the top. A warning to hikers, especially with children: This trail is known for having rattlesnakes. Ask a ranger for more information.

⑫ La Verkin Creek Trail For a unique reward, experienced hikers can take the La Verkin Creek Trail to **Kolob Arch.**

At the end of this strenuous, 7-mile (one way) trek is the second longest natural arch in the United States (287.4 feet) after Arches National Park's Landscape Arch. "For most people it's really tough getting there in one day, especially in summer," Fitzgerald warns. "This is my favorite place to go backpacking. You feel like you have the place to yourself. Even some of the rangers don't know what's out there."

Ponderosa pine at base of Checkerboard Mesa

MORE PARK SECRETS

BLACK CANYON OF THE GUNNISON

PAINTED WALL | 970-641-2337 | *nps.gov/blca*

Deeper than it is wide in some places, the Black Canyon rises more than 2,700 feet above the Gunnison River in Colorado. This plunging, rocky scar is many times steeper than the Grand Canyon and is so forbidding that only the most determined hikers reach the bottom.

But from its rim, you see rare Precambrian rock—at nearly two billion years old, this type of stone normally remains locked up beneath the Earth's surface and rarely sees the light of day. Drive along the South Rim to get a good view of Painted Wall—the highest cliff in Colorado—and divine its secrets.

"It looks like somebody hand-painted it," says Sandy Snell-Dobert, ranger. "There are streaks of pink in the shape of serpents or dragons going across the dark rock background." Or take the longer route to the steep cliffs of the less-traveled North Rim for dramatic vistas that include the river far below.

CARLSBAD CAVERNS

CAVES, FOSSILS & BATS | 575-785-2232 | *nps.gov/cave*

Located in southeastern New Mexico's Guadalupe Mountains, Carlsbad Caverns National Park is mostly known for the 119 caves that lie beneath its rocky slopes and canyons. Aboveground, however, holds wonders as well—265 million years ago the mountains were a reef that edged an inland sea, and the rocks are studded with the preserved bodies of sponges, algae, and nautilus.

People come here to visit the caves, but most forget the fact that there's more than 46,000 acres here, and most of that is wilderness. There's marvelous hiking here, including the **Yucca Canyon Trail,** which runs along the southwestern corner of the park. Accessible by an unpaved road, the trail climbs a side canyon, then levels out on top of an escarpment that offers a dizzying view of the vast **Permian Basin,** all that remains of the inland sea.

Near the end of the 7.7-mile trail, hikers are rewarded with a secret—a stand of ponderosa pines, which is an unusual sight in Carlsbad and a holdover from when this wasn't a desert.

Descending to the caves is, of course, unforgettable. For another memorable experience, stay late for an excellent ranger-led bat-flight program (mid-spring through late fall), and witness hundreds of thousands of Brazilian free-tailed bats swirl from the Natural Entrance into the sky for their nightly feeding.

GREAT BASIN

BRISTLECONE PINE I 775-234-7331 I *nps.gov/grba*

No water drains to an ocean in the Great Basin, a vast area that stretches from the tall Sierra Nevada range in California to Utah's Wasatch Range. Located in eastern Nevada, Great Basin National Park protects a diverse landscape of high-altitude desert valleys, salt flats, and rolling ridges crowned by 13,063-foot **Wheeler Peak.**

Most visitors come for the famed **Lehman Caves,** but for a secret treat, stay aboveground and take the **Wheeler Peak Scenic Drive** to the campground at the mountain's base. Then follow the **Bristlecone & Glacier Trail** 1.4 miles to a grove of magnificent bristlecone pines perched on the slopes of Wheeler Peak. Through the trees, hikers can glimpse magnificent views of the Snake Valley spread out below. Above the grove the trail ends at one of Nevada's few glaciers, a mass of boulders and ice steadily inching its way down the peak.

"Those trees are 5,000 years old," says former park superintendent Andy Ferguson of the bristlecone pines. "They don't fall down, they just weather away. People who go to the grove often all say they have the same feeling—that it's a spiritual visit."

GUADALUPE MOUNTAINS

PERMIAN REEF I 915-828-3251 I *nps.gov/gumo*

For proof that landscapes can change drastically over time, consider the Guadalupe Mountains. Millions of years ago they were part of a marine fossil reef, populated by sponges, algae, and other ocean creatures.

When the water receded, natural forces buried the reef, then pushed it skyward and sculpted the limestone peaks now in the park. The highest part of the more-than-40-mile range is preserved in this West Texas area, where more than 80 miles of trails weave through rocky cliffs, oak and maple forests, and desert scrub.

Many come to admire the park's gorgeous canyons and vistas—**McKittrick Canyon** is popular, with fall colors that rival New England's. But to best appreciate how the landscape came to be, hike the **Permian Reef Trail,** a secret spot that draws geologists from across the world.

The 8.4-mile path climbs 2,000 feet alongside cacti and canyon views. From boulders to rock walls, the limestone along the way is etched with the remains of sponges, cephalopods, ammonoids, and other ancient ocean life. The slopes above the canyon are south facing, and thus treated to full sun—a plus for the Chihuahuan Desert wildflowers but tough for summer hiking. This is considered a difficult trail, so be prepared with water and appropriate footwear.

HOT SPRINGS

TAKING THE WATERS I 501-620-6715 I *nps.gov/hosp*

In the 19th century, a steaming pocket of central Arkansas evolved from a rugged settlement to a glamorous destination for soothing hot water treatments said to cure all sorts of ills. Along **Bathhouse Row,** which is the heart of the park, you can still walk through rooms filled with stained glass and statues and take a dip in traditional baths or at a modern-day spa.

But why stop with just soaking? Come armed with a jug so you can "quaff the elixir," as visitors used to say when they tipped their heads back and gulped the springs' bounty. "Get in line with the locals at one of several jug fountains in the park and take home your share of the 700,000 gallons of thermal spring water flowing daily from Hot Springs Mountain," says Tom Hill, curator of the park's museum. The water comes out hot—the springs average 143°F—but most say it's delicious when chilled.

If you need to stretch those refreshed legs, 26 miles of hiking trails traverse the park's wooded regions amid the Ouachita Mountains. Oak and hickory are the norm here, but you may also spot a few mature examples of shortleaf pine—a tree once abundant in southern Arkansas before being overtimbered.

SAGUARO

ICONIC CACTI I RINCON MOUNTAIN DISTRICT: 520-733-5153
TUCSON MOUNTAIN DISTRICT: 520-733-5158 I *nps.gov/sagu*

With arms reaching upward and a tall, majestic silhouette, it's no wonder the saguaro cactus has become an icon of the Southwest. The plant can grow up to 50 feet tall and weigh as much as 16,000 pounds—and has so captured our imaginations that we protect part of its habitat in Saguaro National Park near Tucson in Arizona.

Just west of the city, the park's **Tucson Mountain District** is widely known for hillsides dotted with the statuesque cacti. Not as many people, however, visit the park's original eastern unit, established in 1933 and now known as the **Rincon Mountain District.** This area, more than twice as big as the park's western district, not only includes saguaros but also features the moister, cooler ecosystems of the Rincon Mountains. Says Natalie Luna Rose, a former spokesperson for the park: "Once you get past a certain elevation here, you lose the saguaros and the cacti, and you start seeing a whole different level of nature."

Andy Fisher, chief of interpretation at the park, notes the Rincon Mountains reach over 8,000 feet in elevation. "Most people don't associate Saguaro National Park with bears, aspen trees, or spotted owls, but those can be found in the designated wilderness if someone is hearty enough to hike up."

WHITE SANDS

GYPSUM DUNES | 575-479-6124 | *nps.gov/whsa*

The redesignation of White Sands from a national monument to a national park in December 2019 was in part acknowledgment of a simple geological fact: The vast sparkling white landscape here comprises the world's largest expanse of gypsum dunes. The unlikely series of events that formed this spectacular terrain date back more than 250 million years, when the region was covered by a shallow sea that deposited thick layers of gypsum (a variety of calcium carbonate) as it continually rose and fell.

Driving the 8-mile (one way) **Dunes Drive** is an immersive experience in itself, but hiking the easy **Playa Trail** or **Dune Life Nature Trail** provides a much more intimate look at White Sands. Says park interpreter Kelly Carroll, "Only coming out at night, White Sands' inhabitants stay away from heat and predators during the day."

"Sunset is the best time in the day to visit White Sands," Carroll adds. "The deep reds and oranges mix with the long shadows on the rolling white dunes as you look west. Looking east, the sun's last light illuminates the Sacramento Mountains with a pink hue, followed by the grayish alpenglow."

Gypsum dunes

4 | ROCKY MOUNTAINS

Sunrise over Swiftcurrent Creek, Glacier National Park, Montana

"There is something profound interwoven into Glacier's majestic peaks. These mountains possess the power to heal and a connection to something greater. Standing in the presence of that power is a necessity our souls desperately crave. It's why these places matter. For when we lose our connection to this earth, it is impossible for us to be whole."

—COLTON SMITH
CO-HOST OF EMMY-WINNING *ROCK THE PARK* ON ABC

View of the Lewis Range, where the Pacific Northwest Trail passes through Stoney Indian Pass

GLACIER

Sprawling across the Continental Divide in northern Montana, Glacier National Park does claim some 26 small alpine glaciers. But in fact, its name refers to the work of much larger glaciers during ice ages of the past. It was heroic business, judging by the monumental results. Attentive visitors soon learn to recognize formations secret to most, with such descriptive names as arêtes, horns, eskers, moraines, cirques, hanging valleys, U-shaped valleys, glacial plucking, and more.

The ice itself comes and goes. The great glaciers melted with the last ice age; the current ones occupy, in a sense, the footprints of their ancestors. Melting ice augments the water from melting snow each year to keep wildflower meadows lush, more than 700 sparkling lakes filled, and waterfalls cascading. Naturalist John Muir perhaps described it best when he called this area the "best care-killing scenery on the continent."

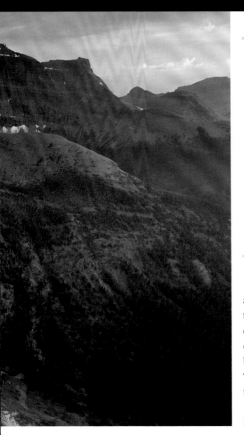

Year-Round Visitor Center

- **Apgar Visitor Center**
  *Apgar Village, 2 miles north
  of West Glacier near foot of
  Lake McDonald*

Seasonal Visitor Centers

- **Logan Pass Visitor Center**
  *Logan Pass, midway along
  Going-to-the-Sun Road*
- **Saint Mary Visitor Center**
  Off US 89, East Entrance

406-888-7800, nps.gov/glac

The east slope is equally spectacular, although being in the rain shadow of the **Continental Divide**, the climate is drier and the vegetation different. Go early in the morning to avoid the crush, but if the road is crowded, no matter. Take the drive, stop often, and revel in the scenery.

Better yet, climb aboard the park's free shuttle; it stops at trailheads and pullouts all along the road. This can be invaluable, especially at Logan Pass where the parking lot is often full at midday. Note, however, that the shuttles themselves may be full at peak times.

GOING-TO-THE-SUN ROAD

The central focus for most visitors to Glacier, and for good reason, is the 50-mile Going-to-the-Sun Road.

There's nowhere in the country quite like it—a two-lane road carved into a stunningly precipitous landscape, it transects the park through its scenic center. There are higher roads in the Rockies, but none better.

From the west side, it climbs out of deep-shadowed forest. Then, clinging to sheer cliffs above deep valleys, it arrives among wildflowers and snowfields at **Logan Pass.**

❶ **Logan Pass** The 1.5-mile hike to **Hidden Lake** overlook is a clear favorite. You'll have plenty of company, but the surroundings make it all worthwhile.

Also popular (again for good reason) is the 7.6-mile **Highline Trail,** accessible from the Highline Trailhead located on the north side of the Going-to-the-Sun Road at Logan Pass. It contours north from the pass, cutting across a near-vertical rock wall, so exposed that the park has strung a hand cable for nervous hikers to clutch. Some people turn

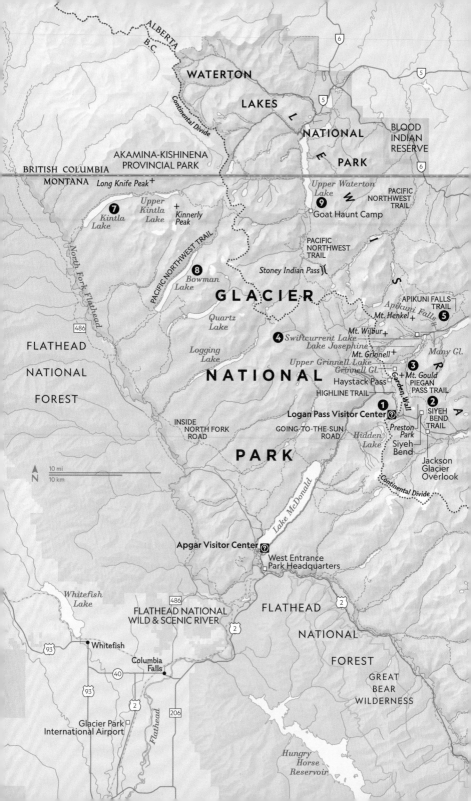

ALBERTA
B.C.

WATERTON

Continental Divide

LAKES

L
A
K
E

NATIONAL

PARK

BLOOD
INDIAN
RESERVE

AKAMINA-KISHINENA
PROVINCIAL PARK

BRITISH COLUMBIA
MONTANA   Long Knife Peak +

Upper Waterton
Lake

PACIFIC
NORTHWEST
TRAIL

9 Goat Haunt Camp

Upper
Kintla Lake

7 Kintla
Lake

+ Kinnerly
Peak

PACIFIC
NORTHWEST
TRAIL

PACIFIC NORTHWEST TRAIL

North Fork Flathead

486

Stoney Indian Pass

8 Bowman
Lake

GLACIER

Quartz
Lake

Logging
Lake

APIKUNI FALLS
TRAIL
Apikuni Falls
Mt. Henkel + **5**

NATIONAL

Mt. Wilbur +

4 Swiftcurrent Lake
Lake Josephine
Upper Grinnell Lake
Grinnell Gl.
Haystack Pass
HIGHLINE TRAIL

Mt. Grinnell +
Many Gl.
3
+ Mt. Gould
Garden Wall
PIEGAN
PASS TRAIL

FLATHEAD

NATIONAL

FOREST

INSIDE
NORTH FORK
ROAD

GOING-TO-THE-SUN
ROAD

Logan Pass Visitor Center **1**

PARK

Hidden
Lake

Preston
Park
Siyeh
Bend

2 SIYEH
BEND
TRAIL

Jackson
Glacier
Overlook

Continental Divide

N
10 mi
10 km

Lake McDonald

Apgar Visitor Center

West Entrance
Park Headquarters

Whitefish
Lake

486

FLATHEAD NATIONAL
WILD & SCENIC RIVER

FLATHEAD

NATIONAL

93

Whitefish

2

Columbia
Falls

40

93

2

Flathead

206

Glacier Park
International Airport

FOREST

GREAT
BEAR
WILDERNESS

2

Hungry
Horse
Reservoir

Map Labels

2

CANADA
UNITED STATES

ALBERTA
MONTANA

17

89

Duck Lake

464

Lake
Sherburne

Continental Divide

Saint Mary
Visitor Center

Saint Mary Lake

BLACKFEET
INDIAN RESERVATION

N

89

G
L
A
C
I
E
R

Cut Bank

North Fork
Cut Bank Cr.

DAWSON-
PITAMAKAN
LOOP TRAIL

89

49

Lower Two
Medicine
Lake

Twin
Falls

Two Medicine

Two Medicine
Lake

6

2

Upper
Two Medicine
Lake

Continental Divide

LEWIS
AND CLARK
NATIONAL
FOREST

FLATHEAD
NATIONAL FOREST

around at the sight of it. Nonetheless, the Highline ranks among the finest high-altitude walks on the planet. **Haystack Pass,** 3.6 miles from the trailhead, offers a scenic climax for the trail.

2 **Siyeh Bend** A less traveled option starts 2.2 miles east of Logan at Siyeh Bend (a shuttle stop). The Siyeh Bend Trail climbs for about a mile through forest, then joins the **Piegan Pass Trail.**

Turning right, you can return to the road at **Jackson Glacier Overlook,** making for a moderate and lovely hike of about 2.5 miles. To the left, about 1.5 miles and some 800 feet higher, is **Preston Park,** featuring one of the park's best wildflower meadows.

MANY GLACIER

Above all, Glacier is a hiker's park, and Many Glacier is the heart of it. Three magnificent valleys converge on **Swiftcurrent Lake.** A series of peaks—**Henkel, Wilbur, Grinnell,** and **Gould**—each one a model of glacial artistry, anchor the sharp ridge that connects the summits and carries the Continental

A mountain goat and kids

Remnants of the vanishing Grinnell Glacier

Divide, separating the Atlantic and Pacific watersheds along its spine.

Streams pour into lakes and tumble over waterfalls in each valley. Wildflowers bloom most of the summer. Distances are not long, and an excellent trail system provides access to it all. You can spend a week exploring here and still want more.

❸ **Grinnell Glacier** Crowding is a relative term. The busiest trail at Many Glacier is a peaceful place compared to almost any park road. So, although Grinnell Glacier is a well-known and popular destination, it's a select group of visitors who make the trip on any given day.

It is worth the effort, not just because the scenery is spectacular, but also because the glacier, perhaps the most famous in the park, won't last much longer. The trend of melting glaciers is wonderfully illustrated on the park website with then-and-now photographs.

NOT TO BE MISSED: *Drive or take the park shuttle along Going-to-the-Sun Road, stopping often for views and hikes.* ▸ *Head into high altitude on the Highline Trail.* ▸ *Explore the waterfalls and wildflowers of Many Glacier.* ▸ *Join a tour or rent your own canoe or kayak and paddle a glacial lake.* ▸ *Head into the forests of the park's northwest corner and send Canada a friendly wave.*

Getting there involves a gentle 3-mile walk on Grinnell Glacier Trail to the head of **Lake Josephine**, and a steady climb of 1,600 feet to the glacier viewpoint at **Upper Grinnell Lake.**

The trail passes through lush meadows filled with beargrass, Indian paintbrush, and, quite likely, a few mountain goats grazing. This is quintessential Glacier. Total distance to the glacier is 5.5 miles each way, or 3.8 miles if you ride the shuttle boat.

❹ **Swiftcurrent Lake** At Glacier, trails may be busy, but the lakes usually aren't. Canoes and kayaks provide a simple way to escape into a zone of privacy.

It might be enough to drift along the shore of Swiftcurrent Lake, soaking up the scenery, but Lake Josephine beckons from the other side of a 400-yard portage. The Park Service and several concession companies offer guided tours that span the lakes or rent kayaks or canoes so you can do the route yourself.

Josephine is often empty of any boats except sightseeing craft that run from one end to the other. Rent a boat at

Apgar, Two Medicine, or Many Glacier. Note: To prevent introduction of invasive water pests (the New Zealand mussel, a primary concern), the park requires inspections for all watercraft.

5 **Apikuni Falls** Short, steep (700 vertical feet in 1 mile), and often overlooked, the **Apikuni Falls Trail** offers a moderately strenuous route to a high, slender, multistaged waterfall. The trailhead is located 1.1 miles east of the Many Glacier Hotel. For some hikers, the main reward for making the climb is the view that opens up as you go higher—**Mount Gould** and the **Garden Wall** framed by the smooth U-shaped valley.

SOUTHEAST CORNER

Two opposite corners of Glacier—the northwest and the southeast—are off the main track and extremely different in character.

The southeast, being on the rain-shadow side of the mountains and bordering the Great Plains, is drier, more open landscape. Like all of Glacier's eastern side, it can be a windy place. But it lacks nothing for scenery, and offers two relatively peaceful places to appreciate it.

One is **Cut Bank,** at the end of a 5-mile dirt road; it offers a primitive campground (bring your own drinking water), a historic ranger station, and little more than the natural surroundings. The other is Two Medicine.

6 **Two Medicine Lake** A glance at Glacier's map shows why lakes are the focus of most activities. There are many, almost all of which occupy glacier-carved valleys. The main ones are long and narrow, and reach deep into the

Sunset over Two Medicine Lake

Waterton Lakes in fall

mountains like the ice rivers that made them. It's natural that visitors want to see what lies at their upper ends.

Two Medicine Lake is no exception. Overlooked by a ring of peaks, it was a busier place in early years, before construction of the scenic and popular Going-to-the-Sun Road shifted visitors' attention northward.

It remains a fine place if you have a canoe or kayak and the wind is not blowing too hard. Rental boats are available, as is a boat tour that also serves visitors as a hiker shuttle.

From the boat dock at the upper end, a gentle trail (2.2 miles each way) leads past **Twin Falls** to Upper Two Medicine Lake. And there is another option for the more adventurous: the not-gentle 18-mile **Dawson–Pitamakan Loop Trail** from near Two Medicine.

NORTHWEST CORNER

The northwest portion of Glacier is on the way to nowhere but itself. This is just fine with visitors looking to get away and seek serenity.

The North Fork Flathead River flows out of Canada to form the park boundary. Two roads flank the river. One road is outside the park, the other is inside and sensibly named the **Inside North Fork Road,** a rough and winding route not recommended for RVs or trailers.

The drive offers few mountain vistas. The theme here is deep, luxuriant forest, moist meadows, two magnificent fjord-like lakes—Bowman and Kintla—and solitude. (Note that in peak season access to these lakes is often restricted to prevent overcrowding.) Two additional lakes, also large and splendid, are even farther removed; Logging Lake and Quartz Lake are accessible only on foot.

❼ Kintla Lake Although the road is rough and the driving slow, getting to Kintla Lake, the most remote vehicle-accessible place in Glacier, is worth the effort. It's possible to get there from **Lake McDonald** and back in a day, but the far better idea is to camp out a night or two. The campground is old-fashioned (with pit toilets and no hookups). It almost never fills up.

Take a paddleboat if you can (remembering that you will need to have your boat inspected at Apger first). No motors are allowed on the water; the loudest sound could be the dip of your paddle.

Of course, the mountain views are excellent and only get better the farther up the lake you go. From Kintla's head,

it's a 3-mile hike to Upper Kintla Lake, which lies in the embrace of Kinnerly and Long Knife Peaks.

❽ Bowman Lake Bowman Lake is practically a twin to Kintla. Of similar size, also reached by a rough dirt road, and girded by mountains, Bowman is only a little less remote.

❾ Waterton Lakes Located in Canada, Waterton Lakes National Park adjoins Glacier, protecting an equally grand landscape; together they form **Waterton–Glacier International Peace Park**, the first such trans-border park in the world. **Upper Waterton Lake** extends across the border like a neighborly hand. In summer a sightseeing boat motors down to the remote American end, and backpackers with identification can hike from there.

LOCAL INTELLIGENCE

Visiting Glacier takes planning for a range of contingencies. Going-to-the-Sun Road, for example, underwent a multi-year rehabilitation project that affected all traffic, and road closures are still a possibility for a variety of reasons. Today Going-to-the-Sun's schedule is driven by weather, and snow also complicates any attempt at trip planning. The park starts to plow the route in April; beware, however, that cold weather can strike even in the summer months. (In 2011, the Going-to-the-Sun Road did not open until July 13.) Keep up with the bulletins posted on the park's website.

Trails are also affected. Steep, slippery snowfields can be a deadly hazard for the unskilled or unprepared. Says Denise Germann, a park ranger who used to work at Glacier: "People need to evaluate their own skills, and sometimes it means not doing something you want to do."

She adds that although snow might block the pass or make hiking difficult, "the valley bottoms can be 60 or 70 degrees and beautiful, warm and green. Even without **Logan Pass** there are plenty of opportunities to enjoy the park in peaceful, scenic places."

As with many national parks, visitation to Glacier has surged in recent years, and the park may feel very different to someone who wandered these trails a decade ago. This just means giving a bit more advance thought to timing and where you want to explore. Check the park's official website, where the "Plan Your Visit" section is loaded with helpful information; Glacier also has a presence on social media, where others can provide tips from their trips.

Balsamroot in bloom below the Tetons

GRAND TETON

The Teton Range demands immediate attention. From first sight, it's hard to tear your eyes from these towering crags. Pushed up along a sharp fault line, they rise in a single, audacious wall of granite 6,000 to 7,000 feet above Jackson Hole, the valley at their feet, which makes an ideal viewing platform. There are no foothills to speak of, nothing to block the view of coniferous forest, alpine meadows, bare granite, and light blue glaciers.

No matter what you do here—boating, hiking, bicycling, wildlife-watching, or simply gazing upward—the peaks are ever present and never far from your consciousness, hiding secrets in their shadows.

Their true magic lies in juxtaposition. Something small, a bird perhaps, or a cluster of wildflowers, captures your interest. For a moment, you forget the mountains, but then you lift your eyes and there they stand—high and distant but at the same time too close to be believed.

Seasonal Visitor Centers

▪ **Colter Bay Visitor Center**
   25 miles north of Moose

▪ **Craig Thomas Discovery &
   Visitor Center**
   *Moose, 12 miles from Jackson on
   Teton Park Road*

▪ **Flagg Ranch Information Station**
   *2 miles south of Yellowstone's
   south boundary on the John D.
   Rockefeller, Jr. Memorial Parkway*

▪ **Jenny Lake Visitor Center**
   7 miles west of Moose

▪ **Laurance S. Rockefeller Preserve
   Center**
   *Moose-Wilson Road, 4 miles south
   of Moose*

   307-739-3300, nps.gov/grte

US 89

The main road through the park is US 89, which leads north from the town of Jackson to Yellowstone National Park. Leaving town, it passes the **National Elk Refuge,** then climbs a small rise to emerge suddenly in full view of the Tetons and head into this national park.

For the next 30 miles to Moran Junction, the views are well worth stopping for and taking in, despite traffic that includes long-haul trucks headed east across Wyoming.

❶ **Gros Ventre Road** Leave the highway at Gros Ventre Junction for a bucolic cruise through sagebrush-covered meadows on the east side of the park. The road follows cottonwood-lined **Gros Ventre River,** a spot to see bald eagles, moose, and waterfowl. On the open sagebrush flats, look for pronghorn, elk, and bison.

A mile beyond the hamlet of Kelly, the Gros Ventre Road climbs over aspen-covered hills toward **Lower Slide Lake,** outside of the park. The lake was created by a giant landslide in 1925 that blocked the Gros Ventre River. This road goes miles farther through untraveled country, for those with time to explore.

Return for now to Kelly Road, and continue north 2.5 miles to Antelope Flats Road, which leads back to US 89. On the way, it passes **Mormon Row,** the location of two historic barns built by pioneer settlers John and Thomas Moulton. Seen at dawn, with the peaks behind them, the barns are among the most photographed objects in the Tetons.

JOHN D. ROCKEFELLER, JR., MEMORIAL PARKWAY

↑ To Yellowstone National Park, and Flagg Ranch Information Station

TETON

JEDEDIAH SMITH WILDERNESS

89
191
287

Jackson Lake

Colter Bay Visitor Center **3** Colter Bay Village

LAKESHORE TRAIL

HERMITAGE POINT TRAIL

Elk Island

Jackson Lake Junction

Jackson Lake Dam

CARIBOU-

TARGHEE

NATIONAL

FOREST

GRAND TETON

Mount Moran + 12605 ft

Leigh Lake

LEIGH LAKE TRAIL **9**

Signal Mt. 7727 ft **10**

SIGNAL MOUNTAIN ROAD

NATIONAL

Lake Solitude

String Lake

Inspiration Point

Cascade Canyon

Cascade Cr. Hidden Falls

PARK

Jenny Lake

TETON PARK RD.

South Fork Cascade Cr.

Grand Teton +13770 ft

Jenny Lake **7** **Visitor Center**

Snake River Overlook

Disappointment + Peak **8**

Lupine Meadows

Shadow Mt. 8252 ft +

Amphitheater Lake

Bradley Lake **6**

TETON PARK ROAD

2 Schwabacher's Landing

SCHWABACHER RD.

Taggart Lake

SHADOW MOUNTAIN ROAD

VALLEY TRAIL

ANTELOPE FLATS RD.

DEATH CANYON TRAIL **5**

Death Canyon

Craig Thomas Discovery and Visitor Center

Moulton Barns

Moose

GROS VENTRE RD.

Phelps Lake

MORMON ROW

1 Kelly

JEDEDIAH

26

SMITH

Laurance S. Rockefeller **4** **Preserve Center**

Jackson Hole Airport

89

WILDERNESS

191

GROS VENTRE RD.

Gros Ventre

NATIONAL

Jackson Hole Mountain Resort

MOOSE-WILSON RD.

Gros Ventre Junction

ELK

BRIDGER-TETON NATIONAL FOREST

390

Snake

↓ To Jackson

REFUGE

WILDERNESS

BRIDGER-TETON

NATIONAL

FOREST

Two Ocean Lake

Emma Matilda Lake

Oxbow Bend

Snake

Moran Junction

26 287

26

89

191

N 4 mi
   4 km

BRIDGER-TETON

NATIONAL

FOREST

Lower Slide Lake

GROS VENTRE WILDERNESS

Fog rising over the Snake River

2 **Schwabacher's Landing** US 89 stays above the braided, fast-moving **Snake River** for miles, affording a fine view of cottonwood forest and sparkling water. For a closer look, take the short Schwabacher Road down to the river bottom (four-wheel drive recommended), where woods and shrubby meadows alternate with meandering streams, beaver ponds, and mirrored views of the mountains.

Looking for those classic views of the craggy Tetons at sunrise reflected warmly in dark waters? This is the place. Fishermen's trails lead in all directions (note fishing is seasonal in this location). Otters, beavers, osprey, mergansers, and trout live here. So do moose. Take care not to stumble upon a grazing moose; the animals appear placid but can be dangerous as they defend their territory.

3 **Colter Bay** Some 25 miles farther north and home to an excellent visitor center, a marina, and other facilities, Colter Bay is a bustling place. Several trails, though, provide quick escape through pine forest to the

Jackson Lake with Grand Teton and Mount Moran

smooth-cobbled beaches of **Jackson Lake.** During midsummer and later, the water can be warm enough for swimming. Look for pelicans, gulls, and other waterfowl.

The **Lakeshore Trail** is an easy 2-mile jaunt around a small island—an ideal excursion for kids who want to skip stones on the water. For a longer, more secluded hike (9 miles), the **Hermitage Point Trail** leads to a treeless outlook with sweeping views.

MOOSE-WILSON ROAD

For those not driving RVs or pulling trailers, the Moose-Wilson Road is the back way into the park. It starts near the town of Wilson as Wyo. 390 leading to Jackson Hole Mountain Resort.

Beyond the resort, it enters the park and becomes a winding, partly gravel and often bumpy byway for 8 miles to park headquarters at Moose. Because it snakes through forest much of the way, it offers few mountain views; rewards here go to those with keen eyesight.

"Moose-Wilson Road is one of the best areas in the park to view wildlife," says Denise Germann of the park's public affairs office. "Forests mixed with riparian [wetlands] boast prime habitats for moose, beavers, bears, elk, and owls." Germann reminds visitors throughout their stay to "always maintain at least 100 yards from bears and wolves, and 25 yards from other wildlife." She also advises bringing bear spray, and making sure you know how to use it.

The park has plans to pave a 7-mile unpaved section of the road, prompting closures; check the website or a visitor center for up-to-date information at the time of your visit.

❹ Laurance S. Rockefeller Preserve
In the 1930s, John D. Rockefeller, Jr., purchased some 35,000 acres of Jackson Hole, which he donated to the nation in 1943 for the creation of the Jackson Hole National Monument. In 1950, the original

1929 Grand Teton National Park, which consisted only of the mountains and the glacial lakes at their base, combined with the Jackson Hole National Monument to become the present-day park.

The family retained the **JY Ranch** at the south end of secluded **Phelps Lake** as a private retreat until Laurance S. Rockefeller transferred it to public ownership in 2007. Subsequently, cabins used by the Rockefellers were moved to other locations, a visitor center was built near the road, and once exclusive trails were opened to everyone. An invitation is no longer required to visit the lakeshore or walk the quiet forest paths, but it still feels like a privilege to be there.

❺ Death Canyon Trail A popular 1.7-mile trail leads from the Death Canyon Trailhead to a breezy viewpoint above **Phelps Lake.** Hikers stop here to enjoy the terrific view of the lake on one hand and Death Canyon on the other. Many continue to the canyon, which, belying its name, is a delight of cascading water and fragrant woods. Note, however, that parking is limited.

"For an awesome adventure, try biking the 16 miles of paved, multi-use pathway within the park," Germann recommends.

NOT TO BE MISSED: *Watch (from a safe distance) for wildlife along Moose-Wilson Road. ▸ Wander the Laurance S. Rockefeller Preserve. ▸ Bike the park's multi-use pathways. ▸ Visit scenic Jenny Lake, then head to Inspiration Point. ▸ Stroll along Leigh Lake. ▸ Take a geology lesson from the summit of Signal Mountain.*

"It's a great family activity and just incredible to ride at the base of the Teton range."

TETON PARK ROAD

The Teton Park Road begins at Moose and runs northward, as close to the mountains as you can go without hiking. It rejoins US 89 near the **Jackson Lake** dam, a distance of 20 miles.

Along the way, it takes in **Jenny Lake,** the most popular single place in the Tetons, along with numerous opportunities for mountain gazing and private excursions. Some trails scramble steeply upward; others stroll through gentle country on the valley floor. Four

LOCAL INTELLIGENCE

Dawn is the best time to see the Tetons from almost any viewpoint, but particularly Schwabacher's Landing near Moose and **Oxbow Bend** near Jackson Lake Junction. Because the mountains face east, they catch the first light of day while the valley floor remains in misty shadow, and wildlife are more likely to be out in the open. The morning air is often calm, allowing mirrored reflections on the park's many lakes and ponds.

The trademark image is of a morning moose standing in that rose-colored reflection at the center of concentric ripples in the water. It's not a common sight, but it's possible almost any day. Also, pay attention to the lunar cycle. Once every month, a full moon sets behind the dawn-lit Tetons as the sun rises in the east—spectacular compensation for getting up early.

Hidden Falls, near Jenny Lake

lakes—Jenny, **String, Leigh,** and Jackson—offer boating in addition to easy lakeside walking.

❻ Bradley & Taggart Lakes When glaciers plowed down from the peaks, they not only carved the steep canyons between mountains, they also created piles of rock rubble—called moraines—that today hold a string of alpine lakes at the base of the Tetons.

A few, including Jenny and Jackson, can be reached by road. Others, equally beautiful, lie beyond pavement. Bradley and Taggart are two such bodies of water, cupped in morainal hills, fringed by pines, and overshadowed by grand summits.

It's about 4 miles round-trip from the trailhead to Taggart Lake, and double

that if you include Bradley. Check the map for several options, all good.

❼ Jenny Lake Almost everyone stops to appreciate Jenny Lake, where a multi-year, public-private partnership with the Grand Teton National Park Foundation has improved accessibility for all visitors. There's also a scenic boat ride to the western shore, where a 1.1-mile trail climbs through deep forest to **Hidden Falls** and beyond to **Inspiration Point.**

This stop is worthwhile any time, no matter the crowds—which at midday can fill the trail. For some privacy, carry on into **Cascade Canyon**, if only for a couple of miles. The trail ascends gradually along sparkling **Cascade Creek.** Crowds drop away as the mountains leap upward.

Although not exactly undiscovered, 7.5 miles (via the shuttle boat) in, **Lake Solitude** offers stunning views of the central Tetons. An easier way to find some privacy is to ride the boat only one way, then to walk back along the shore of Jenny Lake; either way is about 3 miles.

❽ Amphitheater Lake The trail to Amphitheater Lake (10.1 miles round-trip) is a different beast from its more moderate cousin located in Cascade Canyon.

Beginning at **Lupine Meadows,** this one steams relentlessly up and up through steeply pitched meadows filled with the yellow flowers of balsamroot. Views of the valley become ever more expansive as altitude is gained.

After climbing 3,150 more vertical feet, the trail tops out near timberline beside the icy lake. **Disappointment Peak** towers overhead, and the valley below seems impossibly distant. There will be other hikers at the lake, but usually not a lot.

9 **Leigh Lake Trail** Not many walks in the Tetons can be called strolls, but this one qualifies. It begins along the shore of **String Lake**, a narrow channel popular for swimming as its shallow waters warm up earlier than the bigger lakes.

At 1.5 miles, the trail crosses a short divide where paddlers must portage their canoes, and it emerges on Leigh Lake.

Some locals say that the best thing is to come with a boat and paddle close beneath the stunning wall of **Mount Moran**. Others vote for walking the flat trail along the eastern shore, where sand beaches provide sweeping views of the peaks and pleasant picnic sites; the total distance from String Lake Trailhead to the far end of Leigh Lake is about 4 miles.

10 **Signal Mountain** Geology instructors know this place well, but most visitors pass it by. The best single place from which to view the physical structure of Jackson Hole and the Tetons is the summit of Signal Mountain.

A relatively humble peak, it stands away from the great mountains and near to Jackson Lake, offering a unique perspective on the park.

The short Signal Mountain Summit Road cruises smoothly to the top at 7,727 feet, no hiking boots needed. From here, with panoramic views of Jackson Hole and the Teton Range, you can see that the valley floor tilts down toward the west as the mountain block rises. The two are going in opposite directions.

Along the Lupine Meadows Trail

Fall aspens in Rocky Mountain

ROCKY MOUNTAIN

The highest elevation national park in the United States, Rocky Mountain protects more than 415 square miles of some of the most spectacular scenery in Colorado. Almost a third of the park lies above the tree line, a harsh alpine environment reaching its summit on 14,259-foot Longs Peak. Rugged mountains dominate vistas from anywhere in the park, which encompasses more than 70 peaks above 12,000 feet in elevation.

The lure of the high country is understandably irresistible, and nearly all visitors feel the urge to immerse themselves in the alpine scenery. The park makes it easy to do just that. Famed Trail Ridge Road crosses the park from east to west, climbing up and over the Continental Divide at a maximum elevation of 12,183 feet. Bear Lake Road offers access to many popular destinations, and the mighty Colorado River begins its journey here.

TRAIL RIDGE ROAD

This route (US 34) is the highest continuous paved road in the United States, and quite literally every turn along its 48 miles brings a new and awe-inspiring panorama.

Open from about late May to late October (depending on snow cover), Trail Ridge Road is heavily traveled, with stops at numerous scenic overlooks and the **Alpine Visitor Center.** But it's far more rewarding to leave your vehicle and experience the environment up close.

Be advised, however, that this is now the third-most-visited national park, and that may mean full parking lots, long lines, and restricted areas. Consult the

Year-Round Visitor Center
◼ Beaver Meadows Visitor Center
On US 36 at East Entrance
◼ Kawuneeche Visitor Center
Just north of Grand Lake

Seasonal Visitor Centers
◼ Alpine Visitor Center
At Fall River Pass
◼ Fall River Visitor Center
On US 34, 5 miles west of Estes Park
◼ Holzwarth Historic Site
Trail Ridge Road, 7 miles north of the Grand Lake Entrance
◼ Moraine Park Discovery Center
On Bear Lake Road, 1.5 miles from Beaver Meadows

970-586-1206, nps.gov/romo

park website and plan ahead to make the most of your visit.

❶ **Beaver Ponds** Eager to reach those postcard mountain views, nearly all visitors pass by the Beaver Ponds along **Hidden Valley Creek,** between **Deer Ridge Junction** and **Hidden Valley.** Stop to see them, and watch for wildlife including such birds as the mountain chickadee and MacGillivray's warbler, which may be glimpsed from the accessible boardwalk.

❷ **Tundra Communities Trail** Once above the tree line on Trail Ridge Road, where severe weather means trees can't grow, the landscape looks barren at first glance. Yet gorgeous wildflowers, delicate grasses, and colorful lichens abound in summer. An excellent place to enjoy the alpine habitat is the 0.5-mile Tundra Communities Trail at **Rock Cut,** a parking area west of the **Forest Canyon Overlook.**

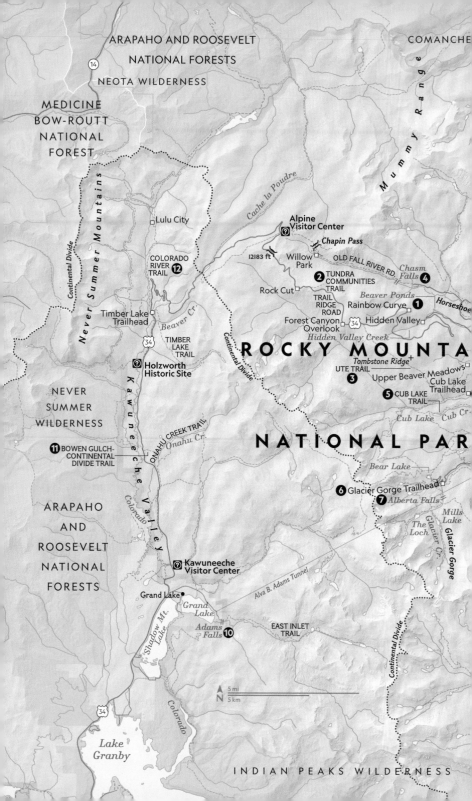

ARAPAHO AND ROOSEVELT
NATIONAL FORESTS

NEOTA WILDERNESS

COMANCHE

MEDICINE
BOW-ROUTT
NATIONAL
FOREST

14

ARAPAHO
AND
ROOSEVELT
NATIONAL
FORESTS

NEVER
SUMMER
WILDERNESS

Never Summer Mountains

Continental Divide

Lulu City

COLORADO
RIVER
TRAIL **12**

Timber Lake
Trailhead

34

TIMBER
LAKE
TRAIL

Beaver Cr.

Holzworth
Historic Site

ONAHU CREEK TRAIL
Onahu Cr.

BOWEN GULCH-
11 CONTINENTAL
DIVIDE TRAIL

Kawuneeche Valley

Colorado

Kawuneeche
Visitor Center

Grand Lake

Shadow Mt. Lake

Grand
Lake

Adams
Falls **10**

34

Lake
Granby

Colorado

Mummy Range

Cache la Poudre

Alpine
Visitor Center

Chapin Pass

12183 ft   Willow
Park

OLD FALL RIVER RD.

*Chasm
Falls* **4**

2 TUNDRA
COMMUNITIES
TRAIL

Rock Cut

TRAIL
RIDGE
ROAD

Rainbow Curve **1**

Beaver Ponds

Horseshoe

Forest Canyon
Overlook

34

Hidden Valley

Hidden Valley Creek

ROCKY MOUNTA

Tombstone Ridge

UTE TRAIL
3   Upper Beaver Meadows

Continental Divide

Cub Lake
Trailhead

5 CUB LAKE
TRAIL

Cub Lake   Cub Cr.

NATIONAL PAR

Bear Lake

6 Glacier Gorge Trailhead

7 *Alberta Falls*

*The
Loch*

Glacier Cr.

*Mills
Lake*

Glacier Gorge

Alva B. Adams Tunnel

EAST INLET
TRAIL

Continental Divide

N   5 mi
     5 km

INDIAN PEAKS WILDERNESS

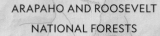

PEAK WILDERNESS

ARAPAHO AND ROOSEVELT

NATIONAL FORESTS

N. Fk. Big Thompson

Park
Fall
Deer Ridge
Junction
34

Fall River
Visitor Center

Big
Thompson
River

Estes
Park

34

I N

Beaver Meadows
Visitor Center
& Park Headquarters
36

36

Moraine Park
Discovery Center

Moraine
Park

7

K

66

BEAR
LAKE
ROAD

8 Estes Cone
11006 ft

Eugenia
Mine

Longs Peak
Trailhead

+Longs Peak 14259 ft

+Mt. Meeker
13911 ft

7

ARAPAHO

AND

ROOSEVELT

NATIONAL

FORESTS

Wild Basin 9

Ouzel
Falls

Calypso
Cascades

Allenspark

Alpine sunflowers, snow buttercups, and alpine avens bloom, and a lucky hiker might spot the elusive white-tailed ptarmigan, a chicken-like bird that camouflages itself by changing color from winter white to summer brown.

This path ascends only moderately, although people with heart or breathing problems should use caution at this lung-straining altitude.

❸ **Ute Trail** To experience the tundra, walk the section of the Ute Trail that leaves Trail Ridge Road between **Rainbow Curve** and Forest Canyon Overlook.

Remaining fairly flat as it passes below the striking rocks called **Tombstone Ridge**, the Ute Trail quickly makes hikers feel far removed from civilization. Named for the Ute Indians who used the path to cross the mountains centuries ago, the route was later followed by other tribes and early European explorers. Imagining the long heritage of travelers here makes a walk more meaningful to modern hikers, who have access to equipment and resources unimaginable to ancient peoples.

Though alpine plants must be tough to survive, they're highly vulnerable to careless hikers. With the short growing

Yellow-bellied marmot

season at this elevation, many small plants are actually years or even decades old—yet they can be destroyed with one wrong step of a boot.

This means that on the tundra, even more than other parts of the park, it's vital to stay on the trail. Look for moss campion, a low-growing "cushion" plant that colonizes disturbed soil and displays beautiful pink flowers. With luck, you might also spot bighorn sheep.

OLD FALL RIVER ROAD

A less traveled and more adventurous drive to the tundra is Old Fall River Road, an 11-mile unpaved route that in places is twice as steep as Trail Ridge Road. Following Indian paths and built in part by convict labor, this route has been making drivers nervous since its completion in 1920. Lacking guardrails, with many tight switchbacks, the road demands attention. Drivers should obey the 15-mile-per-hour speed limit and keep their eyes on the road, rather than the scenery.

❹ **Chasm Falls** Open for a relatively short summer season, the Old Fall River Road is one-way ascending only: Once you start, you can't turn around and must continue to the Alpine Visitor Center on Trail Ridge Road.

Stop often at overlooks, beginning at striking Chasm Falls, where **Fall River** roars through a chute in the rocks. Watch for elk at **Willow Park**, just before a series of switchbacks up to **Chapin Pass.** Beyond is a fine example of an alpine cirque, or glacier-carved bowl, at the head of the valley.

The primitive nature of Old Fall River Road sends most motorists to more sedate Trail Ridge Road, with the result that the former seems a trip to an earlier era of park exploration.

BEAR LAKE ROAD

Driving Bear Lake Road to beautiful **Bear Lake** ranks among the most popular activities at Rocky Mountain National Park—so much so that traffic can often be dismaying. The large parking lot at Bear Lake fills up early on summer mornings, and the park encourages visitors to take the popular shuttle bus from the Estes Park Visitor Center. (Note an entrance pass is required to board the shuttle.) The attraction: a gorgeous high-elevation lake that can be reached by a paved road, and trailheads to many other scenic sites.

LOCAL INTELLIGENCE

Here and there in Rocky Mountain National Park (at **Moraine Park,** for example) you'll notice tall fencing around areas such as willow or aspen groves. These "exclosures" keep elk and moose out of places suffering from overgrazing, allowing natural vegetation to recover.

As Michele Simmons, a former Rocky Mountain National Park interpreter, points out, "Many visitors don't know that they're allowed to enter these fenced areas, as long as they close gates behind them. They can be excellent places for bird- and butterfly-watchers." Wildflower enthusiasts and photographers, too, will be pleased to see the substantial difference in flora in habitats where grazing is limited.

Bear Lake autumn reflection

5 **Cub Lake Trail** In a hurry to get to Bear Lake, many people pass by a trail that offers a fine natural experience for minimal effort.

A short side road in **Moraine Park** leads to the Cub Lake trailhead, starting point for an easy 2.3-mile one-way hike that goes through meadows, wetlands, and woods of ponderosa pine and aspen where wildlife and wildflowers abound. Passing through willow thickets along the **Big Thompson River**, the flat trail rounds large rock outcrops to the pretty valley where Cub Creek flows.

Mule deer are seen often here, beaver and ducks may swim in the shallow pools, and elk sometimes come down from the forests at dusk to feed. (Muddy edges of ponds are good places to look for animal footprints.) Broad-tailed hummingbirds sip nectar from trailside flowers, making a distinctive buzzing noise as they zip from bloom to bloom.

The Cub Lake Trail showcases some of the park's geological features, as well. In the distant past, glaciers slowly flowed down this valley, pushing rocks to the side as they moved. The upland to the south is a moraine: a long hill formed by glacial debris. The large boulders along the trail are called "glacial erratics." Picked up and shaped by moving ice, they were carried down the valley and left in new positions when the glacier finally melted.

6 **Glacier Gorge Trailhead** It pays to heed the words of Kent Dannen, author of several excellent guides to the park: "The easy and spectacular hikes from Glacier Gorge Trailhead or Bear Lake are, of course, very popular. Nonetheless, by exploiting the philosophy of 'No pain, no gain,' hikers can experience beyond-normal benefits on these trails in relative seclusion. The pain comes from rising early to be on the trail by 6 a.m. in summer. Yes, kids and adults hate early rising, but the gain is the peace, joy, and beauty of dawn on the trail, which are beyond description."

7 **Alberta Falls** From the Glacier Gorge trailhead, near the end of Bear Lake Road, another short trail leads to one of the park's most welcoming waterfalls. From the trailhead it's a walk of less than a mile, with just a mild elevation gain, to Alberta Falls, a thunderous cascade on **Glacier Creek.** The sight of Alberta Falls, combined with its easy access, makes this a very popular hike; this is another place to heed Dannen's advice about a dawn start.

From the falls, consider continuing to either **Mills Lake** or **The Loch,** both in rugged alpine settings, and both among the park's most majestic mountain lakes.

SOUTHEASTERN CORNER

If you'd like to climb to the summit of a national park mountain without hours of approach hiking and strenuous elevation gain, consider heading to Estes Cone or, for flatter alternatives, try the hikes of Wild Basin.

❽ Estes Cone Located on the east side of the park, the nicely symmetrical Estes Cone provides plenty of reward at the end of a 3.3-mile hike. With a height of 11,006 feet, Estes Cone is a bit of a runt compared to its towering neighbors, but thanks to its isolated location it offers clear vistas of the park's giants.

The route begins at the **Longs Peak** trailhead, and along the way passes **Eugenia Mine,** the tumble-down remains of a failed mining operation from the 19th century. Traversing forest and open areas, the trail ascends Estes Cone and requires a small amount of rock scrambling at the end, though it's nothing a moderately fit person can't handle. The summit is a place to relax, enjoy a snack, and take in the view of Longs Peak and **Mount Meeker** to the southwest.

NOT TO BE MISSED: *Follow in the footsteps of past explorers on the Ute Trail.* ▸ *Stop for amazing views along Old Fall River Road.* ▸ *Watch for wildlife on the Cub Lake Trail.* ▸ *Leave the crowds behind on the park's west side.* ▸ *Discover a hidden viewpoint beyond Adams Falls.* ▸ *Head back in time at Holzwarth Historic Site.*

❾ Wild Basin The Wild Basin area, in the southern part of the park, once was a relatively untrafficked destination. No more: The park now warns that parking lots fill up early in summer and, as elsewhere in the park, access may be restricted to prevent overcrowding.

One of the closest and most popular Wild Basin sites is **Calypso Cascades,** a long and lovely waterfall named for an equally lovely orchid species blooming in July. Once you're at Calypso Cascades, you might as well continue to roaring **Ouzel Falls,** just 0.9 mile farther.

WEST SIDE

Park areas west of the Continental Divide see fewer visitors than do sites to the east (more than 80 percent of people arrive through the park's east entrances). That's just fine with many experienced travelers who prefer this area, enjoying greater solitude on trails as well as excellent wildlife viewing. This is also where the mighty Colorado River makes its start, in a wet meadow at La Poudre Pass.

❿ Adams Falls One spot where you won't be alone, though, is Adams Falls, reached by an easy walk along the **East**

Headwaters of the Colorado River, Kawuneeche Valley

Inlet Trail near the town of Grand Lake. This roaring waterfall is less than 0.5 mile from the trailhead.

"Most people go to the falls, turn around, and go right back to their car," observes Michele Simmons, a former district interpreter. "But if folks go about another quarter mile, they get to a meadow with views up into the high mountain peaks. It's fairly level, it's a beautiful walk, and it leads to this gorgeous viewpoint. And if they're willing to go one more mile, they get to a second meadow, which again opens up into some beautiful views."

Wildflowers can be abundant along the **East Inlet Trail**, and if you didn't see a moose along the main park road north of Grand Lake, you may spot one here.

⓫ Bowen Gulch–Continental Divide Trail Farther north, take the **Onahu Creek Trail** 0.3 mile to reach a connector path to the Bowen Gulch–Continental Divide Trail (30 miles). A short walk here leads to a bridge over **Onahu Creek** and a meadow Simmons calls "a little gem of a spot."

Or head back in time a century or so at the **Holzwarth Historic Site,** where several buildings dating back to a 1917 homestead bring alive the challenges of early settler life. A former saloonkeeper from Denver, John Holzwarth, Sr., made a new start here during prohibition, eventually establishing a popular guest lodge amid these towering peaks.

⓬ Colorado River Trail As another alternative to the bighorn-viewing site at **Horseshoe Park**, take a walk up the 3.1-mile Colorado River Trail, which begins near the **Timber Lake Trailhead** and heads north toward **Lulu City.** While sheep sightings aren't guaranteed on the cliffs above, there's a good chance of one in early summer.

Dawn at Castle Geyser, Upper Geyser Basin

YELLOWSTONE

Arguably the world's most famous national park, Yellowstone would appear to hold few secrets. Every year, millions of visitors pour through the park's entrances. Surely they must cover it all? Nope. They do not. The park's nearly 3,500 square miles are filled with places rarely visited and sights seldom seen.

It is said that 99 percent of visitors see only 1 percent of the park. This is true in essence, if not a precise statistical fact. Most travelers stay close to the paved roads and gather at major sights—Old Faithful, Yellowstone Lake, and the Grand Canyon of the Yellowstone River. There's also a time factor. Most visitors tour the park in midday, and in midsummer. They miss the magic of dawn, dusk, and even the dark of night. Nor do they experience the pleasures of spring and autumn, to say nothing of winter, which is perfect for anyone seeking solitude.

GEYSER BASINS

Thoughts of geysers lead naturally to **Old Faithful**, the park's number one attraction, drawing some 30,000 people a day in summer. Yet Old Faithful is not alone. It stands surrounded by hundreds of other geysers and hot springs, large and small, spread across the Upper Geyser Basin. There are numerous other such concentrations of thermal activity—some along the road, dozens in the backcountry, many with no official names. There's much to see beyond the main sites.

The ongoing restoration of overlooks and trails may mean closures; check the park website for current information.

Year-Round Visitor Center
▪ Albright Visitor Center
Mammoth Hot Springs

Seasonal Visitor Centers
▪ Canyon Visitor Education Center
Canyon Village complex
▪ Fishing Bridge Visitor Center & Trailside Museum
East Entrance Road
▪ Grant Visitor Center
1 mile off main park road at Grant Village Junction
▪ Madison Information Station
Madison Junction, Madison Picnic Area
▪ Museum of the National Park Ranger
1 mile north of Norris
▪ Norris Geyser Basin Museum & Information Station
West of Norris Junction, off Grand Loop Road
▪ Old Faithful Visitor Education Center
Upper Geyser Basin
▪ West Thumb Information Center
Western shore of Yellowstone Lake, north of Grant Village
▪ West Yellowstone Visitor Information Center
West Yellowstone Chamber of Commerce

307-344-7381, nps.gov/yell

❶ Upper Geyser Basin Midday crowds are no reason to avoid the Upper Geyser Basin. Privacy is possible, especially at dawn, before the park wakes up. The nearest campground is 16 miles away at Madison Junction and most campers are happily snoozing at first light.

"Crowds don't start pouring in until 10:30 a.m. or so," says Orville Bach, park ranger. "Hardly anyone is out at seven or

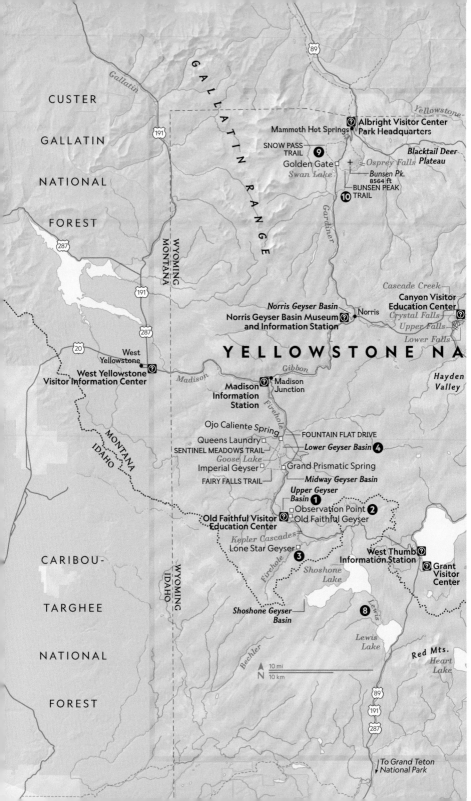

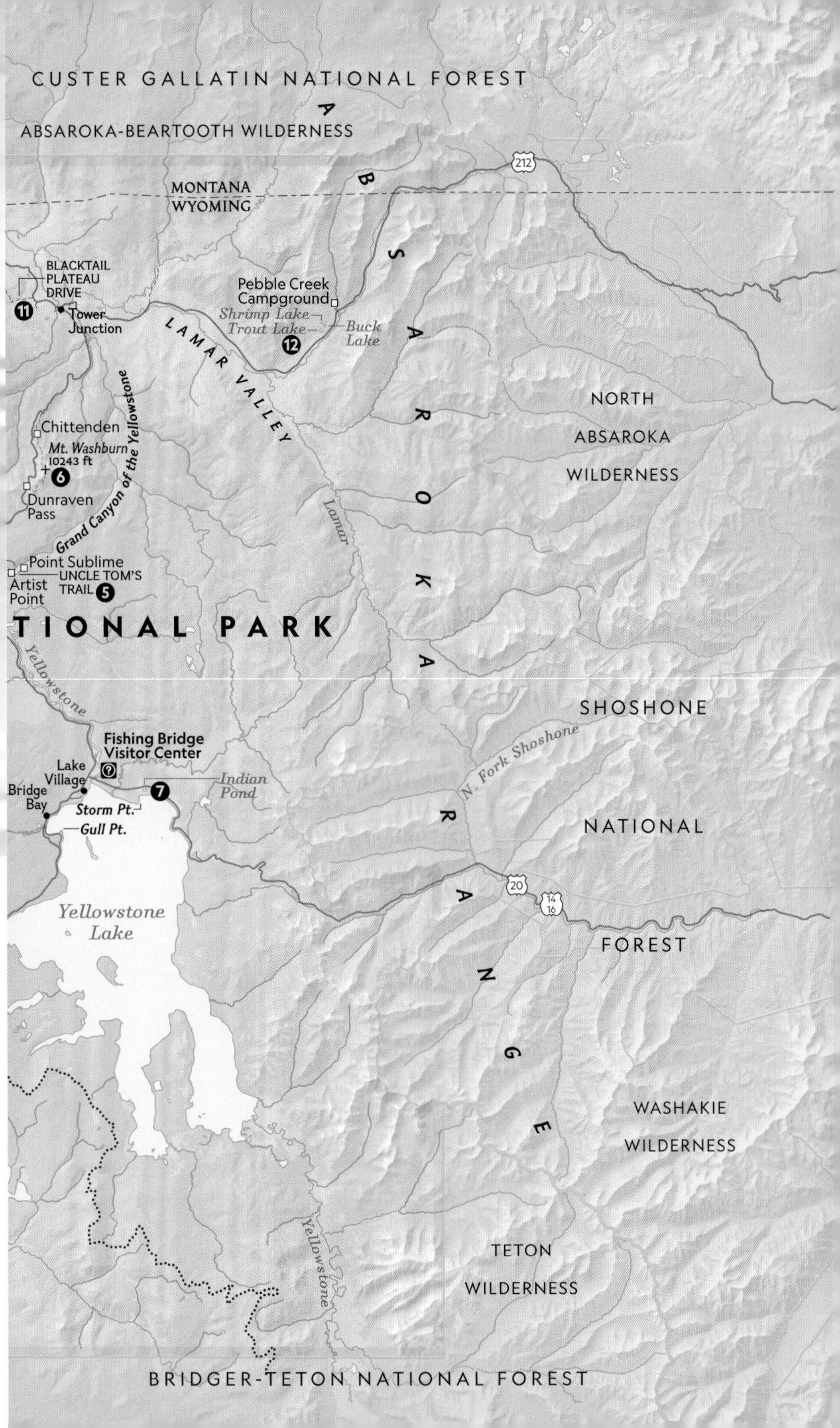

CUSTER GALLATIN NATIONAL FOREST

ABSAROKA-BEARTOOTH WILDERNESS

MONTANA
WYOMING

212

BLACKTAIL
PLATEAU
DRIVE

11

Tower
Junction

Pebble Creek
Campground

Shrimp Lake
Trout Lake

Buck
Lake

12

LAMAR VALLEY

NORTH

ABSAROKA

WILDERNESS

Chittenden

Mt. Washburn
10243 ft

6

Dunraven
Pass

Grand Canyon of the Yellowstone

Lamar

A B S A R O K A   R A N G E

Point Sublime

Artist
Point

UNCLE TOM'S
TRAIL

5

TIONAL PARK

Yellowstone

Fishing Bridge
Visitor Center

Lake
Village

Bridge
Bay

7

Storm Pt.

Gull Pt.

Indian
Pond

SHOSHONE

N. Fork Shoshone

NATIONAL

20

14
16

FOREST

Yellowstone
Lake

WASHAKIE

WILDERNESS

Yellowstone

TETON

WILDERNESS

BRIDGER-TETON NATIONAL FOREST

Chromatic Spring, Upper Geyser Basin

eight in the morning." Even guests at hotels beside the geysers tend to sleep late. They are missing the best time of day. In the cool morning air, steam from geysers and hot springs looks more dense, lending a sense of primeval mystery to the valley. Large animals are more likely to be seen. Vegetation is touched by dew, and in spring and fall, delicate frost shapes appear during the night, then quickly melt away as day breaks.

Bach also recommends the "neglected parts of the basin, just off the main track." This includes the trail past **Daisy Geyser** to **Punch Bowl Spring** and **Black Sand Pool.** Also **Artemisia Geyser:** "It's just past Morning Glory Pool, where most people turn around. Artemisia is beautiful, but almost no one knows it's there. With a little imagination, I think you can always have a quality time in the basin."

❷ **Observation Point** This is another example of a worthwhile side trail. It turns off the paved trail close to **Geyser Hill** and climbs about 200 vertical feet to a viewing platform standing atop the volcanic bluff, from where you can watch an eruption.

The trail continues through the woods, whose trees are scarred by bison rubbing against them (look for scraps of their wool), to **Solitary Geyser.** Alone in the forest, it is more pool than geyser, and it erupts frequently a few feet high.

Once a nonerupting hot spring, it changed its character after being tapped for hot water to supply a swimming pool near the hotel. That pool was removed long ago when the park realized that exploiting thermal features damaged them, but Solitary still erupts.

❸ **Lone Star Geyser** To see a truly wild geyser in its natural setting, walk the easy, partly paved trail to Lone Star Geyser, a 5-mile round-trip from the trailhead near **Kepler Cascades.**

An old service road that is also open to bicycles, the trail follows a placid stretch of the **Firehole River** (watch for trout in the clear water) through a section of forest that did not burn in the great fires of 1988.

If you want a classic Yellowstone walk in the woods, it's 6 miles farther to **Shoshone Geyser Basin;** this is best done as an overnight hike.

❹ **Lower Geyser Basin** The old road through Lower Geyser Basin and **Midway Geyser Basin**, once the main route, is now a quiet foot-and-bicycle path.

Fountain Flat Drive leads to a trailhead at the north end; there's another parking area at the south end. Between the two is an easy 4-mile walk through open meadows dotted with trees and numerous thermal features.

The trail passes **Ojo Caliente Spring,** Goose Lake, and the back side of **Grand Prismatic Hot Spring,** the largest in the park. Even less traveled is the **Sentinel Meadows Trail,** which loops 3.8 miles through a large thermal-studded meadow past a hot spring called **Queens Laundry** and the ruins of a simple bathhouse begun in 1881 but never completed, which is now a historic structure.

Another good hike at Yellowstone is **Fairy Falls Trail,** a 5.4- or 6.7-mile loop leading to a misty 200-foot-high

Grizzly bear

waterfall. Beyond lies **Imperial Geyser,** which erupts frequently and feeds an unusual warm stream.

CANYON

At Canyon, Yellowstone's two grand waterfalls plunge into a spectacular yellow-rock gorge, attracting almost as many visitors as Old Faithful.

Popular overlooks are jammed at midday, yet even here there are options, says Bach: "Park at Brink of the Upper Falls and walk to **Crystal Falls** on **Cascade Creek.** Almost no one goes there."

❺ **Uncle Tom's Trail** In 1898, "Uncle" Tom Richardson built a rough trail to the base of the Lower Falls, and he sold

LOCAL INTELLIGENCE

Every morning, a ranger at Old Faithful makes rounds of the Upper Geyser Basin to check the status of geysers and predict when the big ones might erupt. If you're on the boardwalks early, keep an eye out for the ranger uniform; ask for the first estimates of the day, among other tips. Also, a squad of volunteers known as "geyser gazers" monitor nearly every aspect of every thermal feature in the place. Most of them work at the general stores or hotels; some have spent summers here for decades and know the basin better than anyone. They do it because they love geysers, and they like to share their knowledge with anyone who shows interest. Recognize them by their bicycles, calculators, and notepads, and be prepared for encyclopedic answers.

guided trips that involved clinging to ropes in the steep places.

Later, the park built a more substantial path with paved switchbacks and steel stairways (500 feet down from the rim) to a superb face-on view of the falls. Note: As of 2019, the trail is closed due to metal fatigue in the staircase.

❻ Mount Washburn For another chance to trade sweat equity for a splendid uncrowded viewpoint, hike to the fire lookout on top of Mount Washburn. The road goes partway; then it's a walk through alpine meadows strewn with wildflowers and frequented by bighorn sheep.

Two trails provide access to the lookout tower, either from **Dunraven Pass** picnic area 3 miles away (one way) or from **Chittenden** parking area 2.25 miles away (one way). The latter is an old roadbed on which cars once drove all the

NOT TO BE MISSED: *Wake up early and have the attractions of Upper Geyser Basin almost all to yourself.* ▸ *Ask a ranger or volunteer "geyser gazer" what's active the day of your visit.* ▸ *Hike or bike into the forest to Lone Star Geyser.* ▸ *Explore Lower Geyser Basin along the Sentinel Meadows Trail.* ▸ *Spot (from a distance) huge bison and moose.* ▸ *Seek out the many unnamed thermal features beyond Old Faithful.*

way to the summit, sometimes having to do it backward because of the better reverse gear ratio.

Washburn marks the rim of the Yellowstone caldera. On a clear day you can see the **Red Mountains** 40 miles south marking the far rim; the mountains were once continuous, until the great volcano blew everything within that 40-mile distance sky high.

YELLOWSTONE LAKE

Located in the southeastern part of the park, this is the largest alpine lake in North America above 7,000 feet, and with 110 miles of shoreline it could be a park in its own right. Roads running along the north and west shores burrow through old-growth forest, past cobbled beaches and small wetlands where streams pour into the lake. In the remote southeastern part of the lake, several fjordlike arms extend deep into wilderness country, reachable only on foot or by boat.

At **Gull Point,** near **Bridge Bay,** the highway cuts inland a short distance, but the original road stays close to shore,

The Grand Canyon of the Yellowstone

Lone Geyser, Yellowstone Lake

offering one of many chances to find a private spot by the lake.

Bison gather at the meadow near Bridge Bay, while moose like the ponds along the Gull Point Road.

7 Indian Pond & Storm Point Activity centers on the lake's outlet, where the Yellowstone River pours cold and smooth on its way to wildlife-rich **Hayden Valley.**

Hotels, campgrounds, general stores, and other services cluster at Fishing Bridge on one side of the river, and Lake Village on the other. Three miles east, a stretch of secluded shoreline can be found at **Storm Point** near the deceptively ordinary-looking **Indian Pond.**

The 2.3-mile loop begins at a pond created by a steam explosion near the end of the last ice age; the park has a dozen or so such features. Reaching the lakeshore, the path turns west through deep forest to the point. Alternatively, wander the open meadows to the east.

8 Lewis River Channel Two neighboring lakes to the southwest of Yellowstone Lake—**Lewis** and **Shoshone**—are appealing in their own right, and receive less attention than their large cousin.

Shoshone is a wilderness lake, reachable on foot or by paddling a canoe upstream on Lewis River, which connects the two lakes. Anyone inclined toward canoe camping should put Shoshone at the top of their list. Day hiking is also good.

The channel is renowned among fishermen for the autumn spawning run of brown trout. One trail goes straight to Shoshone from the trailhead, while another closely follows the Lewis Lake shore and the river.

MAMMOTH & THE NORTH

The central and southern parts of the park were shaped by the great volcano

LOCAL INTELLIGENCE

Yellowstone is a wildlife park as much as it is a geologic wonderland. A lot of animals can be seen simply by cruising the roads, especially early and late in the day. If there's something good to see, traffic piles up; cars stopped in the middle of the road are good indicators.

Skilled wildlife-watchers, however, don't rely on chance alone. They know that animals favor certain areas, varying with the season and the time of day. Food has a lot to do with it.

For example, elk go where the grazing is good, and wolves follow the elk. Terrain is also a factor. Bison take the easiest route from place to place. They avoid dense woods if possible; but of course forest creatures like pine martens shun the open meadows that bison prefer. Each species has its place and time. Those who learn where to look, and when, are soon able to mystify the uninitiated with their apparently uncanny ability to find critters.

and its aftermath, but the region north is different. Landscapes here are more typical of the northern Rockies with glaciated valleys, high peaks, and limited thermal activity.

The terraces at **Mammoth Hot Springs** draw most visitors, and the crowd generally continues south. Smaller numbers head east, past **Tower Junction** to the mountain-rimmed valleys of the **Lamar River.**

❾ Snow Pass For a hike that takes in a variety of sights, including hot spring terraces that few visitors see—and is downhill most of the way—start at the

Bison cow and calf

Glen Creek trailhead (you'll need to catch a shuttle there) on the edge of **Swan Lake Flat.**

The trail skirts huge meadows before joining the 4.2-mile **Snow Pass Trail.** Cutting through a gap in the mountains, it drops back down to Mammoth through mixed forest. Until the current road was built through **Golden Gate**, horse-drawn coaches brought visitors on this route. It was a hard steep pull for horses.

In late summer and autumn, the woods ring with the sound of bugling elk. Before emerging at the **Upper Terrace Drive**, the trail passes several hot springs that might or might not be active; things change fast here.

❿ Bunsen Peak If you bring a bicycle, the **Bunsen Peak Road** is a fine place to use it. Starting just south of Rustic Falls, this 6.3-mile route is a favorite among mountain bikers. It follows the back side of Bunsen Peak and ends on the main highway about a mile south of Mammoth Hot Springs.

If you prefer to explore by foot, this route intersects with a few somewhat strenuous hikes, including one to the

Bull moose grazing

Aspens along Blacktail Plateau Drive

summit of Bunsen Peak and another down **Gardner Canyon** to the base of **Osprey Falls.** Lacking a shuttle, or someone to drop you off at the start, you can still get the best of this trail by going out some distance and back the same way.

11 **Blacktail Plateau Drive** East of Mammoth, **Blacktail Deer Plateau** is mostly open country broken by strips of pine and aspen forest—the sort of place grazing animals prefer. A gravel road (one way, eastbound) meanders over it for 7 miles.

This is easy walking country, no trails needed. A short trip away from the car, perhaps to the top of a nearby hill, is bound to turn up something interesting. If you have binoculars, a scan of the distant slopes may reveal elk, bison, wolves, and bears.

12 **Trout Lake** Perched 200 feet above the Lamar Valley road, out of sight but only 0.5 mile away, Trout Lake is a hidden gem with a reputation for good fishing and lovely mountain views.

Formerly called Fish Lake, it was a hatchery for cutthroat and rainbow trout until the 1950s, when fish-stocking operations were ended throughout the park. Otters are commonly seen here, catching fish and chasing each other playfully among the partially submerged tree trunks along the shore. You might also see a moose in the shallows; bison and other wildlife roam the surrounding meadows.

The trailhead is not marked, but it's easy to find the vehicle turn-out 1.2 miles south of **Pebble Creek Campground.** From there, it's less than 0.5 mile to the lake. You can walk around it, and also visit nearby **Buck Lake** and **Shrimp Lake.**

MORE PARK SECRETS

GREAT SAND DUNES

SAND, SURGES & STARS | 719-378-6399 | *nps.gov/grsa*

Climbing up to 750 feet and softly undulating in the shadow of the Sangre de Cristo Mountains, Colorado's Great Sand Dunes are spectacular on their own. This park, however, also includes 13,000-foot mountain peaks, fragrant piñon-juniper woodlands, open grasslands, alpine tundra, and **Medano Creek,** which generates waves up to a foot high—a rare phenomenon called "surge flow"—from snowmelt in late May to early June. You can sail down the dunes on special sand sleds or sandboards (rented in town), and in spring and early summer, kids can use inner tubes to bob in Medano Creek's unusual waves. For both activities, head to the main **Dunes Parking Area.**

"The real secret here," shares park ranger Patrick Myers, "is not so much the unusual location, but timing. Visitors should plan their sledding and hiking for early morning or evening hours to better avoid 150°F sand, thunderstorms, or potential high winds."

Another secret attraction that most visitors miss? The night sky. "We have excellent dark night skies due to high elevation, dry air, and distance from cities," says Myers. "Plan your visit on a moonless night to see the most stars, or on a full-moon night to enjoy the dunes in a bright, surreal light."

Sunset at Great Sand Dunes

"The American West is one of the most vast and inspiring landscapes on earth—I know because I've spent the better part of the last decade living in my van and exploring the various cliffs and mountain ranges. There is a grandeur here that reminds us of our place in the world. The mountains reveal our own insignificance."

—ALEX HONNOLD
PROFESSIONAL ROCK CLIMBER

5 | PACIFIC SOUTHWEST

Rare *ʻāhinahina* (silversword plants), Haleakalā National Park, Hawaiʻi

Santa Cruz Island, famous for its sea caves

CHANNEL ISLANDS

Discovering the Channel Islands is like tumbling through a time warp into a California everyone assumed had vanished long ago. While mainland southern California has burgeoned, with more than 24 million people filling every beach and crowding every canyon, the islands have been idling in the Santa Barbara Channel—as close as 17 miles to the mainland, but rarely visited. A true secret.

When the National Park Service took over management of the islands in 1980, they found a reasonably intact mirror of old mainland California, plus a few surprises. Years of private ownership created some ecological problems, but the Park Service has worked diligently to eradicate invasive animal and plant species and to restore the islands to what they truly are: a wild slice of southern California, a place of solitude and beauty.

Year-Round Visitor Centers

▪ **Robert J. Lagomarsino Visitor Center**
1901 Spinnaker Drive, Ventura

▪ **Island Visitor Contact Stations**
Santa Barbara, Anacapa & Santa Cruz islands

▪ **Outdoors Santa Barbara Visitor Center**
113 Harbor Way, 4th Floor, Santa Barbara

805-658-5730, nps.gov/chis

SANTA CRUZ ISLAND

Santa Cruz is the largest of the Channel Islands and by far the most visited. Don't let that put you off—there's never a sense of crowding on any of these islands. As with all the islands except **Santa Rosa** and **San Miguel**, the only way to visit Santa Cruz is by boat with the park's concessionaire, Island Packers *(islandpackers.com)*.

The island is famous for its sea caves —some of the world's largest—which make it a world-class destination for sea kayaking. Some come to snorkel and dive in the chilly (55°F to 68°F) water or to sun on the beach near the landing site. But most visitors simply arrive to walk and enjoy the island's serenity.

❶ Cavern Point & Potato Harbor Once you've landed on Santa Cruz, received an orientation from a park ranger, and taken in the visitor center, you'll want to make the 1-mile walk to Cavern Point.

As you ascend the hill above **Scorpion landing**, you'll note the view just keeps getting better as you near the point. From which you can see migrating gray whales in season (December to April).

Most people stop here and loop down to the campground to return, but the 2-mile coastal-bluff hike on the **North Bluff Trail** from Cavern Point to Potato Harbor is even more spectacular—vast ocean and mainland views from 350 feet above the water surface. Try it out.

Notice occasional piles of seashell fragments? "Those are shell middens," explains Bill Faulkner, a park ranger. "They're everywhere on the island. They indicate where native Chumash people camped thousands of years ago."

❷ Scorpion Canyon If you follow the basic, signed **Scorpion Canyon Loop Trail**, you'll enjoy a 4.5-mile walk in the

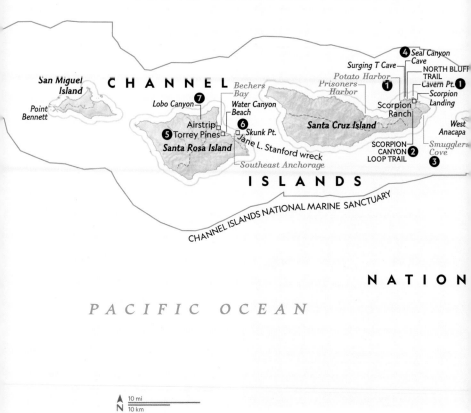

SANTA BARBARA CHANNEL

CHANNEL

San Miguel Island

Point Bennett

Lobo Canyon **7**

Airstrip
5 Torrey Pines
Santa Rosa Island

Bechers Bay

Water Canyon Beach

6 Skunk Pt.
Jane L. Stanford wreck

Southeast Anchorage

Surging T Cave
Potato Harbor **1**
Prisoners Harbor

Scorpion Ranch

SCORPION CANYON **2**
LOOP TRAIL

Santa Cruz Island

4 Seal Canyon Cave

NORTH BLUFF TRAIL

Cavern Pt. **1**
Scorpion Landing

West Anacapa

Smugglers Cove **3**

ISLANDS

CHANNEL ISLANDS NATIONAL MARINE SANCTUARY

NATION

PACIFIC OCEAN

N ▲ 10 mi / 10 km

interior of the island, but you might miss the chance of seeing one of the world's rarest bird species, the island scrub-jay—a type of jay that lives only on Santa Cruz Island. To see (or hear) this bird, walk through the upper campground, but continue straight (west) up a rocky dry wash. Look for the small groves of oaks and endemic ironwoods, where the jays are most likely to be spotted—or their screeches heard.

You may also see another rare species, the endemic island fox, in the park campgrounds on the way to or from Scorpion Canyon.

"They're cute, but *don't* feed them," warns Faulkner. "We don't want them to get habituated to human food."

3 Smugglers Cove The 7.5-mile round-trip hike to Smugglers Cove is one few visitors make. It crosses the island south on an old ranch road from **Scorpion Ranch**, climbs high enough to yield good views of **Anacapa Island**, passes a historic grove of cypress trees (a nice spot for a picnic), and lands you at a secluded beach.

"It's at the mouth of an incredible little valley," says Yvonne Menard, chief of interpretation. "Ranchers here had

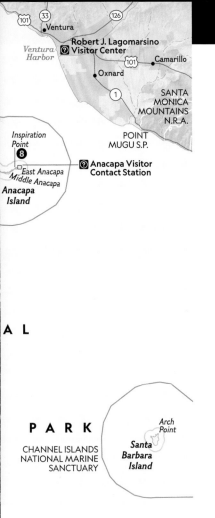

Aquasports. "I take people out who have never seen the ocean before."

A typical trip is a half day—an early boat out to Scorpion, a safety briefing, and a few hours of exhilarating paddling. Harbor seals may accompany you as you traverse the cliffs.

The experience inside the caves is as much auditory as visual—the sound of surge, swash, and blowholes. A helmet and headlamp are musts to avoid contact with barnacle-encrusted walls and ceilings. Some caves are so narrow that you have to back in. One called **Seal Canyon Cave** is about 6 feet wide, 10 feet high, but goes back at least 600 feet.

SANTA ROSA ISLAND

The second largest of the Channel Islands, Santa Rosa offers one thing none of the others do—an airstrip. You can go either by boat with Island Packers or by plane from the town of Camarillo with Channel Island Aviation. Some visitors fly in to surf, fish, and hike—and fly right back, though there's plenty on the island to justify more than a day trip.

groves of olive trees, and you'll see their adobe ranch buildings from the 1880s."

4 The Sea Caves The north coast of Santa Cruz Island is riddled with sea caves, many of them huge—of the 100-some caves, 72 are more than 200 feet long.

Exploring them by kayak is thrilling, though best done with a guide who can read the tides and swell and know which caves are safe to enter. The park website has a list of authorized outfitters.

Not that the paddling is difficult. "It takes no skill," says Eric Little, kayak guide for Santa Barbara–based

An endangered island fox

5 **Torrey Pines** A grove of Torrey pines on a bluff above **Bechers Bay** is one of those Channel Islands time-warp experiences. These leftovers from the Pleistocene age occur only here and on the California mainland around La Jolla.

6 **Water Canyon Beach & Skunk Point**
Water Canyon Beach is probably Santa Rosa's most obvious feature—2 miles of white-sand beach arcing southeast from the landing pier. But don't just walk the beach; keep going to **Southeast Anchorage** and beyond to Skunk Point.

You'll see tide pools, blowholes, coastal cliffs with views of Santa Cruz Island, and the offshore wreck of the four-masted lumber schooner *Jane L. Stanford*. (Note that access to Skunk Point is restricted to the area below the main high tide. To protect nesting Snowy Plovers, you can't visit the back beaches and sand dunes from March 15 to September 15.)

7 **Lobo Canyon** Lobo Canyon is a sandstone cliff cut by a perpetual stream of water and equally perpetual wind that would be right at home in a place like Utah. The canyon runs 2.5 miles from an old ranch road down to the ocean, and it takes a side turn into a true slot canyon. Its walls are lined in smooth faces of purple and yellow sandstone, and toyon and wild cherry trees spring from the banks of the stream.

It's an 8-mile round-trip from the campground to the start of Lobo Canyon, but the Park Service often provides guided hikes for overnighters.

ANACAPA

Anacapa, composed of three small islands, is the closest of the Channel Islands to the mainland, making it ideal for a quick day trip.

8 **Inspiration Point** This is the must-see place on East Anacapa. In the clear water, bat rays dart amid a forest of giant kelp. Unsurprisingly, it invites diving and snorkeling. "The diving is amazing," says Faulkner. "The giant kelp is like the rain forest of the marine environment."

A hidden cove near the East Point of Santa Rosa Island

"In the Channel Islands, a lot of work goes into restoration and recovery of the native and endemic plants and animals that call these islands home," says Bill Faulkner, interpretive ranger.

Faulkner cites examples of recent park projects that have helped island natives resurge: eradication of rats on Anacapa that benefited nesting sea-birds; and removal or eradication of sheep, cattle, elk, golden eagles, and feral pigs from Santa Cruz and Santa Rosa, resulting in saving the endemic island fox and the return of nesting bald eagles. The outlawing of the pesticide DDT helped bring back the brown pelican, which breeds on West Anacapa and Santa Barbara Islands, from near extinction.

Now the park is focusing on restoring native vegetation. "A lot of seabirds rely on native plant species," reports Laurie Harvey, park biologist. "The more intact the ecosystem, the better for key species like the Xantus's murrelet, ashy storm-petrel, and Cassin's auklet."

Anacapa is also home to a working lighthouse, whose horn sounds every 18 seconds. This is also a good place to watch out for impressive bald eagles, which have returned to the island after a 60-year absence.

SAN MIGUEL ISLAND

A warning: San Miguel, 58 miles from **Ventura Harbor**, is only for the determined and hardy.

First, it's a four-hour boat trip just to get there. Island Packers makes runs to the island from spring to fall for both day and camping trips but advance planning is required. Second, be prepared for the weather: The island is frequently hammered by fierce 30-knot winds.

It's all worth it, though, for the 16-mile round-trip guided hike to **Point Bennett** to view one of North America's prime wildlife spectacles—some 30,000 seals and sea lions hauled out on the point's beaches.

On the way you'll see the caliche forest —strange sand castings that amount to a petrified forest of ancient vegetation.

NOT TO BE MISSED: Dive among the bat rays off Inspiration Point. ▸ Kayak into the huge sea caves of Santa Cruz Island. ▸ Spot the endemic island scrub jay or island fox. ▸ Try a strenuous guided hike on San Miguel Island to marvel at some 30,000 seals and sea lions sunning at Point Bennett.

SANTA BARBARA ISLAND

The smallest and most southerly of the Channel Islands, Santa Barbara has great snorkeling at its **Landing Cove**—where sea lions cooperatively congregate for photographers—and 5 miles of hiking trails. Be sure to make the 4-mile round-trip hike to Arch Point to view the sea lion rookery.

Island Packers runs a few trips to Santa Barbara late summer and fall. The boat schedule generally requires a three-day stay at the island's fine little campground—call ahead for reservations.

Full moon rising over Zabriskie Point

DEATH VALLEY

Death Valley, which spans California and Nevada, is desert and mountain laid bare and dissected. You might not think such a barren place would have secrets—but you would be wrong. Extremes and oddities are everywhere. A shimmering salt pan of a desert floor. The lowest and hottest place in North America. Mountains largely bereft of trees, but presenting geology lessons written in stony hues of red, blue, green, and yellow. Sand dunes, volcanic craters, and critters that live nowhere else on Earth. The most improbably sited castle you'll ever see.

Much of Death Valley can seem ferocious and forsaken, but the National Park Service has done a brilliant job of making it highly visitable. From fall through spring, short walks can take you beyond the intimidating veneer. It's then that a park labeled death truly comes to life. But heed the warnings: Don't hike in summer, don't feed the wildlife, and don't drive off road.

Year-Round Visitor Centers

■ **Furnace Creek Visitor Center**
On Calif. 190, Furnace Creek resort area

■ **Scotty's Castle Visitor Center & Museum**
On Nev. 267, north end of park

760-786-3200, nps.gov/deva

Walk out on that extraordinary valley floor until you can no longer read the sea level sign tucked into a palisade of the **Black Mountains** above Badwater and can barely see the parked cars.

Enjoy a surface that is both crisp and pliant, like strolling on chocolate-chip cookies. Observe the geometric patterns of the floor plates, lifted by expanding salt crystals.

"There might be water out there," says Patrick Taylor, Death Valley interpretive ranger. "That alone is kind of fascinating." So is the sense of solitude—but you're not alone. "There's life, too: microscopic extremophiles growing under the salt," Taylor adds.

❶ **Devils Golf Course** A few miles up the road from Badwater, the valley floor gets even stranger. Trying to hit a seven iron out of the extensive rough that is ironically named Devils Golf Course would be hellish; not that there's a green anywhere near.

Here crystallized minerals reacting with groundwater have lifted themselves into tightly packed ridges and globules up to 2 feet high. You can walk out as far as you wish—most of the ridges will support your weight, though the going is clumsy, a bit like walking across crunchy broken glass.

BADWATER & THE VALLEY FLOOR

Two miles out into Badwater Basin is the lowest place in North America, 282 feet below sea level. Yet most people know only the puddle of foul-tasting water beside **Badwater Road**, an attraction that takes two minutes to see (and that's exactly how long most visitors spend there).

But **Badwater Basin**—that vast, cracked, parched-looking, bright white salt flat that extends clear across the valley floor to the base of the **Panamint Range,** distills everything that is wonderful about Death Valley.

BLACK MOUNTAINS

The rugged range that rises above Death Valley's eastern flank holds the park's most fabled drive-up viewpoints. Spaced apart by about a 30 minute drive, **Zabriskie Point** and **Dantes View** are both off Calif. 190.

The first, Zabriskie Point, looks out over barren badlands that glow in early morning light, making it a popular place to gather for sunrise. The second, Dantes View, stares nearly 6,000 feet straight down onto Badwater.

2 Artists Drive This one-way scenic loop off Badwater Road climbs steeply into the mountains south of Zabriskie Point, giving you an up-close look at side canyons whose minerals shine in shades of ocher, red, and tan.

But don't just drive; get out and walk. You can park at the second dip (the dips are obvious) and walk a mile or so up an unnamed, unsigned canyon—you're likely to have it to yourself—until it narrows to about 15 feet and becomes impassable without rock-climbing gear.

At the apex of Artists Drive is **Artists Palette,** where an easy walk starts from

---

NOT TO BE MISSED: *Stroll upon the crisp-cookielike surface of Badwater Basin.* ▸ *Experience the magic of the Red Cathedral within Golden Canyon.* ▸ *Learn about the lure of borax at the Borax Museum.* ▸ *Get a taste of Mars at Ubehebe Crater.* ▸ *Hike the park by moonlight and see the colors of the rock glow.*

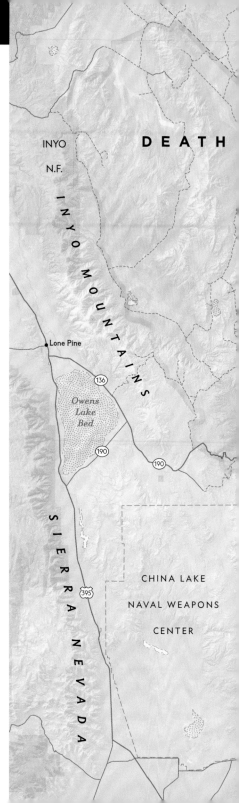

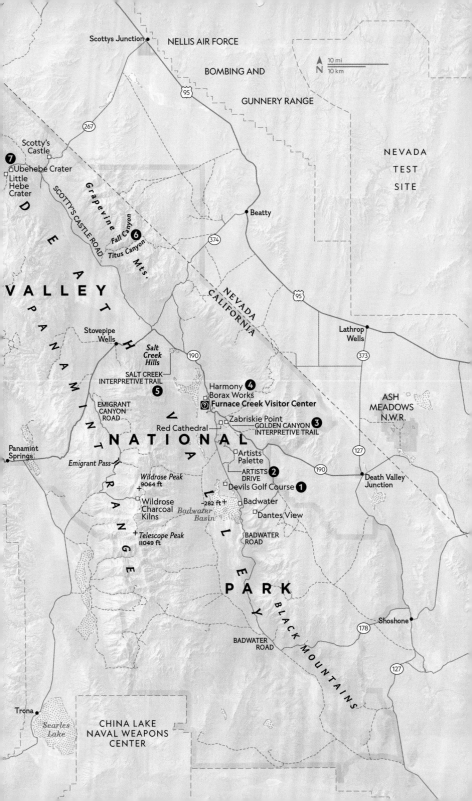

Scottys Junction

NELLIS AIR FORCE

BOMBING AND

GUNNERY RANGE

95

267

NEVADA

TEST

SITE

Scotty's
Castle

7 Ubehebe Crater
Little
Hebe
Crater

D

E

A

T

H

SCOTTY'S CASTLE ROAD

Grapevine

Fall Canyon

Titus Canyon **6**

Mts.

Beatty

374

NEVADA

CALIFORNIA

V A L L E Y

P A N A M I N T

95

Stovepipe
Wells

Salt
Creek
Hills

190

Lathrop
Wells

373

SALT CREEK
INTERPRETIVE TRAIL **5**

Harmony **4**
Borax Works

ⓟ Furnace Creek Visitor Center

ASH
MEADOWS
N.W.R.

EMIGRANT
CANYON
ROAD

Red Cathedral

Zabriskie Point

GOLDEN CANYON **3**
INTERPRETIVE TRAIL

Panamint
Springs

N A T I O N A L

Emigrant Pass

R

Artists
Palette

ARTISTS **2**
DRIVE

127

190

Death Valley
Junction

A

Wildrose Peak
9064 ft

Devils Golf Course **1**

N

Wildrose
Charcoal
Kilns

-282 ft

Badwater

G

*Badwater
Basin*

Dantes View

E

Telescope Peak
11049 ft

BADWATER
ROAD

P A R K

B L A C K

Shoshone

178

M O U N T A I N S

127

BADWATER
ROAD

Trona

*Searles
Lake*

CHINA LAKE
NAVAL WEAPONS
CENTER

N
10 mi
10 km

LOCAL INTELLIGENCE

What keeps a park naturalist in love with Death Valley for 21 years? "It's akin to the prospectors of the old days," says Alan Van Valkenberg, a retired ranger who served that long at the park. "The freedom to explore."

While most national parks admonish visitors to stick to established footpaths, Death Valley permits cross-country walking. "You think, 'Hey, it's a national park and I'm supposed to stay on trails,'" says Van Valkenberg, "but once you get past that, you realize you can wander anywhere your feet will carry you. That's pretty liberating. You never run out of discoveries." A caveat, of course, is to use your common sense.

Van Valkenberg also encourages prepared explorers to hike by night, when a bright moon or a star-filled sky provides ample illumination in light-colored open spaces. "Under a full moon you can see all the colors—the reds, yellows, oranges, and purples," he says.

a parking area and leads up a wash whose bordering rock faces are painted in reddish shades as well as lavender and blue.

❸ Golden Canyon Here is one of the park's popular interpretive nature walks—a brochure available at the trailhead off **Badwater Road** explains the canyon's geological phenomena at ten stops along the way.

Its secret, though, lies beyond stop No. 10, well past the point most people turn around. It's a 400-foot, red fluted wall known as the **Red Cathedral,** 1.25 miles from the trailhead. Walk this in late afternoon, when the low rays of the sun set the towering wall glowing with a brilliant red.

FURNACE CREEK AREA

Furnace Creek is the heart of the park, site of park headquarters, a visitor center, the country's lowest golf course, three campgrounds, and two inns—**Furnace Creek Ranch** and **Furnace Creek Inn.**

Even if you're not staying in Furnace Creek, take the time to park at the ranch and check out the huge steam engines

and other equipment outside the **Borax Museum,** as well as exhibits set within the oldest structure in Death Valley.

These explain the history of borax mining and display some nifty rock specimens. The museum also helps answer the inevitable question: Why in the world would pioneers endure the hardships of living here?

❹ Harmony Borax Works With a bit of borax lore under your belt, you'll appreciate the short walk around the well-preserved ruins of Harmony Borax Works, just north of Furnace Creek. Check out the adobe masonry surrounding the borax-refining machinery, and the big-wheeled 20-mule team wagon dozing in the sun just below the plant.

❺ Salt Creek A boardwalk nature trail along Salt Creek is a perfect platform for viewing one of the park's rarest denizens, the Salt Creek pupfish. The tadpole-size critters are especially active in spring—mating season—darting about in the clear saline water.

For a sense of solitude, take a short off-trail walk from the end of the boardwalk into the Salt Creek Hills—the dry-mud mounds that soon give way to small dry-mud canyons.

SCOTTY'S CASTLE

Scotty's Castle is hardly a secret—the ornate villa is the park's most popular attraction—but there's an alternative way to see the castle that's worth sticking around for after the main tour.

The hour-long **Underground Tour** literally plumbs the subterranean world beneath the home, whose owner, Albert Johnson, was a civil engineer with a penchant for technology. The tour starts in a basement and proceeds through a system of tunnels.

You see such innovations for the period —1930s and 1940s—as hollow insulation tiles, massive nickel-iron batteries for storing electricity generated by a Pelton wheel, and (outside) a solar water heater.

Note: As of 2020, Scotty's Castle is closed due to massive flood damage. Check the park website before visiting for up-to-date information.

6 **Titus & Fall Canyons** Walking up either of these side-by-side canyons off **Scotty's Castle Road** gets you quickly into a spectacular, steep-sided defile carved into the **Grapevine Mountains.**

Each walk is lined with steep walls of twisted, metamorphosed marble and dolomite. Titus is easier going as you're walking up a road, but you might meet vehicles coming toward you on the one-way passage.

You'll also reach narrow sections just 15 feet wide in less than a mile. Because it follows a road, this is the rare trail in the park that you can take dogs on. "But keep them on a leash," warns Taylor.

"There are bighorn sheep up there."

A signed trail at the mouth of Titus Canyon leads over to Fall Canyon, whose floor is coarse sand—slower going, but you're almost guaranteed solitude for whatever portion of the 3.5-mile hike you opt for. Early morning is the best time to explore either canyon.

7 **Ubehebe Crater** Just west of Scotty's Castle is a little slice of Mars known as Ubehebe Crater, a maw of a volcanic crater a half-mile wide and 600 feet deep. Geologists once assumed it was thousands of years old, but they now estimate that the blast could have occurred as recently as 800 years ago.

To best appreciate the crater and the alien landscape that surrounds it, follow the 1.5-mile (round-trip), signed trail that leads above Ubehebe's west rim and climbs to **Little Hebe Crater.**

You get great views of both craters and two other smaller ones as well as of some dramatic gullies carved into the gray, cinder-strewn landscape.

Aerial view of Ubehebe Crater

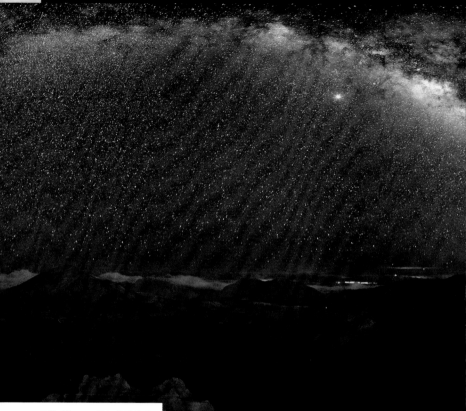

Milky Way over Haleakalā Crater

HALEAKALĀ

Covering 33,265 acres—some 24,000 of which is designated wilderness—and named for the dormant volcano Haleakalā (meaning "house of the sun") that dominates Maui's skyline, Haleakalā National Park has two access points. The more popular leads to the crater rim (9,740 feet) from the tourism-heavy side of the island between Wailea and Kahului; the other is from Kīpahulu, on the remote eastern shore near the town of Hāna.

There are no highways or trails connecting the upper and lower parts of the park. Although more than one million people visit Haleakalā each year, many in organized tour groups to watch the sun rise, the park is beautiful throughout the entire day, and sunrise from the summit is a very different experience than sunset from the beaches. If you seek a more in-depth exploration of the secrets of Haleakalā, embark on any of the web of hiking trails that start near the visitor centers.

Year-Round Visitor Centers

▪ Park Headquarters
  Visitor Center
  *On Hawaii 378, park summit
  entrance*
▪ Haleakalā Visitor Center
  *11 miles south (uphill) of Park
  Headquarters*
▪ Kīpahulu Visitor Center
  On Hawaii 31

  808-572-4400, nps.gov/hale

entering," requests Bennadette Duman, interpretation and education specialist at the park. This is to prevent accidentally introducing unwanted plant seeds and disease that could contribute to the rapid death of the ohi'a.

In addition to having an elevation (6,750 feet) well suited to viewing the unique flora of the park, **Hosmer Grove** is an exceptionally good area for bird-watching, with several native forest birds—including Hawai'i's endangered honeycreepers—regularly spotted. At night, the Hawaiian hoary bat, called the *'ōpe'ape'a,* sometimes makes an appearance.

PARK HEADQUARTERS VISITOR CENTER

Park Headquarters Visitor Center is the place most people start their visit. Interpretive guides are available here to answer questions, make suggestions, and help you get your bearings.

❶ **Hosmer Grove Loop** This is an easy but rewarding hike that starts 1 mile below the Park Headquarters Visitor Center.

Next to the drive-in campground, a short trail leads through a non-native forest past ohi'a lenua trees and native shrubland. "Please be sure to clean all gear and hiking shoes of all debris before

❷ **Halemau'u Trail** Considered moderate in difficulty because of its terrain and high elevation, this trail begins at the 8,000-foot level (3.5 miles upslope from the Park Headquarters Visitor Center) and leads 1.1 miles through native shrubland to the rim of **Ko'olau Gap**.

Here, the cliffs drop off 1,000 feet and you are treated to extraordinary views across the upper reaches of the park. If you are looking for a short walking experience, this is a good one.

Pressing forward from the rim, though, a longer trail descends 1,400 feet down a sometimes steep (and narrow)

series of switchbacks to the valley floor. The views along this portion of the trail are remarkable, revealing a valley that shows various shades of muted rust and brown, is punctuated by lava flows and lava cones, and is in many places covered in cinder ash.

At the 3.7-mile mark of this trail, you'll run across **Hōlua Cabin** and campsite for overnight stays (with permit). Less than a mile beyond the cabin, a cursory jaunt off the Halemau'u Trail, the 1-mile **Silversword Loop** leads through an area displaying one of the greatest concentrations of 'āhinahina (silversword plants)

in the park. A mature 'āhinahina can stand 8 feet tall, with misty silver fingers emanating from a spiny center stalk.

The Halemau'u Trail is one of the park's primary hiking arteries. It extends 10.3 miles from the trailhead to the **Palikū Cabin** and the **Kaupō Trail**. The trail also branches off to **Keonehe'ehe'e (Sliding Sands) Trail.**

For a longer (11.2 mile) day hike, plan ahead and leave a car at the start of Halemau'u. Then walk out to the hiker pick-up area where you can catch a ride to Keonehe'ehe'e, hiking back along the trail to your waiting vehicle.

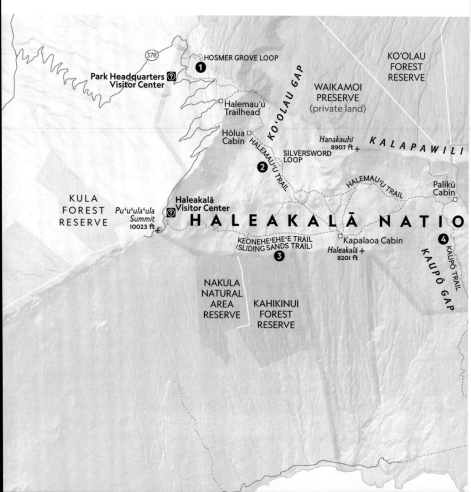

HALEAKALĀ VISITOR CENTER

Haleakalā National Park preserves the volcanic landscape of the upper slopes of the mountain and protects its unique and fragile ecosystems that include many rare and endangered plants and forest birds. But this is not the jungle-covered Hawai'i portrayed in Hollywood movies. Instead, you'll get a glimpse into the geologic history of the island chain and its fiery volcanic past.

Start at the Haleakalā Visitor Center and hike from there. Trails range from 10-minute strolls to overnight trips. Three rustic cabins are available by reservation.

3 Keonehe'ehe'e Trail This trail sets out from the visitor center and descends 2,500 feet through a cinder desert to the crater floor and a vast wilderness area. "The crater is one of the quietest places on earth," shares park superintendent Natalie Gates.

The trail's descriptive Hawaiian name, Keonehe'ehe'e, refers to how a *he'e*—or octopus—moves across the reef. In the soft cinders, hikers experience a trail that slides octopus-like underfoot. The

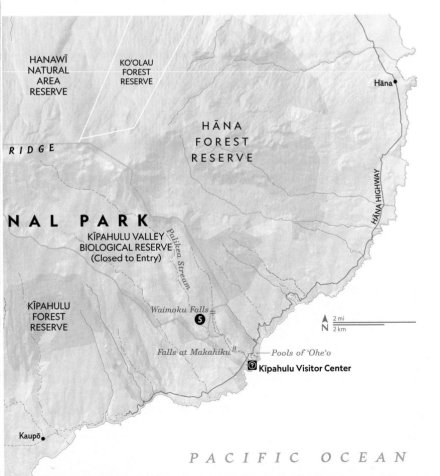

A boardwalk through a bamboo forest at Haleakalā

footing is safe, but it adds to the challenge of hiking back up the steep trail to the visitor center. It also takes twice as long to hike up.

The first portions of the Keonehe'ehe'e Trail are beautifully desolate, with little shrubbery and no trees or greenery of any sort. But the red-hued cinder ash is otherworldly, particularly as you pass the frequent *pu'u* (cinder cones) along the way.

Kapalaoa Cabin is found 5.6 miles from the trailhead, and **Palikū Cabin** is 9.3 miles from the trailhead. Both require permits for overnight stays.

4 Kaupō Trail One of the less traveled and most spectacular trails in the upper regions of the park is the Kaupō Trail. Considered one of the premier hikes in Hawai'i, the upper trailhead is found near Palikū Cabin. Visitors will be rewarded with lush scenery and frequent waterfalls visible from the trail.

Many find hiking up the rugged and steep Kaupō Trail from the ocean easier than hiking downhill from the cabin. The trail traverses the outer wall of the verdant pali, with broad views toward the **Big Island of Hawai'i** and down toward the southeastern shore of **Maui.**

LOCAL INTELLIGENCE

Haleakalā figures prominently in Hawaiian mythology. One of the most widely told stories recalls an achievement of Māui, an ancient Polynesian sailor and navigator with many feats and tales to his credit. One of his many accomplishments, as the legend has been told for generations, was to climb to the summit of Haleakalā and lasso the sun's rays in order to slow the sun's passage and prolong the day.

Throughout Polynesia, this tale is most prominent in Hawai'i and Aotearoa (New Zealand), the two portions of the "Polynesian Triangle" farthest away from the Equator, which share seasonal changes in day length—important knowledge for island mariners.

NOT TO BE MISSED: *Bird-watch at Hosmer Grove.* ▸ *Travel the Halemau'u Trail to the valley floor, branching off to see the park's rare silversword plants.* ▸ *Waterfall-watch along the rugged Kaupō Trail.* ▸ *Drive the scenic Hāna Highway, stopping often for spectacular views.*

The trail actually goes beyond park boundaries through privately owned lands. While the property owners have granted hikers permission to pass through, provided they stay on the designated trails, the park advises against this, noting that the Kaupō Trail outside park boundaries is rugged and unimproved. Visitors go at their own risk.

KĪPAHULU

The other park entrance is via Kīpahulu. To get to the **Kīpahulu Visitor Center,** you'll take one of the most dramatic drives in the Hawaiian Islands, the **Hāna Highway,** a 68-mile route along the scenic east coast of Maui. With 620 hairpin curves, 59 bridges, and numerous turnouts to snap photos, it often takes more than 2.5 hours to get to the town of Hāna from Kahului.

Another 30 minutes (10.7 miles) past Hāna is the Kīpahulu Visitor Center and the coastal area of Haleakalā National Park. Far different than the more barren upper reaches, at Kīpahulu the terrain is green with rain forest vegetation and waterfalls are common.

Hāna and Kīpahulu were once densely populated and farmed. The Kīpahulu portion of the park was added not only to preserve scenery, but also to

allow a glimpse into traditional Hawaiian lifestyles. Walter Pu, park guide, says that for him, "Kīpahulu is living the past, sustaining the future."

⑤ Waimoku Falls Stop first at the visitor center to enjoy cultural demonstrations and get hiking advice. Short trails branch out from here to the coast and upslope to Waimoku Falls (4 miles round-trip) and **Falls at Makahiku** (2 miles round-trip).

While many are tempted to swim in the **Pools of ʻOheʻo,** wise visitors will just take pictures while keeping their feet dry. Those who disregard the warning signs can easily slip on the smooth rocks or be swept out to sea by sudden "freshets"—flash floods that come without warning.

And even clear, calm, fresh waters can be home to parasites such as *giardia* and *spirulosis* in modern Hawaiʻi. A spontaneous swim can lead to months of medical care.

ʻOheʻo Gulch, aka Seven Sacred Pools

Hōlei Sea Arch

HAWAI'I
VOLCANOES

It may be that the greatest secret to appreciating Hawai'i Volcanoes National Park involves understanding and accepting it as a place of near-constant change—as an example of the power of volcanism to transform our planet in profound ways. This was explicitly demonstrated in 2018, when a series of lava eruptions and earthquakes closed the park for more than four months, with a limited reopening beginning in 2019.

The impact of this volcanic activity was huge: New lava flows, which covered more than 13 square miles, contributed to the destruction of more than 700 houses, and more than 800 acres of land was added to the island of Hawai'i. Not surprisingly, the landscape at the park's summit area, especially Halema'uma'u Crater, took on a very different aspect.

Year-Round Visitor Center

■ Kīlauea Visitor Center

On Hawaii 11, Crater Rim Drive,
between mile marker 28 and 29,
southwest of Hilo

808-985-6000, nps.gov/havo

KĪLAUEA VISITOR CENTER

The park entrance is located near the small town of Volcano, where you'll find restaurants and lodging. Here also is the **Volcano Arts Center,** which oversees the adjacent Niaulani rain forest, a small patch of old-growth forest of the type that's rarely accessible elsewhere.

"I really love going in there," says local tour leader Rob Pacheco. "So much of the area around has been either affected by volcanic activity or deforested, but here's this little area that never got developed and has never been overrun by lava. There are giant koa and ohi'a trees and giant tree ferns. They have a short trail, so you can spend 15 or 20 minutes and see it all."

Just minutes away is the park entrance and visitor center. It's especially appropriate to check with staff at this park, where conditions continue to change rapidly and areas may be closed temporarily.

Keep in mind the advice of local resident and birding guide Nick Shema: "I would say from sunrise to about 10 a.m. is the best time to visit the park. After that things get a bit crowded and parking becomes an issue at certain locations." Buses with passengers from cruise ships often arrive at midday, and "it gets pretty crazy," Shema adds.

Near the visitor center, sites such as the **Steam Vents** and **Sulphur Banks** demonstrate aspects of volcanism; the **Halema-'uma'u Trail** passes through rain forest and by formations of pahoehoe lava (identifiable by its smooth, undulating surface). Gerrit van der Plas, an astronomer and founder of *lovebigisland.com,* recommends **Steaming Bluff** at sunrise "for spectacular views of Mauna Loa and Mauna Kea, the Halema'uma'u Crater, and a good start of your day for exploring the park."

The crater itself looks very different from before the 2018 activity, having increased greatly in both depth and diameter, and without (at this writing) any glowing lava flows.

One reason parking is sometimes an issue is the closure of the park's Jaggar

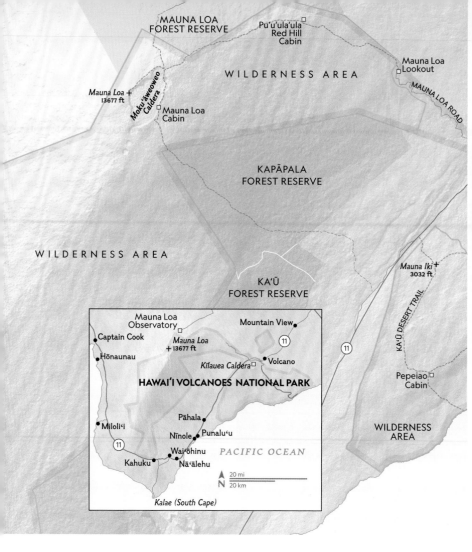

Museum, which once provided a fine view into Halema'uma'u Crater. (Some of the artifacts from the museum are now housed at the **Lava Zone Museum** in the small town of Pahoa, about 30 miles east of the park.)

CRATER RIM DRIVE

Crater Rim Drive, which once circled Halema'uma'u, has been partially closed since the 2018 eruption as well, terminating just west of the Steam Vents area.

① Kīlauea Iki Trail Following Crater Rim Drive clockwise from the entrance station leads to several of the park's most popular areas. The 4-mile loop Kīlauea Iki Trail passes through an area of rain forest to the **Kīlauea Iki Crater**, a solidified lava lake. Van der Plas calls this "one of my favorite ways to get a good feel of the park." Hikers here will see formations such as steam vents, cinder cones, and spatter cones, many dating from a massive 1959 eruption. This event produced spectacular volcanic activity,

HAWAI'I VOLCANOES NATIONAL PARK

PACIFIC OCEAN

10 mi
10 km

including lava fountains shooting 1,900 feet into the sky, the highest recorded in Hawai'i during the 20th century.

A half-mile farther along the road is **Thurston Lava Tube** (Nāhuku), where a short trail leads through a forest of tree ferns to a "tube" where molten lava once ran; when the outside solidified before the inside, a tunnel was left, 450 feet long and up to 20 feet high. Electric lights help guide the way through. Note: This trail was closed following the 2018 eruption; check with the park for its current status.

CHAIN OF CRATERS ROAD

Dropping 3,700 feet to the Pacific Ocean in 19 miles, Chain of Craters Road passes through forest to vast expanses of old lava flows, with many enticing sights along the way.

❷ Crater Rim Trail Not far from the intersection of Chain of Craters Road with Crater Rim Drive, watch for the Crater Rim Trail. From here, a rewarding 1-mile trek west leads to **Keanakako'i Crater**.

"You walk through beautiful native forest, then across an old lava flow with interesting formations along the way," says park volunteer Cindy Granholm.

PACIFIC VIEWS

Back on the road, continue 2 miles farther and turn west on Hilina Pali Road. "Many visitors miss the spectacular **Hilina Pali Overlook,** just 9 miles along the road at a beautiful covered picnic area," says park ranger Dean Gallagher. "A short walk toward the ocean offers breathtaking panoramic views looking over 2,000 feet down to the blue Pacific crashing waves onto the rugged lava coastline far below."

❸ Mauna Iki Trail Gallagher also recommends walking part of the Mauna Iki Trail, starting near the Kulanaokuaiki campground. "Approximately 3 miles out, you'll see a sign for the **Twin Pit Craters** on your right. Nothing will prepare you for these spectacular formations hundreds of yards deep into the lava flows. The secret nesting sites of the native

NOT TO BE MISSED: *Let your senses take in the sights and smells at the Sulphur Banks site.*
▸ *Walk across the surface of an old lava lake on the Kīlauea Iki Trail.*
▸ *Explore a tunnel through lava at Thurston Lava Tube (Nāhuku).*
▸ *Marvel at Pacific coastline views at Hilina Pali or Kealakomo overlooks.* ▸ *Decipher the petroglyphs at Puʻu Loa.*

white-tailed tropicbirds are within these crater walls. Be sure to bring a camera because this just may be your once-in-a-lifetime Hawaiian experience."

❹ Nāpau Trail Farther along Chain of Craters Road is the 18-mile round-trip Nāpau Trail, which van der Plas calls his "favorite long hike in the park, although not a trek for the faint of heart!"

Beginning at the Mauna Ulu parking area, the trail takes you past many different geologic features such as lava trees, pit craters, and lava channels from

LOCAL INTELLIGENCE

National parks can be spiritual places, but not many have their own resident goddess. Count Hawaiʻi Volcanoes National Park as an exception. Here, Pele, Hawaiʻi's powerful fire goddess, is said to live in **Halemaʻumaʻu Crater,** near the park's main entrance. In ancient Hawaiʻi, people displayed great respect for their deities, calling on them to bless food crops and bring success in fishing, good tidings for family, or strength in battle.

Today, "We look at Pele as a grandmother figure," explains Danny Akaka, one of Hawaiʻi's most respected elders and cultural ambassadors. "She takes care of our land. When we go visit Tutu Pele, we take an offering and lay it on the edge of the crater in respect. We want our children to grow up with a strong connection to our cultural past."

Most often, the offering is an open *maile* lei—made from the vines and leaves of Hawaiʻi's maile plant. Akaka explains: "It represents an umbilical cord that connects us to the spiritual side."

recent eruptions. Hikers will also go by the remains of a 19th-century factory that harvested pulu (fibers) from tree ferns to use as stuffing for pillows and mattresses.

As Chain of Craters Road descends, expansive panoramas of the ocean stretch before you. Keep a lookout for the **Kealakomo overlook**, located at the edge of an escarpment with a view of what was once a village, now buried by the massive Mauna Ulu lava flows of 1969 to 1974.

Six miles farther along the road, watch for the sign for **Pu'u Loa.** Here, a walk of less than a mile leads to Hawai'i's largest collection of petroglyphs, with thousands of sacred images dating from 1200 to 1450. Chain of Craters Road ends beside the Pacific Ocean at the **Hōlei Sea Arch**, varied layers of lava shaped by erosion.

MAUNA LOA ROAD

Since 2018, the park has entered a quiet period, with no eruptions or lava flows—part of the cycle of activity and dormancy that has continued for millennia.

❺ Kipukapuaulu Trail "A kipuka is formed when the flowing lava goes around and spares an area," explains Granholm. A fine example can be seen along the 1.2-mile Kipukapuaulu loop trail located 1.5 miles north of Hwy. 11 on Mauna Loa Road.

The resulting "island" of native vegetation, including old-growth koa and ohi'a trees, is "the densest stand of native plants anywhere in the park," Granholm adds. Kipukapuaulu is also among the best spots in the park to see native birds such as 'elepaio, 'apapane, and 'amakihi. Look too for the Kamehameha butterfly, one of only two native species of Hawaiian butterflies.

Beyond Kipukapuaulu, follow a narrow road toward a dead end below the 13,679-foot summit of the massive Mauna Loa volcano. A few cabins are available here, and backcountry camping is allowed with a permit. Hiking the upper slopes requires preparation, proper equipment, and extreme caution. In the sobering words of park personnel, "Be prepared for severe winter conditions, including blizzards, high winds, and whiteouts. Snow or driving rain are possible at any time of year. High altitude storms can occur without warning. Temperatures are below freezing at night year round."

New life amid the lava

The park's namesake Joshua trees

JOSHUA TREE

To the untrained eye, Joshua Tree National Park in California looks like a vast expanse of desert wilderness littered with gigantic piles of rusty brown rocks and punctuated by scraggly trees. Ironically, to the trained eye of a desert aficionado, it looks the same way. Desert lovers hold deep affection for Joshua Tree's spaciousness, its amazing rocks—fabled among rock climbers—and its signature Joshua tree, but they also understand that secrets lurk behind the scenes, particularly evidence of human residents.

Curious travelers willing to go afoot in Joshua Tree receive all sorts of rewards—bighorn sheep and desert tortoises; weathered remains of the mines and abodes of dreamers and desperadoes; pictographs and bedrock mortars left by Native Americans; and countless members of the yucca family, which put Mormon pioneers in mind of prophets with upraised arms.

Year-Round Visitor Centers

▪ **Oasis Visitor Center**
   *At Twentynine Palms,
   Oasis of Mara*
▪ **Joshua Tree Visitor Center**
   *6554 Park Boulevard,
   Joshua Tree Village*
▪ **Cottonwood Visitor Center**
   *At Cottonwood Spring,
   8 miles north of I-10*

Seasonal Visitor Center

▪ **Black Rock Nature Center**
   *At Black Rock Campground,
   Yucca Valley*

760-367-5500, nps.gov/jotr

HIDDEN VALLEY

Hidden Valley is about as close as Joshua Tree comes to a hub, yet many visitors miss the rock-ringed enclave for which it's named. This is what climbers call "Real Hidden Valley," adjacent to Hidden Valley picnic area and across the street from the campground.

"It encapsulates what the park is all about," says Joe Zarki, the park's chief of interpretation—meaning Hidden Valley combines natural and human history with the presence of rock climbers.

A popular 1-mile nature trail slithers through a portal of gigantic boulders, loops among huge rock formations, and leads to a secluded natural arena that was once lush with native bunchgrass—and hence a favorite spot for cattle rustlers to graze their contraband.

For fewer crowds, head across the street to **Intersection Rock** to watch the climbers challenging cracks and faces on formations such as **Sports Challenge** and **Gateway Rock.**

A branch trail on the east side leads to an impressive spire called **Hidden Tower,** a popular climbing spot because it harbors near-vertical routes that are not as difficult as they look.

❶ **Keys Ranch** Scads of dreamers—not to be confused with Native Americans—ambled through Joshua Tree in the 19th and 20th centuries, but rancher Bill Keys stands out as Edison of the Mojave Desert, the rare man to stake a claim, eke out a living, and even raise a family there.

Keys worked his Desert Queen Ranch from 1917 until his death in 1969. Today the well-preserved cattle ranch is open

only to ranger-led tours (book up to 30 days in advance at recreation.gov). It's worth it to make arrangements to visit. The 1916–1917 family home is still lovely. A windmill towers over orchards and all manner of carts, gizmos, trucks, and gold-mining machinery. Watch for bighorn sheep on nearby rocky promontories.

❷ Barker Dam & Petroglyphs Keys's stamp is on another popular Hidden Valley site called Barker Dam. Keys fortified and extended a mortared-stone barrier to catch winter rain that would pour through a usually dry wash.

It worked then—supplying much of the water for his ranch, cattle, and **Desert Queen Mine**—and still does. Hence the improbable sight of a lake (if there's been sufficient winter rain) in the heart of the bone-dry park.

The trail departs from a parking area just east of Hidden Valley. On the return part of the 1.3-mile loop, look for an alcove with the most vivid pictographs in the Mojave. Native? Yes, but enhanced (read: vandalized) by a Disney film crew in the early 1960s for that epic: *Chico, the Misunderstood Coyote.*

NOT TO BE MISSED: *Travel back in time at Keys Ranch.* ▸ *Visit Wall Street Mill and the site of a gunfight.* ▸ *Climb the stone steps to Ryan Mountain.* ▸ *Explore the desert oasis of Cottonwood Spring.* ▸ *Spy desert tortoises along Indian Cove Nature Trail.*

❸ Wall Street Mill A separate trail leads 1.1 miles from the Barker Dam parking area to yet another Keys site.

Wall Street Mill was a stamp mill for processing ore from Desert Queen Mine. The mill itself is one of the best preserved of its ilk in the desert, as is a windmill en route, while some old utility trucks lie decaying in the desert sand. Zarki, however, suggests another reason to make this easy hike.

"It's the place where Keys got into a gunfight with his neighbor Worth Bagley. It was a law-of-the-desert kind of

Barker Dam

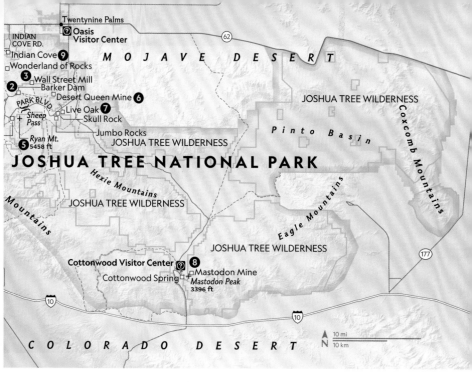

thing; Keys felt he should be able to cross Bagley's property to get to his."

A stone marker beside the trail reads: HERE IS WHERE WORTH BAGLEY BIT THE DUST AT THE HAND OF W.F. KEYS. MAY 11, 1943. Keys ended up serving five years in prison. The intercession of a part-time desert rat named Erle Stanley Gardner—yes, author of the Perry Mason mysteries—got him a hearing and eventually a pardon.

PARK BOULEVARD EAST OF HIDDEN VALLEY

Park Boulevard east of Hidden Valley climbs **Sheep Pass** between two mountainous regions of the park. **Skull Rock** is "the best place to park if a visitor wants to experience the amazing rocks of the area," says park ranger Christian Derlich.

He adds, "**Split Rock Trail** is a highlight as well. I consider this 2.5-mile loop to be the best hike in the park after Ryan Mountain." Although Split Rock does

have its own parking lot, signage for a connector trail from Skull Rock is just across the road.

4 Ryan Ranch Ryan Mountain was named for homesteaders Jep and Tom Ryan. The Ryans sited their home here for its water, which they pumped 3.5 miles cross-desert to their gold mine. What's left of their cattle ranch lies just to the west of there; a half-mile trail leads to it from Park Boulevard. Remains of gorgeous rust-colored adobe masonry only hint at what a fine stand this ranch was in its time.

5 Ryan Mountain If you're up for a bit of elevation gain, the 1.5-mile hike to the top of Ryan Mountain (5,458 feet) delivers the best view of the heart of the park.

It's also an outstanding piece of trail building—lots of stone steps assure firm footing for the 1,100-foot ascent. Do it early in the morning and you'll have

Wildflowers in the Live Oak area

shade most of the way up. From the top you can see all of the west side of the park and beyond to **Mount San Jacinto,** the **Wonderland of Rocks** to the north, and vast **Pinto Basin** to the east.

From the same trailhead parking area, a short trail leads to the **Indian Cave**—a natural rock lean-to on which you can see the effects of years of campfire smoke.

❻ Desert Queen Mine A smooth dirt road leads north from Park Boulevard to the trailhead for Desert Queen Mine, where you can see the ghostly remnants of tailings, cyanide tanks, machinery, and shafts that composed the most productive gold mine in Joshua Tree, yielding 3,845 ounces of gold from 1894 to 1961. A 0.25-mile walk leads to an overlook directly above the ruins.

❼ Live Oak You might think Live Oak is simply a name for a picnic area—not a secret site. Wrong. Drive west on the dirt road past the main picnic area until it

ends, then follow a short trail down to, yes, a towering live oak—a tree you'd expect to see on the coast or in the central valley of California, but not in this world of cactus, mesquite, and Joshua trees. How does it survive? "Deep roots," answers Zarki.

COTTONWOOD SPRING

The entire Cottonwood Spring area, 7 miles north of the park's southern entrance, is something of a secret as most visitors stick to the north, or whiz by if they enter from the south.

The spring itself waters a desert oasis shaded by native desert fan palms towering 75 feet above. It's a pleasant, restful spot just a short walk from the trailhead, filled with the sound of birdsong. Nearby are some bedrock mortars—smooth cavities in stone left by native Cahuilla women who crushed and ground seeds and piñon nuts with stone pestles.

⑧ Mastodon Mine If you've done some exploring in Joshua Tree, you might think, "Why visit another mine?" But the point of seeing Mastodon Mine is the walk in, because in the Cottonwood area you're in the Colorado Desert, entirely different from the Mojave Desert of the northern part of the park.

Instead of Joshua trees you'll encounter palo verde trees and tall, spindly ocotillo, which burst into red blossoms March through June. The 2.3-mile loop trail leads to **Mastodon Peak** and great views, then passes by mining ruins and the Winona stamp mill on the way back to Cottonwood.

INDIAN COVE

You don't just happen upon Indian Cove, a popular camping area at the northern end of the Wonderland of Rocks. It's not on the way to anywhere else in the park, but rather accessed by those in the know from Indian Cove Road 7 miles west of the town of Twentynine Palms.

⑨ Indian Cove Nature Trail Off by itself at the far west end of Indian Cove Campground is the Indian Cove Nature Trail, which leads into the secret world of a desert wash—"a corridor of biodiversity," as one interpretive sign puts it. Among the highlights along the 0.5-mile walk are flowery desert willows and desert almonds, whose fruit natives dried for food. In spring and fall, keep an eye out for desert tortoises.

Cholla cactus in bloom

LOCAL INTELLIGENCE

Over the centuries Joshua Tree National Park's human denizens included Native Americans, miners, and cattle ranchers.

"I have a deep appreciation and respect for their way of life," says Jeff Ohlfs, the park's chief ranger, who has lived here for more than 20 years. "They knew how to survive off the land. Chester Pinkham [a miner] saw more of this park than anyone who's ever worked here, and he traversed it all by mule."

Although the native presence dates back at least 5,000 years, traces of their lives aren't widely evident. "That's because they were nomadic," explains Ohlfs. "There are no pueblos or ancestral Puebloan ruins here."

More recent human arrivals, however, left plenty behind. Miners recorded thousands of claims in the area. Not all were worked, but many were, accounting for the abundance of mining ruins. Cattle ranchers went where the water was, staking claims at many watering holes and seeps. Of the settlers, prospectors get Ohlfs's vote as the toughest. Their creature comforts? Only a bedroll. "But that's just how they lived. They knew nothing else," he observes.

Moonrise at sunset, Pinnacles National Park

PINNACLES

After approaching through rolling central California landscape devoted to ranching and agriculture, Pinnacles National Park is a surprising world of spires, huge boulders, and towering peaks, all eroded into endlessly varied shapes. This terrain was born from volcanic eruptions 23 million years ago—not here, but 200 miles to the southeast. That ancient volcanic field lay across the San Andreas Fault, and as the western side of this active fracture moved north it carried the rocks of today's Pinnacles with it.

The park's 26,000 acres are popular not just for scenery but for wildflowers, wildlife (especially birds), hiking, and rock climbing. Visitors should be aware that although Hwy. 146 enters the park from both east and west, it does not connect. To drive from one side of the park to the other requires a trip of more than 50 miles. Most development, including the main visitor center and the park's only campground, is on the eastern side.

Year-Round Visitor Centers

◼ **East Pinnacles Visitor Center**
*Cal. 146, eastern side of park,
2 miles from Cal. 25*

◼ **West Pinnacles Visitor Contact
Station**
*Cal. 146, western side of park,
10 miles from Soledad*

831-389-4486, nps.gov/pinn

beautiful weather, peak wildflower bloom, and spring breaks," says ranger Elizabeth Hudick. "If people plan to visit during those months, they might consider arriving at off-peak times like early morning or late afternoon."

Park wildlife biologist Gavin Emmons has another suggestion for avoiding crowds at Pinnacles: "Rainy days in winter and spring can be very nice for visitors to see creeks flowing and waterfalls cascading over cliff faces," he says. "These are the only seasons we reliably have running water, and the threat of rain keeps away most people. Both **Bear Gulch Cave Trail** and **Moses Spring Trail** offer some wonderful opportunities."

THE EASTERN PARK

First stop is the park visitor center for information on trails and ranger-led programs. It's another 3 miles to the popular **Bear Gulch** area, with picnicking and a nature center (seasonal).

Pinnacles is famous for its wildflowers, especially in spring, when species such as California poppy, monkeyflower, shooting star, penstemon, Indian warrior, suncup, sage, larkspur, and lupine create a colorful display. During these months, the park can become extremely crowded, with road congestion and delays in entering. "March and April are our busiest months because of the confluence of

❶ **Condor Gulch Trail** Leaving from Bear Gulch, the Condor Gulch Trail ranks among the park's most popular. A climb of just 1 mile reaches an overlook with long-range views of dramatic rock formations and distant ridgetops. From here, many hikers continue to the **High Peaks Trail,** where loop routes of up to 6 miles are possible, offering even more views of rock spires eroded into an infinitude of picturesque shapes. Lucky hikers may spot a critically endangered California condor, reintroduced to the park as part of a recovery effort (see page 222).

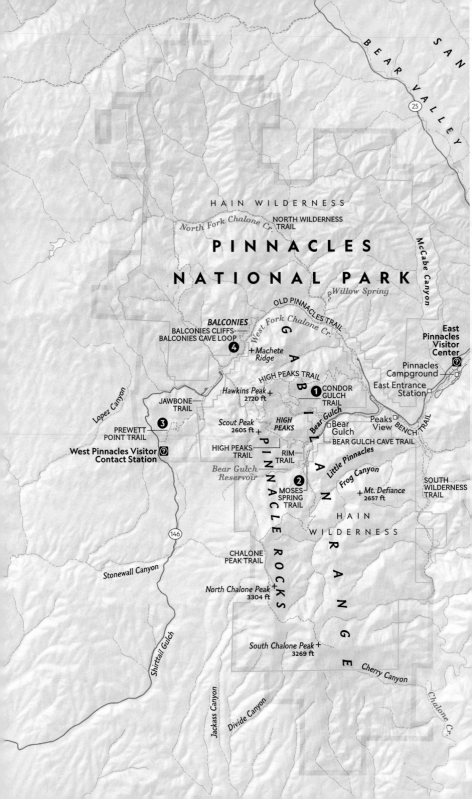

SAN
BEAR VALLEY

25

HAIN WILDERNESS

North Fork Chalone Cr.

NORTH WILDERNESS
TRAIL

PINNACLES
NATIONAL PARK

Willow Spring

McCabe Canyon

OLD PINNACLES TRAIL

BALCONIES
BALCONIES CLIFFS—
BALCONIES CAVE LOOP ④

West Fork Chalone Cr.

+ Machete
Ridge

G A B I L A N

East
Pinnacles
Visitor
Center

Pinnacles
Campground

HIGH PEAKS TRAIL

Hawkins Peak +
2720 ft

① CONDOR
GULCH
TRAIL

East Entrance
Station

JAWBONE
TRAIL

Scout Peak +
2605 ft

*HIGH
PEAKS*

Bear Gulch

Bear
Gulch

Peaks
View

BENCH TRAIL

Lopez Canyon

③

PREWETT
POINT TRAIL

HIGH PEAKS
TRAIL

RIM
TRAIL

BEAR GULCH CAVE TRAIL

Little Pinnacles

**West Pinnacles Visitor
Contact Station**

P I N N A C L E

Bear Gulch
Reservoir

② MOSES
SPRING
TRAIL

Frog Canyon

+ Mt. Defiance
2657 ft

SOUTH
WILDERNESS
TRAIL

H A I N

R A N G E

W I L D E R N E S S

146

R O C K S

CHALONE
PEAK TRAIL

Stonewall Canyon

North Chalone Peak +
3304 ft

South Chalone Peak +
3269 ft

Cherry Canyon

Shirttail Gulch

Chalone Cr.

Jackass Canyon

Divide Canyon

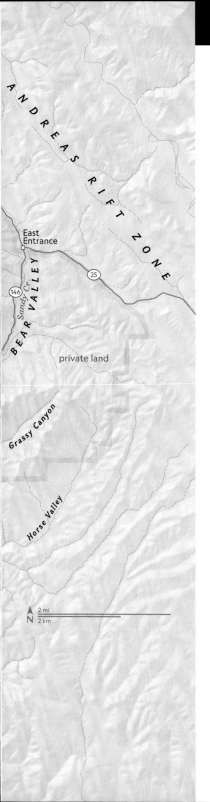

East
Entrance

A N D R E A S   R I F T   Z O N E

25

146

B E A R   V A L L E Y

Sandy Creek

private land

Grassy Canyon

Horse Valley

2 mi
2 km
N

❷ Moses Spring-Rim Trail Loop

Heading south from Bear Gulch, the Moses Spring Trail passes through a narrow valley of cottonwood and sycamore trees under scenic rocky bluffs, to reach **Bear Gulch Cave,** one of the park's two fascinating talus caves.

Here, trails wind beneath massive boulders that have fallen into gorges and wedged above the valley floor, forming narrow passageways where flashlights are required for entry. This cave, and the similar **Balconies Cave** to the north, may be closed at various times to protect bat colonies or because of seasonal flooding.

Just past Bear Gulch Cave lies **Bear Gulch Reservoir,** a scenic pool surrounded by tall rock formations. A trip here makes for perhaps the park's most appealing short hike (just 0.7 mile one way), especially for families.

"The edges of the day—at sunrise and sunset—can be quite special at the reservoir," Emmons says, "with early morning light and calm water in the morning providing some excellent opportunities for reflections in photos."

A return via the Rim Trail finishes the popular Moses Spring–Rim Trail Loop, a

Lupine in Bear Valley

LOCAL INTELLIGENCE

The near-mythic California condor soars on wings spanning 9 feet or more. In the 1980s, the population of this magnificent vulture had dropped to fewer than two dozen, making it one of the world's most endangered birds. Since then, breeding and conservation efforts have increased the number of captive and wild birds to more than 460, with nearly 100 individuals in the reintroduced central California population. The first nest of a condor was found at Pinnacles in 2010. For a chance to see these birds, recommended sites are the High Peaks region in early morning or early evening and the ridge just southeast of the campground.

2.2-mile round-trip hike with close-up views of cliffs and spires along the way. This walk, as elsewhere in the park, can be very sunny and hot summer through fall. Dehydration is a serious issue for many—carry plenty of water (no water is available on trails), and use sunscreen.

THE WESTERN PARK

Entering the park from the west, Hwy. 146 is extremely narrow and winding—not suitable for large recreational vehicles or trailers. Although facilities are limited in this part of the park, it's a good choice for those not hiking into the interior.

❸ Prewett Point Trail "The 1-mile Prewett Point Trail, which leaves from the West Pinnacles Contact Station, is flat and easy and wheelchair accessible," shares Hudick. "And it offers some of the best panoramic views of the park."

NOT TO BE MISSED: *Explore Balconies Cave.* ▸ *Visit Bear Gulch Reservoir in early morning.* ▸ *Spot a California condor.* ▸ *For a real thrill, try your hand at climbing the High Peaks—with a guide.*

---

❹ Balconies Cliffs–Balconies Cave Loop One of the park's most rewarding walks, this 2.4-mile loop begins at the Chaparral parking area. Hikers can first explore Balconies Cave (flashlight required) and return by the higher cliff route, which offers fantastic views of the park's largest rock formations. (Balconies Cave can also be reached from the east via the longer **Old Pinnacles Trail**, a 5.3-mile hike round-trip.)

The striking cliffs and towers of Pinnacles make it a very popular destination for rock climbers, with dozens of designated routes. "The east side of the Pinnacles has popular and easily accessible formations such as the **Tourist Trap, Discovery Wall,** and the **Monolith**," says local expert climber Bruce Hildenbrand. "The west face of the **First Sister** at the Bear Gulch Reservoir has been the first-ever rock climb for many. But it's the soaring spires of the **High Peaks** where the true Pinnacles climbing experience occurs, with sweeping summit vistas and the ever present California condors keeping watch."

However, the volcanic rock in the park can be brittle and weak, so caution and experience are vital. "Undoubtedly the best way would be to go with a gym excursion or a guide," Hildenbrand says.

California condor soaring

Giant Forest, Sequoia National Park

SEQUOIA

"Sequoias," wrote John Muir, "towering serene through the long centuries, preaching God's forestry fresh from heaven." The Scottish-American naturalist was one of the primary forces behind this California park's creation in 1890. A week after its designation, Congress summarily tripled the preserve's size. Over the years, Sequoia has expanded into one of the nation's largest parks, and it lies side by side with Kings Canyon National Park.

The Giant Forest area and its leafy legends—such as the General Sherman Tree—get plenty of visitors, especially with recent enhancements to the road network. The rest of Sequoia remains refreshingly devoid of apparent human impact, in particular a vast backcountry that includes Kern Canyon and 14,494-foot Mount Whitney. While it might take a backpack and good pair of hiking boots to explore Sequoia's secrets, there are plenty of secluded spots near the park's heart.

GIANT FOREST

Generals Highway meanders through Sequoia's western regions between the Foothills Visitor Center and the Grant Grove section of Kings Canyon National Park (page 239). Along the way are Giant Forest's celebrated sequoias. Start your visit at the Giant Forest Museum for an excellent introduction to the park's natural and human history.

❶ General Sherman Tree From the museum you can drive, hop the shuttle, or hike (roughly 2 miles) to the General Sherman Tree. At 275 feet, the tree has an estimated volume of more than

Year-Round Visitor Center
▪ Foothills Visitor Center
  On Generals Highway, 1 mile north of Ash Mountain Entrance

Seasonal Visitor Centers
▪ Lodgepole Visitor Center
  On Generals Highway, 2 miles north of the General Sherman Tree
▪ Mineral King Ranger Station
  On Mineral King Road, 28 miles from Three Rivers

  559-565-3341, nps.gov/seki

52,000 cubic feet, making it the largest living thing on Earth—and the most photographed plant in the park. Nearby Congress Trail can be crowded, but Giant Forest is laced with other less trafficked routes.

"There's a maze of trails that connect in different ways in the Giant Forest," says park ranger Becky Satnat. "Any trails in the middle of the grove are good for avoiding the crowds." To explore these routes, she suggests purchasing a detailed trail map of Giant Forest (available at the museum and visitor centers).

❷ Trail of the Sequoias Satnat says the most challenging (and rewarding) secret hike is Trail of the Sequoias, a 5-mile loop that starts beneath the Chief Sequoyah Tree.

The path climbs over several ridges and down into secluded Log Meadow, coined for the hollowed-out sequoia cabin built by pioneer rancher Hale Tharp in the 1860s, the oldest European structure in the park. From there, the trail loops around to Crescent and Circle Meadows, with plenty of giants such as Chimney Tree and the Pillars of

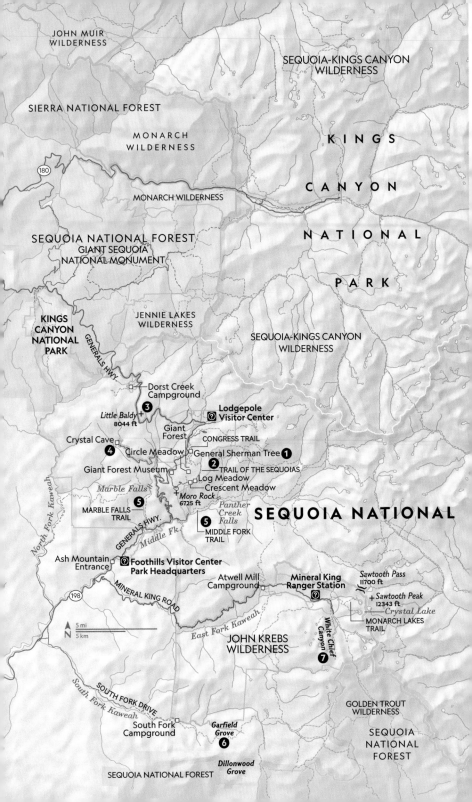

JOHN MUIR
WILDERNESS

SEQUOIA-KINGS CANYON
WILDERNESS

SIERRA NATIONAL FOREST

MONARCH
WILDERNESS

K I N G S

180

MONARCH WILDERNESS

C A N Y O N

SEQUOIA NATIONAL FOREST
GIANT SEQUOIA
NATIONAL MONUMENT

N A T I O N A L

P A R K

KINGS
CANYON
NATIONAL
PARK

JENNIE LAKES
WILDERNESS

SEQUOIA-KINGS CANYON
WILDERNESS

GENERALS HWY.

□ Dorst Creek
Campground

3 ✛

Little Baldy
8044 ft

Lodgepole
ⓘ **Visitor Center**

Giant
Forest

CONGRESS TRAIL

CRYSTAL CAVE ═

4

Circle Meadow

General Sherman Tree **1**

2 TRAIL OF THE SEQUOIAS

Giant Forest Museum □

□ Log Meadow
□ Crescent Meadow

Marble Falls

✛ *Moro Rock*
6725 ft

*Panther
Creek
Falls*

SEQUOIA NATIONAL

5

MARBLE FALLS
TRAIL

GENERALS HWY.

Middle Fk.

5
MIDDLE FORK
TRAIL

North Fork Kaweah

Ash Mountain
Entrance

ⓘ **Foothills Visitor Center**
Park Headquarters

Atwell Mill
Campground □

Mineral King
Ranger Station

ⓘ

Sawtooth Pass
11700 ft

✕

✛ *Sawtooth Peak*
12343 ft

Crystal Lake

198

MINERAL KING ROAD

MONARCH LAKES
TRAIL

▲
N

5 mi
5 km

East Fork Kaweah

White Chief
Canyon

7

JOHN KREBS
WILDERNESS

SOUTH FORK DRIVE

GOLDEN TROUT
WILDERNESS

South Fork Kaweah

South Fork
Campground □

*Garfield
Grove*

6

SEQUOIA
NATIONAL
FOREST

*Dillonwood
Grove*

SEQUOIA NATIONAL FOREST

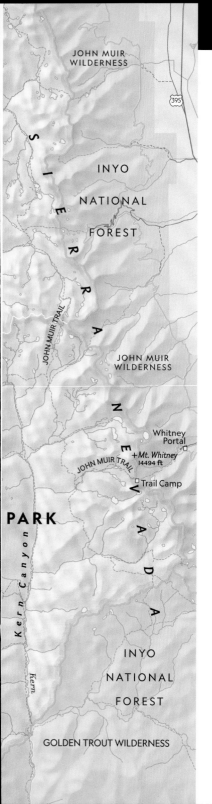

JOHN MUIR
WILDERNESS

INYO

NATIONAL

FOREST

S I E R R A

JOHN MUIR TRAIL

JOHN MUIR
WILDERNESS

N

E

JOHN MUIR TRAIL

Whitney
Portal

+Mt. Whitney
14494 ft

Trail Camp

V

PARK

A

Kern Canyon

D

A

Kern

INYO

NATIONAL

FOREST

GOLDEN TROUT WILDERNESS

NOT TO BE MISSED: *Hike among giant trees on the Trail of the Sequoias.* ▸ *Belly-crawl into Crystal Cave.* ▸ *Scale Little Baldy.* ▸ *Check out the rocks at Mineral King.*

Hercules along the way. It takes about four hours to complete the circuit back to the General Sherman parking lot.

❸ **Little Baldy** Although **Moro Rock** is a popular summit in the Giant Forest area, in summer the steep trail morphs into a highway of camera-clad hikers. An alternative is the granite dome called Little Baldy, about a mile east of **Dorst Creek Campground.** Little Baldy "is a little gem, and it's not too far from the road," says Erika Jostad, park ranger.

The total round-trip distance is 3.6 miles with some elevation gain, so plan about 90 minutes for the hike.

THE FOOTHILLS

The far western part of Sequoia National Park offers a contrast in landscape and temperament to the redwood belt and the High Sierra. Ranging between 500 and 5,000 feet in elevation, the region is clad in oaks and chaparral vegetation, and it is perforated by valleys and caves. **Foothills Visitor Center** near the Ash Mountain Entrance offers an overview of the park's diverse biosphere.

Unlike higher elevations of Sequoia that are often snowed in, the foothills area is open year-round. Summer temperatures can hit triple digits, but during the other seasons the hiking weather is sublime.

"This area is characterized by bands of limestone and marble," says Jostad.

"The marble is that same [geological] feature that **Crystal Cave** is in, the lower end of it. So this is where a lot of our cave features are.

"But you also get unique vegetation. In the springtime you might see yucca blooming. The buckeye trees are there, which have nice blossoms. It's also a great place for spring wildflowers. And really, spring starts in February down in the foothills."

❹ **Crystal Cave** One of the park's major landmarks, Crystal Cave perches on the upper edge of the foothills. The 45-minute daily tours (between Memorial Day and Labor Day) are a park staple. Less known are tours by the Sequoia Parks Conservancy *(sequoiaparksconservancy .org)*: the historical candlelight walk, the junior cave adventure for kids, and the four- to six-hour cave tour that involves belly-crawling through muck, mud, and tight places.

❺ **Middle Fork & Marble Falls Trails** Satnat recommends a couple of day hikes in the area. Middle Fork Trail leads 3 miles up **Kaweah River** to **Panther**

Climbing Mount Whitney

Creek Falls. "People can just walk on it as long as they want and then come back," Jostad explains. "But it does continue many miles into the Sequoia backcountry."

Even tougher is Marble Falls Trail, leading 3.9 miles to the cascade of the same name. Both trails are easily doable in a single day for anyone in good physical condition. Bring water.

SOUTH FORK

Another lush foothill area is South Fork, in Sequoia's southwest corner. Exit the park via the Ash Mountain Entrance, drive 6 miles south along Calif. 198, and then 13 miles east along South Fork Drive.

❻ **Garfield & Dillonwood Groves** Just inside the national park boundary on the South Fork Drive is a small campground. This is the jumping-off point for hikes to secluded Garfield and Dillonwood Groves, home to such giant sequoias as the **King Arthur Tree**, the ninth largest tree in the world by volume.

"Garfield is a pretty good-sized giant sequoia grove," says Jostad. "It's a very nice place to visit in the spring and fall. In the spring, for instance, you get a lot of wildflowers in that area. Getting into Dillonwood is a lot more challenging."

MINERAL KING

The Mineral King area in south-central Sequoia became part of the national park only some four decades ago. The moment you first lay eyes upon this striking highland valley, you wonder what took so long.

Mountains climb up from the meadow-strewn valley, carved by bygone glaciers and the East Fork Kaweah River. The vegetation is an eclectic blend of sequoia, pine, and fir trees, with alpine plants at higher elevations. Giant sequoias cluster on either side of the river at **Atwell Mill Campground** and are easy to reach from the main road.

"Mineral King wasn't even added to the park until 1978," explains Satnat, "because Walt Disney wanted to build a ski resort there." An epic environmental battle that raged for nearly a decade thwarted Disney and kept the valley pristine—not the first time that mankind tried to conquer the valley.

"The name Mineral King comes from an 1870s mining boom," says Satnat. "It was mostly silver, but other minerals, too. There's still a lot of old mines up that way."

"It's unique in the Sierra," adds Jostad. "A true alpine valley. A lot of rock types that you don't see elsewhere in the park and different plant associations. It's the old rock of the Sierra Nevada before it was transitioned into granite or metamorphic rock. It's also got marble outcrops and caves. And it's got its mining history."

The only road into Mineral King is a steep 25-mile drive from Calif. 198, which starts outside the Ash Mountain Entrance. (Note: No RVs or oversize vehicles permitted.) Its proximity to the **John Muir Trail** and **Mount Whitney** make the valley a prime starting point for backpacking. But there are plenty of day hikes to lakes and overlooks above the valley. The trail density is the highest in the park—11 different routes start from Mineral King.

❼ White Chief Canyon Jostad also likes the hike up to White Chief Canyon. "White Chief was one of the mines, so you see some of the mining history that was there," she observes. "It's also possible to get up close and personal with the marble, and you see polished marble in the streambed." The round-trip is about 8 miles, with an elevation gain of almost 1,800 feet.

LOCAL INTELLIGENCE

At 14,494 feet, Mount Whitney is the highest mountain in the lower 48 states. The western slope lies inside Sequoia National Park, the eastern slope in **Inyo National Forest.** Despite its height and intimidating façade, Whitney is comparatively easier to scale than other ultrahigh mountains (but still very difficult). "I've climbed Mount Whitney more times than I'd like to admit," says Erika Jostad, the ranger who oversaw the far eastern sector of Sequoia National Park for 18 years.

The mountain is most often conquered from **Whitney Portal,** near the town of Lone Pine in the Owens Valley east of the national park. "It's about 11 miles from Whitney Portal up to the summit," says Jostad. "And it's extremely strenuous. The elevation changes a lot and you should adequately acclimate yourself to the altitude before attempting the climb. The trail starts at 8,361 feet, which is high to begin with for most people. And then you're talking about adding 6,130 more feet on top of that."

The United States Forest Service offers an excellent online guide to climbing Mount Whitney from the eastern side, including checklists for planning and equipment. See *fs.usda.gov* for more information. From here, the trail climbs more than 6,000 feet in 11 miles.

The Tunnel View of Yosemite Valley

YOSEMITE

"Into this one mountain mansion," wrote Yosemite's great bard and advocate John Muir, "nature had gathered her choicest treasures, to draw her lovers into close and confiding communion." In light of the California park's visitation statistics, Muir's eloquence can sound ironic—more than four million visitors a year make the pilgrimage to the park, and the communion can seem a bit too close. Still, the majesty and ultimate spaciousness of Yosemite override its occasional crowds and protect its secrets. The granite cathedrals still soar above the valley, the Sierra peaks rise even higher, and waterfalls fill the air with the sound of liquid thunder, no matter how many people are there to witness it.

It's easy to avoid too-close communion if you go at the right time. July and August see more than twice as many visitors as the months of May and October—and dawn is almost exclusively yours anywhere in the park.

YOSEMITE VALLEY

Many equate Yosemite Valley with Yosemite National Park, yet the 7-mile-long valley represents just 3 percent of the park's total land area. Still, the valley does pack in the park's most fabled sights and is rightly its center stage.

Using the valley's free shuttle service and avoiding popular sights at peak hours during peak months are the best ways to avoid feeling crowded in the valley.

❶ Valley Floor Loop The great secret of Yosemite Valley is the hidden-in-plain-sight Valley Floor Loop. It sounds almost too good to be true: The 13-mile hiking trail (no bikes allowed) circles the valley and links such major sights as **Yosemite Falls**, **El Capitan**, and **Bridalveil Fall**—yet it sees very little foot traffic.

Using the park shuttle at its two stops along the way—**El Capitan Bridge** and the **Four Mile Trail** trailhead—allows you to hike half the loop or even less. But doing the full distance is surprisingly easy, as the trail is virtually flat, with just a few rises. As you walk, you can fancy yourself a sojourner in Muir's day, experiencing the beauty of Yosemite in solitary splendor.

"The trail was very popular until 1997," says park ranger Kari Cobb, "when a flood washed away the pavement, and people kind of forgot about it."

Remnants of the pavement remain, but most of the trail is dirt. And although you can hear the sound of cars and shuttles on the valley roads much of the time, you're too enthralled with the woods, meadows, waterfalls, and cliffs to pay the noise much attention.

Start at Yosemite Falls, shuttle stop No. 6, look for the sign for **Upper**

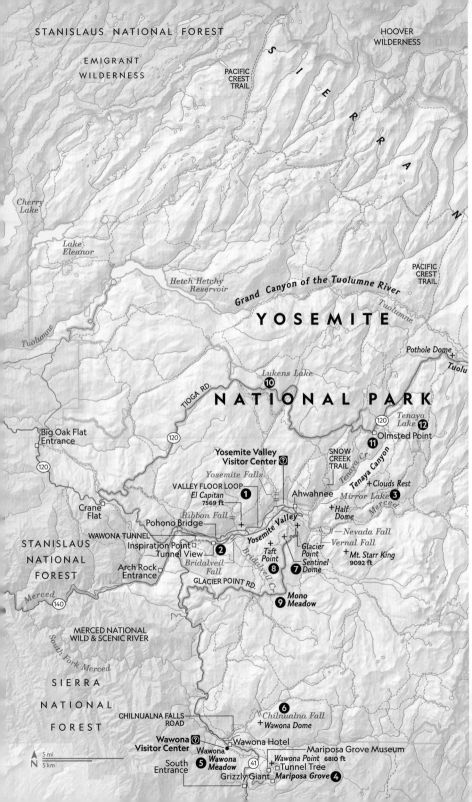

STANISLAUS NATIONAL FOREST

EMIGRANT WILDERNESS

HOOVER WILDERNESS

PACIFIC CREST TRAIL

S I E R R A

Cherry Lake

Lake Eleanor

Hetch Hetchy Reservoir

Grand Canyon of the Tuolumne River

Tuolumne

YOSEMITE

Tuolumne

Pothole Dome +

+ Tuolu

N

PACIFIC CREST TRAIL

Tuolumne

TIOGA RD.

Lukens Lake

10

N A T I O N A L   P A R K

120

Tenaya Lake

12

Big Oak Flat Entrance

120

Olmsted Point □

11

SNOW CREEK TRAIL

Tenaya Cr.

Crane Flat

Yosemite Valley Visitor Center ⑦

Yosemite Falls

VALLEY FLOOR LOOP
El Capitan 7569 ft **1**

Ribbon Fall +

Pohono Bridge

WAWONA TUNNEL

Inspiration Point □

Tunnel View

Arch Rock Entrance □

Ahwahnee

Tenaya Canyon

+ Clouds Rest

Mirror Lake

Merced

3

Half Dome

Yosemite Valley

Nevada Fall

Vernal Fall

Bridalveil Cr.

Bridalveil Fall

2

Taft Point

8

Glacier Point Sentinel Dome

7

+ Mt. Starr King 9092 ft

GLACIER POINT RD.

Merced

140

Mono Meadow **9**

STANISLAUS NATIONAL FOREST

MERCED NATIONAL WILD & SCENIC RIVER

South Fork Merced

SIERRA

NATIONAL

FOREST

Chilnualna Fall **6**
+ Wawona Dome

CHILNUALNA FALLS ROAD

Wawona Visitor Center ⑦

Wawona

Wawona Hotel

Mariposa Grove Museum

Wawona Point 6810 ft □
□ Tunnel Tree

△ 5 mi
N   5 km

South Entrance

Wawona Meadow **5**

41

Grizzly Giant □

Mariposa Grove **4**

HUMBOLDT-
TOIYABE
NATIONAL
FOREST

395

HOOVER WILDERNESS

INYO NATIONAL
FOREST

120

S I E R R A N E V A D A

Tuolumne
Meadows
Visitor
Center
TIOGA RD.

Tioga Pass
9945 ft

mne Meadows

PACIFIC
CREST
TRAIL

INYO
NATIONAL
FOREST

ANSEL ADAMS
WILDERNESS

SIERRA NATIONAL
FOREST

Yosemite Fall and Camp 4, and proceed walking west. You're quickly in a magic world of boulders and sheer cliffs, and it becomes obvious why the walk-in Camp 4 is known as the climbers' camp.

The trail proceeds west and occasionally crosses the park road, but that's a good thing—it puts you out into lovely El Capitan Meadow and skirts the north bank of the Merced River, sights that are hidden from the park road by trees. That's the beauty of this hike: You see the whole valley, not just its highlights.

After El Capitan, the trail crosses the Merced River on Pohono Bridge and passes by Bridalveil Fall. If Bridalveil Creek is flowing high, you might need to hike up to the road to cross it.

The trail then climbs a bit, opening onto great views of El Capitan Meadow and the monolith itself, as well as Ribbon Fall right next door to El Cap. After a long, quiet stretch in the woods, it passes by the backside of lovely Yosemite Chapel, where you can cross Sentinel Bridge to return to your starting point—or, if you're staying in Curry Village or one of the

Resident coyote

Half Dome in the majestic Sierra Nevada

campgrounds, you can extend your walk another couple of miles.

2 Above Tunnel View Back to the west toward the park entrance, it was the glorious vista from **Tunnel View** that inspired photographer Ansel Adams—as it has about 50 million other shutterbugs. Visitors stop where the park road emerges from **Wawona Tunnel,** and suddenly they see much of the grandeur of Yosemite Valley—El Capitan, Clouds Rest, Half Dome, Bridalveil Fall, and Cathedral Rocks.

But it's hard to feel like Ansel when you're sharing the view with a few hundred other excited travelers. The solution: Park in (or walk to) the upper parking lot and the trailhead for the route to **Inspiration Point.**

The full hike is 1.2 miles, but you don't have to go far up the steep trail to secure a view all your own, high above the parking lot mob.

3 Mirror Lake & Beyond To the east of Yosemite Village, Mirror Lake is a placid stretch of **Tenaya Creek** that serves as a looking glass for Half Dome. It's not a park secret—the walk up is a very popular paved trail—but doing this 2-mile round-trip hike early in the morning or late in the afternoon means fewer people and prettier light for a beauty shot of Half Dome's reflection.

Take the park shuttle to the trailhead and make the gently climbing walk to the lake, but don't stop there. A dirt (intermittently paved) trail continues east along Tenaya Creek. The secret? Follow it, and very quickly you're in your own world. It's the quietest easy hike in Yosemite Valley.

If you're feeling ambitious, though, hike as far as the junction with **Snow Creek Trail** (another 1.5 miles, basically flat) and proceed up a few switchbacks on a very steep trail. You soon get a dramatic view of Tenaya Canyon and an angle on **Half Dome** that few people see.

| WAWONA

The sights around Wawona, near the southern entrance, may not be as fabled as those in the valley (an hour's drive north), but that's precisely why you should allot some time here.

Generally much quieter than Yosemite Valley, its accommodations are likely to be less crowded. Wawona is home to the classic, Victorian-style **Wawona Hotel**—a far less expensive alternative to the park's hostelry, the **Ahwahnee**—a campground, and some rental cabins that are privately owned.

4 Mariposa Grove & Wawona Point

You don't have to go to Sequoia National Park to see giant sequoias. Yosemite's Mariposa Grove has some 500 specimens of some of the tallest living things on Earth.

The road (closed in winter) to the grove takes off from the park's southern entrance station. But be warned: The parking lot fills up. Either go early, go late, or take the free shuttle from the

NOT TO BE MISSED: *See the main sights from the surprisingly uncrowded Valley Floor Loop.*
▸ *Survey the park's beauty from Inspiration Point.* ▸ *Walk among the giant sequoias of Mariposa Grove and the Upper Grove beyond.* ▸ *Take the shortcut to Chilnualna Falls and stand face-to-face with that roaring cascade.*
▸ *Soak in the amazing views from Glacier Point.* ▸ *Stare down The Fissures, then admire El Capitan from Taft Point.*

Mariposa Grove Welcome Plaza. Then be sure to proceed past the closest trees.

One called the **Grizzly Giant** is visible in about 0.8 mile, and the **California Tunnel Tree** is nearby. Keep going another 1.5 miles to the Upper Grove, where the crowds thin out and you get beyond the reach of the tram tour.

You'll see many more giants as you crest the hill, just before you reach the

LOCAL INTELLIGENCE

Although encounters between bears and humans are much less frequent than they used to be in Yosemite—thanks to visitor education and the strategic placement of food-storage lockers—somewhere between 300 and 500 bears still live in the park and meeting bears is possible.

"We have only black bears; no grizzlies," says Kari Cobb, park ranger. "Black bears are more scavengers than predators." Meaning that Yosemite bears prefer to patrol campgrounds looking for half-open food lockers—they'll enter a site even when people are present—and sniff cars for the presence of food. That includes canned food. The park requires that all food and anything scented (shampoo, bug spray) be stored in lockers at night.

If you encounter a bear, or any animal in the park, Cobb says, most will simply walk away. If you inadvertently find yourself close to a bear, make some noise and perhaps throw a pinecone.

And what if you want to see a bear? "Try any meadow in the park around sunset," says Cobb. Just keep your distance.

Deer in a field of wildflowers

Mariposa Grove Museum, which interprets the life of these amazing trees. More giant sequoias stand on the hill above the museum.

If your climbing muscles feel strong, continue by trail to Wawona Point (elevation 6,810 feet) for a dizzying view of Wawona Meadow and **Wawona Dome.** If you return via the **Outer Loop Trail,** you won't have to retrace your steps on the 3-mile hike back down.

❺ Wawona Meadow Here's another hidden-in-plain-sight Yosemite walk. The golf course across the road from the Wawona Hotel is obvious, but what is not is the trail that encircles it and proceeds all the way around Wawona Meadow.

"It's a nice evening stroll with a glass of wine in your hand," says Cobb—although the full loop is 3.5 miles, so you might want to bring a water bottle as well.

Early on you get some nice views across the golf course to the hotel, but soon you leave civilization behind and it becomes a solitary walk in the woods—

just you, scads of birds, and the odd mule deer.

Occasionally the trees open up to reveal the wildflower-strewn meadow, especially at the far end of the loop, where you'll be glad you decided to go all the way.

❻ Chilnualna Fall The full hike to Chilnualna Fall is a challenging one—4.1 miles one way, 2,400 feet of gain. But don't write this one off due to lack of time or ambition; a mini version of the hike is less than 0.5-mile round-trip.

The road to the trailhead, **Chilnualna Falls Road,** is just off Wawona Road north of the hotel. It leads 2 winding miles through a residential section of Wawona.

The hike up takes only about 15 minutes, yet you still get the rush of standing face-to-face with a roaring cascade that would be a major attraction if it were in Yosemite Valley. In Wawona, the secret is all yours.

GLACIER POINT ROAD

Glacier Point, at the end of Glacier Point Road (closed in winter), is one of Yosemite's must-see wonders—the overlook is perched 3,000 sheer feet above the floor of Yosemite Valley and the views down and across are amazing.

You get a great look at both **Upper** and **Lower Yosemite Falls, Vernal** and **Nevada Falls, Half Dome,** and **High Sierra peaks** in the distance.

If you just hop out of your car, have a look from the nearest viewpoint, and be on your way, you might miss the actual Glacier Point. It requires a short walk downhill past the geology exhibit to another viewing platform, from which you can see a distinctive overhanging slab.

Though it gives most people (rangers included) shudders to imagine visitors walking out on this overhang, many old photos depict people posing on it, even a trio of can-can dancers. Do not try this!

Once you've had your fill, head back on Glacier Point Road and stop at some of the other, equally compelling attractions along the way. You'll find far less company at each of them.

7 Sentinel Dome Most of us won't reach the top of Half Dome, but the 1.1-mile hike to the apex of Sentinel Dome serves up a stellar view for somewhat less effort.

You see the backside of the dome as you approach, and it looks steep, but the trail winds around the huge granite mound to a much easier approach.

The slope is still somewhat challenging, but remember, this is Yosemite granite; the traction is superb. And so is the view from the top—the valley, Half Dome, Upper Yosemite Fall (which you can hear)—from a somewhat higher perspective than Glacier Point.

8 Taft Point & The Fissures The trail to Taft Point departs from the same trailhead as the Sentinel Dome trail, but the view and the experience are entirely different. The 1.1-mile trail winds through some forest and meadows, then drops a few hundred feet to the west edge of a steep side canyon whose granite rim is cleaved by deep, sheer fractures that are just a few feet wide—The Fissures—yet plunge 2,000 feet straight down.

Taft Point itself is something of a Glacier Point for El Capitan fans—it looks directly across the valley to the face of the great monolith. You can also see El Capitan Meadow and the Merced River snaking through it.

9 Mono Meadow This meadow, off Glacier Point Road, is a small, secluded glen reached by a 1-mile downhill walk. Much of it is boggy—enjoy it from the perimeter and from the trail—but it's full of wildflowers, bird life, and serenity. It also affords a superb view of **Mount Starr King** (9,092 feet) to the northeast.

Vernal Fall

LOCAL INTELLIGENCE

Photography has a long history in Yosemite, dating back to the images of Carleton Watkins in the 1860s—and later Albert Bierstadt and Eadweard Muybridge—that helped publicize Yosemite and stimulate the movement for its protection.

Ansel Adams, of course, created iconic images of the park in the 20th century. He showed them in the same gallery in Yosemite Valley that continues to bear his name. Every special-edition Ansel Adams print sold there is produced by photographer Alan Ross, who was an assistant to Adams from 1974 to 1979. Today Ross leads photography workshops in the park and creates images of his own.

Ross admires Adams's work for its unpretentiousness. "Every single image is from the heart," he says. "He wasn't trying to impose any meaning in the photograph other than the photograph itself." Ross's advice to today's Yosemite photographers: "Sit down and enjoy the spot. The best way to capture majesty is to soak it up for a bit. Let your feelings guide you."

TIOGA ROAD

Tioga Road is the main artery through Yosemite's high country, climbing from 6,200 feet at its west end, **Crane Flat**, to 9,945 feet at **Tioga Pass** before it exits the park. The road typically closes in November and opens in late May.

Many visitors simply make the drive, stop at a few scenic viewpoints, and move on, while others use its trailheads for backpacking trips. But a number of overlooked short hikes branch off from Tioga Road for a quick but fine taste of the high country.

⑩ Lukens Lake Even though you know you're hiking to a lake, the eventual sight of Lukens provides a pleasant surprise after the 0.8-mile approach. This path ascends a slight forested rise, then leads to a creek at the edge of a long meadow, bright with wildflowers in summer, with the lake shimmering at the far end.

Stay to the left and follow the trail to the far end of the lake—a fine spot to picnic and watch birds.

⑪ Olmsted Point A large turnout and an obvious view of Yosemite high country make Olmsted Point a popular stop on Tioga Road. But be sure to take the stone steps down and the 0.2-mile trail across solid granite to reach the real viewpoint.

From here you look down on **Tenaya Canyon** across miles of mostly bare granite. The most prominent rise on the near horizon is Half Dome, which looks very different from this eastern perspective compared to the familiar views from Yosemite Valley and Glacier Point. Visible on the surrounding slopes are huge boulders, dubbed "erratics," left by long-ago glaciers.

⑫ Tenaya Lake "No one walks to the opposite side of Tenaya Lake," says Kari Cobb. "It's a shame. It's a great loop trail with great views."

Tenaya is very much a high country lake at 8,149 feet, surrounded by granite domes and lodgepole pine forest. A flat, 2.5-mile trail circles it and leads to those terrific views, many of them reflected in the lake's deep blue, very chilly water.

MORE PARK SECRETS

KINGS CANYON

SIERRA NEVADA CANYON | 559-565-3341 | *nps.gov/seki*

Adjoining and mutually operated with Sequoia National Park (pages 224–229), Kings Canyon is often overlooked in favor of its more famous partner. But its glacier-carved canyons and rugged mountains in the southern **Sierra Nevada** offer an equally stunning landscape in central California.

The vast majority of the park is designated wilderness, but visitors can follow the Kings Canyon Scenic Byway, Calif. 180, into the eponymous **Kings Canyon.** "It's the largest canyon in the park into which you can drive," says Becky Satnat, park ranger. The road, open only in summer, winds precipitously down the canyon and runs along the rushing white water of the **South Fork Kings River,** hemmed in by narrow canyon walls. Near its end in **Cedar Grove** the terrain changes from a V-shaped, river-carved canyon to the flatter, gentler U-shape of a glacier-carved canyon and travelers can see peaks in the distance. Grassy meadows, tall trees offering welcome shade, and the **Roaring River Falls** await.

Concludes Satnat about this secret: "People think a dead-end road is boring, but this one ends in an absolutely gorgeous place."

NATIONAL PARK OF AMERICAN SAMOA

ISLAND CULTURE | 684-633-7082 | *nps.gov/npsa*

Traveling thousands of miles to a place where the coconut tree has its own creation myth comes with many rewards: The National Park of American Samoa is a paradise of deep blue waters, secluded beaches, rain forest–covered volcanic islands, and reefs of colorful fish and intricate corals.

These three islands in the southwestern Pacific Ocean are also a cultural park preserving the *fa'asamoa*—the Samoan way. Soak up a secret hospitality by signing up for the park's homestay program, in which you room with the locals. Getting to Samoan hosts can be an adventure itself—you might ride alongside gasoline and groceries on a supply barge or travel in a fisherman's scow.

Once arrived, you may have the opportunity to learn to climb a coconut tree, spear an octopus, or weave leaves into mats. Sundays are observed here as a day for church and rest versus play, with foods such as banana and breadfruit prepared in an oven of heated rocks, an *umu*. At the visit's conclusion, former park ranger Joe Leleua playfully warns, "They're going to make you dance."

6 | PACIFIC NORTHWEST

Wonder Lake, Denali National Park & Preserve, Alaska

"From descending the slopes of Mount Rainier in a snow storm with school pals to joining with hands of young classmates to hug a giant cedar, national parks unlocked a curiosity and sense of wonder that will never leave me. We are blessed that these special places remain, inspiring future generations to experience the secrets of our nation's treasures."

—SALLY JEWELL
FORMER SECRETARY, U.S. DEPARTMENT OF THE INTERIOR
NATIONAL PARK TRUST 2016 RECIPIENT,
AMERICAN PARK EXPERIENCE AWARD

Snow-covered Wizard Island

CRATER LAKE

About 7,700 years ago, a massive eruption—42 times greater than Mount Saint Helens's belch in 1980—emptied the magma chamber of Mount Mazama in southern Oregon, leaving a huge void. The mountain basically imploded, collapsing in on itself to form a vast cliff-lined basin. Imagine a giant thumb pressing down on the top of a 12,000-foot-high volcano, pushing the cone into itself until the top 5,000 feet are gone, leaving a giant basin inside the rim of the collapsed volcano. That's essentially what happened here as the force of gravity pushed the mountaintop down into itself.

Over the centuries, winter snow averaging 524 inches per year flowed into the caldera, and with no outlet to drain the water, Crater Lake was born. Today, it averages 1,500 feet deep, with a maximum depth of 1,932 feet—the deepest lake in the United States. What lies below is a mystery, but aboveground there are a slew of secrets to be found.

Year-Round Visitor Center
■ Steel Visitor Center
Park Headquarters
4 miles north of Oreg. 62,
south of Rim Village Visitor Center

Seasonal Visitor Center
■ Rim Village Visitor Center
Off West Rim Drive, Rim Village

541-594-3000, nps.gov/crla

MAZAMA VILLAGE & RIM VILLAGE AREA

The road linking two small villages and service centers on the south side of the park provides some of the park's best scenery away from the lake itself.

The 7 miles from Mazama Village to Rim Village exposes you to the region's dry pine forest ecology, with some wonderful wildflower meadows tossed in for good measure. Before you start your exploration, do take the time to stroll from Rim Village to the **Sinnott Memorial Overlook** for a long, admiring look at the color, purity, and depth of Crater Lake.

Dave Grimes, park interpretive ranger, also notes that the Rim Village area makes a great destination for winter recreation enthusiasts, with ranger-led snowshoe trips and opportunities for cross-country skiing and self-guided snowshoeing adventures.

❶ **Godfrey Glen Trail** Step out of the car at **Godfrey Glen** to walk a gentle 1-mile loop trail through a spectacular stand of old-growth mountain hemlocks and Shasta red fir. The trail skirts alongside beautiful **Annie Creek Canyon** and the

WIZARD ISLAND

Early on, **Mount Mazama** tried to return to its towering height. A cinder cone grew out of red hot cinders ejected from the caldera floor, rising more than 2,000 feet—but then the mountain lost its power. Scientists say there has been no volcanic activity around Crater Lake for more than 5,000 years.

The cinder cone peak within the mountain stands today as lonely Wizard Island, so named for its resemblance to a sorcerer's hat. Its top rises 767 feet above Crater Lake's surface. For a closer look, the island can be reached by boats operated by park concessionaires.

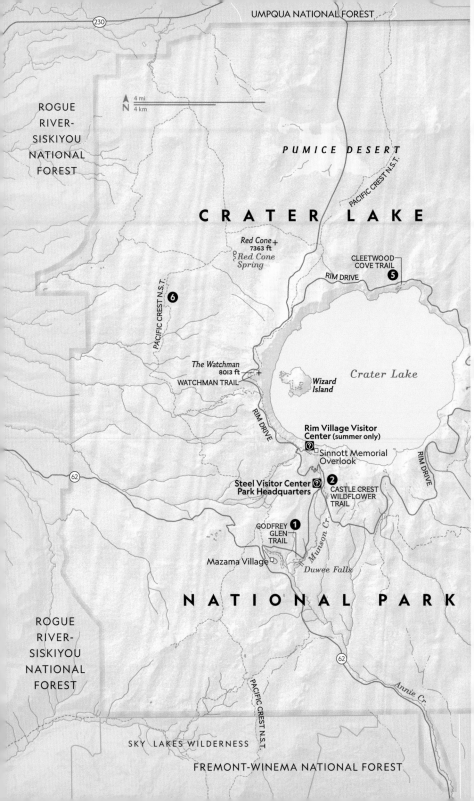

UMPQUA NATIONAL FOREST

230

ROGUE
RIVER-
SISKIYOU
NATIONAL
FOREST

N   4 mi
     4 km

PUMICE DESERT

CRATER LAKE

Red Cone +
7363 ft
Red Cone
Spring

PACIFIC CREST N.S.T.

CLEETWOOD
COVE TRAIL
5

RIM DRIVE

PACIFIC CREST N.S.T.

6

The Watchman
8013 ft   +
WATCHMAN TRAIL

Crater Lake

*Wizard
Island*

RIM DRIVE

**Rim Village Visitor
Center** (summer only)
?   □ Sinnott Memorial
Overlook

62

**Steel Visitor Center
Park Headquarters** ?
2
CASTLE CREST
WILDFLOWER
TRAIL

RIM DRIVE

GODFREY
GLEN
TRAIL   1

Munson Cr.

Mazama Village   □
Duwee Falls

NATIONAL   PARK

ROGUE
RIVER-
SISKIYOU
NATIONAL
FOREST

62

Annie Cr.

PACIFIC CREST N.S.T.

SKY LAKES WILDERNESS

FREMONT-WINEMA NATIONAL FOREST

FREMONT-
WINEMA
NATIONAL
FOREST

MOUNT SCOTT
TRAIL
④ + *Mount Scott*
8929 ft

PINNACLES
ROAD

Wheeler Cr.
❸ *Sand Cr.*
Pinnacles
Overlook
The
Pinnacles

FREMONT-
WINEMA
NATIONAL
FOREST

SUN PASS
STATE FOREST

138

tumbling **Duwee Falls.** Deer, grouse, and rabbits are common here; elk, foxes, porcupines, badgers, and owls also inhabit this emerald forest, although they are seen less frequently. The trail does roll over a few low rises and ridgelines, but the well-maintained tread makes walking relatively easy.

❷ Castle Crest Wildflower Trail

Wildflowers can be found in July and August along this trail near park headquarters, midway between the two villages. The route weaves along a path through a thin subalpine forest and broad wildflower meadows, and alongside **Munson Creek.** The best time to hike this short, exquisite trail is mid- to late summer, when the vast array of wildflower species erupts in a spectrum of colors.

RIM DRIVE

Because of the park's position high in the Cascade Range, winter comes early and lingers long, meaning most of the park's roads, such as Rim Drive, aren't free of snow until late June or early July, and they start gathering new snows in late October. (Note: East Rim Drive is not

Thriving summer fireweed

Wizard Island free of its snowy veil

"These geologic formations are some of the most interesting and photogenic features in the park," says park superintendent Craig Ackerman.

4 Mount Scott Trail Views of the full grandeur of Crater Lake require a climb to a high viewpoint, and the Mount Scott Trail provides just such a challenge.

The 8,929-foot mountain to the east of East Rim Drive holds an old fire lookout tower and provides stunning views west across the breadth of the lake.

The 2.5-mile trail climbs steeply at times, but the route pierces fragrant pine forests and wildflower meadows before reaching the summit. Visitors who get an early start will appreciate the morning light as it illuminates all the coves and creases around the lake.

Perhaps the best secret hike in the park is across the lake—the **Watchman Trail**. Dave Grimes, interpretive ranger, says: "I think the Watchman offers the best of the park in one trail." It is only moderately steep, climbing just 420 feet in 0.8 mile (one way).

5 Cleetwood Cove Trail This trail goes 1 mile from the rim to the lakeshore along a modest grade carved into the wooded slopes of the northern edge of

recommended for trailers.) Rim Drive circles the lake. At least 19 times the road approaches the edge to provide glorious views of the water from a variety of overlooks. But to truly experience the majesty of the lake's beauty, you should take to your feet and hike up.

3 The Pinnacles From the southeast portion of Rim Drive, take Pinnacles Road about 6 miles to see the Pinnacles, an unusual grouping of volcanic pumice spires. As the sides of Wheeler Canyon eroded away, these graceful fossil fumaroles emerged, each marking where volcanic gas rose up through hot ash deposits. There's an overlook from the parking area, but the easy, half-mile trail is well worth the extra steps.

the caldera. Descending its switchbacks is fairly easy, but the return hike to the trailhead can be a real sweat producer and anyone venturing down the trail must be fit enough to come back up under their own power.

The trail ends at a boat dock where a park concessionaire provides tours of the lake—some stopping at Wizard Island.

NORTHERN ACCESS

The road heading north away from Rim Drive leads through forests of lodgepole pines and open meadows. Most impressive are the broad fields of feather-light rocks in the **Pumice Desert.**

This expanse of volcanic debris is a product of the eruption of 7,700 years ago that blasted pumice across this northern plain, creating a deposit nearly 200 feet thick. The porous rock and sand lack nutrients to support life, so the desert remains mostly barren, with just a few tough grasses sprouting from the stone.

NOT TO BE MISSED: *Take a boat to Wizard Island.* ▸ *Walk among old-growth forest in Godfrey Glen.* ▸ *Time your visit to see the park's sea of wildflowers.* ▸ *Cross the lake to climb the Watchman Trail.* ▸ *Seek out the unusual Pinnacles formations.* ▸ *Take a boat tour.*

❻ Pacific Crest Trail The northern blast zone can be explored on foot by walking west on the Pacific Crest Trail from where it crosses the road, 2 miles north of the Rim Drive junction. The trail touches on a pumice-rich lava bed before skirting the flank of **Red Cone**—a 7,363-foot cinder cone—where the low, scraggy vegetation along the early section of trail turns into lodgepole pine and full forest. With virtually no elevation gain along the route, you can hike the 3.8 miles to **Red Cone Springs camp** in the morning, eat lunch beside the spring, and walk out refreshed.

The pumice spires of the Pinnacles

Denali, or "the high one," reflected in Wonder Lake

DENALI

The most impressive, in fact nearly overwhelming, aspect of Denali National Park is simply its sheer scale. At 20,310 feet, the legendary mountain at its heart is the highest peak in North America. Covering more than 6 million acres of Alaska, the park surrounding it is larger than the state of New Hampshire, and well over twice the size of Yellowstone National Park. Vast landscapes—from forest to tundra to glaciers—endure virtually untouched by the modern world, the domain of grizzly and black bears, Dall sheep, caribou, moose, wolves, swans, and scores of other species of wildlife.

The developed area of the park is relatively small and near the main highway between Anchorage and Fairbanks. The park's interior is reached via a 92-mile road spur, mostly closed to private vehicles. Long winters make the major visitation season short, from late May through mid-September. This all means that at Denali, planning is essential.

VISITOR CENTER AREA

Many popular activities are clustered around the park's visitor center and within the first 3.5 miles of the park road, including a large campground, a station of the Alaska Railroad, a store, a post office, an airstrip, and kennels where rangers and Alaskan huskies team up to offer demonstrations of sled dog travel.

Several trails begin here as well, including the popular **Horseshoe Lake Trail,** where wetlands and the Nenana River provide good habitat for spotting wildlife such as moose and beaver. Depending on the starting point, the loop trail ranges from 2 to 3.2 miles.

Year-Round Visitor Centers

■ **Murie Science & Learning Center**
Near Denali Visitor Center
Serves as main visitor center in winter

■ **Eielson Visitor Center**
Mile 66, park road
Accessible only by bus

■ **Walter Harper Talkeetna Ranger Station**
Off Alaska 3 (Parks Highway) in Talkeetna, 120 miles south of main park entrance. Serves as a center for mountaineering, but also offers general park information

Seasonal Visitor Centers

■ **Denali Visitor Center**
Main park road, 1.5 miles off Alaska 3 (Parks Highway); summer only

■ **Wonder Lake Ranger Station**
Mile 86.5; summer only

907-638-9352, nps.gov/dena

❶ **Rock Creek Trail** Jennifer Johnston, an outdoor recreation planner for the park, recommends the 2.4-mile (one way) Rock Creek Trail as an introduction to Denali's woodland wonders. "It takes you through a couple of different forest types, with some really beautiful aspen groves," she says. "There are some great views of the Denali frontcountry area, and if you have just a short time for a hike it's a quick way to make you feel like you're away from other people and the road."

Whether here or elsewhere in the park, hike prepared. "There are very few services in the park and none, including cell reception, beyond mile 3," says Gerald Hitchcock, the park's public affairs officer. "All visitors should carry what they need with them, including bear spray, and pack out what they bring."

THE PARK ROAD

By far the most popular park activity is a bus ride along all or part of the 92-mile park road. A trip along this route offers an overview of the varied landscapes of Denali—its boreal forests, glacial flood-plains, broad tundras, and alpine slopes—and increases the odds of seeing wildlife.

With luck, from the bus it's possible to see all of the park's "big five" mammals: grizzly bear, moose, caribou, Dall sheep, and wolf.

Visitors choose from two bus types: tour or transit. Tour buses feature a guide who narrates the trip, describing geology, vegetation, and wildlife along the way. Transit buses serve primarily to

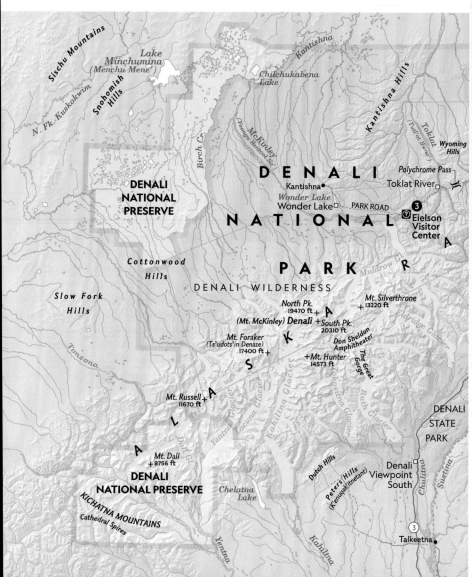

shuttle people from the park entrance to and from various stops along the road, for hiking, camping, and backpacking.

"Visitors actually have greater freedom to roam the wilderness here than at any other national park," says Hitchcock. "Very few established trails means you can set your own path and route, and explore the backcountry as you want."

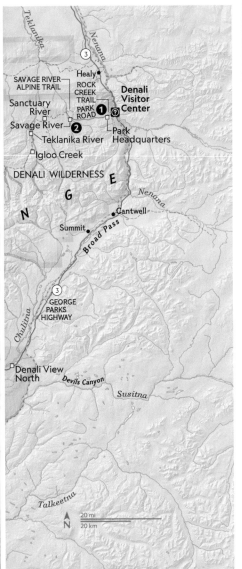

Watery streams

Another option entails putting a bicycle on a transit bus (rentals are available just outside the park), getting off along the park road for a ride, and catching another bus back to the entrance.

2 Savage River Denali backcountry supervisor John Brueck says the Savage River area, 15 miles from the park entrance, makes a great destination for those with limited time. The fairly strenuous 4-mile **Savage River Alpine Trail** ranks as a special favorite. "If it's a clear day you can see Denali from up there," he says. "There's plenty of wildlife, especially Dall sheep, but you could also see moose or grizzly bears or even lynx." A free shuttle bus provides access to both trailheads for the Savage River Alpine route, which makes possible a one-way hike without backtracking.

3 Eielson Visitor Center A visit to the Eielson Visitor Center at mile 66 is a

Caribou in autumn Arctic tundra

popular excursion for both scenery and wildlife, requiring a minimum of eight hours.

Of course, everyone who goes to Denali hopes for a sighting of the namesake mountain, and Eielson offers one of the best postcard-quality viewpoints in the park. But on any given day the odds of a summit view are less than 50-50.

"Eielson is a good destination even if it's not a clear day," Brueck says. "The farther you go on the road the better your chances of seeing wildlife, and there's a good chance of seeing a lot of the iconic species that we have here. It's rare that everybody sees everything, but it's also rare that you have a bus trip out there and don't have at least a couple of quality sightings."

Bus trips into the park can vary from a few hours to a full-day, 12-hour trip out and back. Drivers stop for notable wildlife sightings, but Brueck urges visitors to get out into the landscape for a more intimate experience. "If you're going out to Eielson, it's four hours out and four

hours back," Brueck says. "That's a lot of time to be sitting on a bus for one day."

He recommends spending the night. "There are a number of campgrounds along the park road. You get off the bus with your tent and your gear and you're right there. There are some good ones, like **Igloo Creek**, which has a lot of great day hiking right out of the campground."

Jennifer Johnston agrees. "So much of the focus is on the bus ride and wildlife viewing from the bus," she says. "It's a wonderful way to travel, but at the end of the day you're in a vehicle. Getting off the bus is the best way to check out the park. It doesn't have to be for a long extended hike; if you just go a half-mile off the side of the road it's an entirely different world, whether it's in alpine tundra or in the forest or along a river.

"The big gravel river bars that we have can be great places to see animal tracks in sandy patches. You don't have to be a mountaineer or a serious hiker to just wander off on a river bar. They're usually

NOT TO BE MISSED: *Take a bus out the park road as far as you like, then get out and hike.* ▸ *Spot the park's "big five" mammals.* ▸ *For a different perspective, flightsee over the park and land on a far-flung glacier.* ▸ *Meet the sled dogs at their home kennel.*

flight-seers. "Our visitors say it's far and away their most favorite part of their Alaska visit," she says. "These mountains are just breathtaking. I tell my passengers before we get on the plane that Denali is the most beautiful place on the continent, hands down, and when we get back I've never had anyone disagree with me."

Falley also strongly advocates for the glacier-landing experience. "It really ties the whole landscape to the visitor, because they get to get out of the plane and step onto the glacier," she says. "We turn the engine off and I have my passengers simply be quiet for a moment and listen to the absence of sound other than avalanches. Getting to fly around the mountains is absolutely incredible, but getting to stand on the glacier makes this landscape real instead of just a moving picture outside the window."

pretty flat and pass through scenic valleys, and almost certainly you'll find some caribou tracks or bear tracks, or even wolf tracks if you're lucky."

Bears and moose and mountain peaks are impressive, but so, too, are Denali's smaller wonders, from tiny tundra wildflowers to the vegetation of the forest floor. "In places the moss grows so thick that it's like you're walking on pillows," Johnston says, "and that's something that's really cool to experience."

⏐ FLIGHTSEEING

Many Denali visitors enjoy getting a different perspective of the rugged Alaska Range: from the air. Several companies operate scenic flights over the park, and some are authorized to land on glaciers with ski-equipped aircraft.

Local pilot Leighan Falley enjoys the reaction she gets from first-time

Park bus at Polychrome Pass

Mount Rainier landscape alight with wildflowers

MOUNT RAINIER

Towering over the heart of the Cascade Range, Mount Rainier stands as one of the most recognizable features in Washington's diverse landscape. For centuries, this mighty mountain—viewable from nearly every corner of the state—has filled local culture. Native tribes describe the mountain, "Tahoma" to the western tribes, as a mighty source of power and home to gods. Residents throughout Washington see it today as the icon of their Northwest culture and a wonderful wilderness retreat.

From deep old-growth forests in low valley bottoms to the frosty summit of the peak, Mount Rainier boasts an array of secret terrain and ecosystems to explore and enjoy. Here you'll also find wildflower meadows, more than 100 waterfalls, and nearly 325 lakes.

If possible, visit on weekdays instead of weekends to avoid the crowds. Also note there is no fuel service, and very little cell coverage, in the park.

Year-Round Visitor Center
■ Henry M. Jackson Memorial Visitor Center
At Paradise, 11 miles east of Longmire

Seasonal Visitor Centers
■ Longmire Museum
On Park Rd. 706
■ Ohanapecosh Visitor Center
Wash. 123
■ Sunrise Visitor Center
On Wash. 410, inside the park

360-569-2211, nps.gov/mora

THE ROAD TO PARADISE

The most popular access to the park uses the **Nisqually Entrance** in the park's southwest corner. This route rolls east through the Longmire area before climbing a long, winding road to **Paradise.**

The **Historic Village of Longmire,** nestled at 2,750 feet elevation between **Rampart Ridge** on the north and the **Nisqually River** on the south, cradles the original park headquarters building—still used as the in-park administration hub—the **Longmire Museum,** and the **National Park Inn.**

James Longmire, one of the earliest non-native visitors to the area and the first to build a cabin within what is now the park boundary, discovered mineral hot springs in the meadows and built a hotel and spa to take advantage of those "healing waters."

Later he helped carve the road up the mountain to the broad meadows on the south flank. The awesome splendor of this region earned its name in 1885 from Longmire's daughter-in-law, Martha. On seeing the fields of vibrant wildflowers, she declared, "Oh, it looks just like paradise." The name stuck, and the Paradise meadows today are nearly as pristine as they were 135 years ago.

❶ **Kautz Creek Trail** The Kautz Creek drainage has been ravaged by floods, decimated by fires, and rearranged by mudslides, so it offers a great lesson in the dynamic nature of a Cascade volcano.

The trail leaves from the north side of the road about 3 miles east of the Nisqually Entrance and weaves up the Kautz Creek Valley. It proceeds through a forest killed by the Kautz Mudflow—a massive debris flow in December 1947 that brought millions of cubic yards of liquid rock and soil

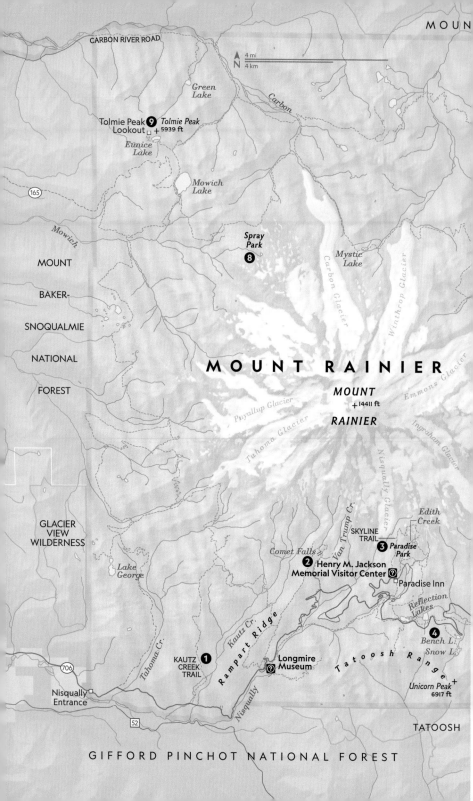

CARBON RIVER ROAD

4 mi
N
4 km

Green
Lake

Carbon

Tolmie Peak **9** *Tolmie Peak*
Lookout □ + **5939 ft**

*Eunice
Lake*

165

*Mowich
Lake*

*Mystic
Lake*

MOUNT

*Spray
Park*
8

Carbon Glacier

Winthrop Glacier

BAKER-

SNOQUALMIE

M O U N T   R A I N I E R

NATIONAL

Puyallup Glacier

MOUNT

Emmons Glacier

FOREST

+ **14411 ft**

RAINIER

Tahoma Glacier

Ingraham Glacier

Nisqually Glacier

*Edith
Creek*

SKYLINE
TRAIL

GLACIER
VIEW
WILDERNESS

Comet Falls

Van Trump Cr.

3 *Paradise
Park*

2
Henry M. Jackson
Memorial Visitor Center ?

Paradise Inn □

*Reflection
Lakes*

*Lake
George*

Kautz Cr.

Bench L.

4
Snow L.

KAUTZ
CREEK
TRAIL **1**

Rampart Ridge

Longmire
Museum
?

Tatoosh Range

Unicorn Peak +
6917 ft

Tahoma Cr.

Nisqually

Nisqually □
Entrance

706

52

TATOOSH

G I F F O R D   P I N C H O T   N A T I O N A L   F O R E S T

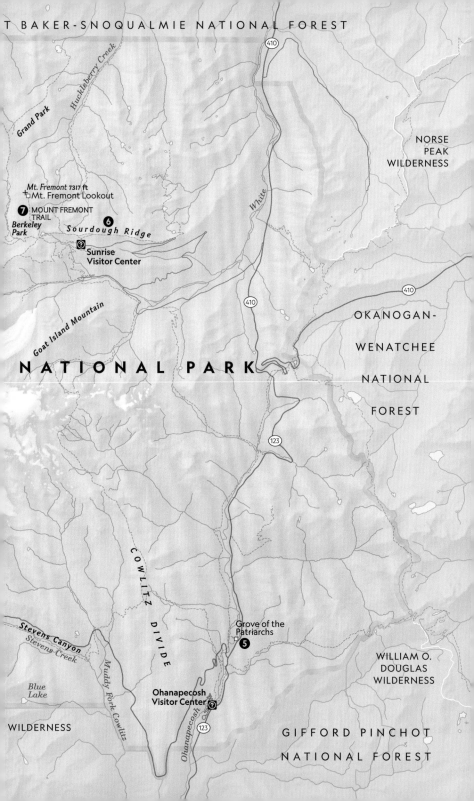

T BAKER-SNOQUALMIE NATIONAL FOREST

410

Huckleberry Creek

Grand Park

NORSE
PEAK
WILDERNESS

Mt. Fremont 7317 ft
Mt. Fremont Lookout
7 MOUNT FREMONT
TRAIL
Berkeley
Park
6 Sourdough Ridge

White

Sunrise
Visitor Center

Goat Island Mountain

NATIONAL PARK

410

410

OKANOGAN-
WENATCHEE

NATIONAL

FOREST

123

C O W L I T Z

D I V I D E

Stevens Canyon
Stevens Creek

Muddy Fork Cowlitz

Grove of the
Patriarchs
5

WILLIAM O.
DOUGLAS
WILDERNESS

Blue
Lake

Ohanapecosh
Visitor Center

Ohanapecosh

WILDERNESS

123

GIFFORD PINCHOT

NATIONAL FOREST

down the creek basin, killing or obliterating everything in its path. This nearly 6-mile one-way route provides proof that a volcano doesn't have to blow its top to unleash destructive power.

❷ Comet Falls Many claim this is the most beautiful waterfall in the park, though the competition is fierce. The 300-foot cascade fans out as it crashes down the andesite cliffs, rolls briefly across a rocky meadow, then drops another 20 feet. The two-stage falls provide a show of force and beauty.

The trail to this natural wonder climbs the steep valley of the **Van Trump Creek,** offering little along the way other than an experience in the forest primeval, but once you reach the waterfall basin at 1.8 miles the average trail turns exceptional.

❸ Skyline Trail This 5-mile trail leaves in front of the newly renovated Paradise Inn—a classic timber-framed lodge—and loops around the broad **Edith Creek Basin.** The pathway leads through alpine flower fields, past a thundering waterfall,

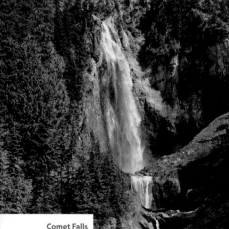

Comet Falls

and finally up onto the ridge above. From there you'll ramble along the high ridgeline above the basin before dropping back into the upper meadows, past arrays of wildflowers, and back to the start.

Throughout, be sure to stay on the paths, as walking through wildflowers is discouraged and even illegal in some areas of the park (see sidebar opposite).

In this one loop you'll experience the best the Paradise region has to offer in terms of scenic beauty, rugged hiking, and varied terrain and ecosystems. The subalpine zone covers more than 54,000 acres of parkland, providing countless opportunities for viewing flowers.

STEVENS CANYON

Stevens Canyon offers access from the park's southeast corner to Paradise. The deep cut of Stevens Canyon separates the wild alpine parklands on the flank of Rainier from the craggy peaks and crystal lakes of the **Tatoosh Range.** Hikers can explore the best of both sides of the canyon, as well as the forest ecosystems of the lower valley.

❹ Bench & Snow Lakes While nearby **Reflection Lakes** get all the tourist attention, hikers willing to spend just a little time getting off the road will find these far more scenic lakes just minutes away.

In less than a mile (0.8 mile), hikers encounter Bench Lake. Though nestled on a broad shoulder of the ridge—or bench—just above the Stevens Canyon Road, the lake has a backcountry feel, thanks to the wild meadows and forests surrounding the basin, and a great view.

Snow Lake fills a narrow, usually snow-filled cirque with fabulous views south to **Unicorn Peak.**

LOCAL INTELLIGENCE

The subalpine and alpine meadows that blanket the slopes of Mount Rainier appear tough and resilient, but in actuality they are very fragile and delicate. Because most reside well above the 5,000-foot level, and the annual snowfall at that elevation exceeds 50 feet per year, the vegetation in the meadows enjoys a very short growing season (mid-June through mid-September). That means any plants damaged by wayward hikers take a long time to recover.

For this reason, rangers insist that hikers stay on the trails, especially around the popular Paradise, Sunrise, and Spray Park areas, where meadows are particularly delicate. Photographers seeking unique shots of wildflowers from within the meadows themselves should ask a park staff member where they may go so that they don't break the law. Options might include north and west of Sunrise in the Berkeley Park and Grand Park areas.

5 Grove of the Patriarchs Some of the biggest, oldest trees in the Cascades stand tall here. These silent old men of moss tower overhead, with a few lying down to show just how massive the trunks really are.

The grove resides in a low boggy area across the **Ohanapecosh River,** with the broad, gentle trail starting just 0.25 mile past the park entrance. The trail crosses the burbling river via a stout suspension bridge, which youngsters either love or hate—there's just enough bounce in the bridge to make it fun and exciting.

The grove itself hosts ancient hemlocks, cedars, and Douglas firs that make the rest of the region's forests appear young and tiny. Some of these ancient monoliths measure nearly 40 feet in circumference and tower more than 300 feet tall—and, in some cases, are at least 1,000 years old.

SUNRISE

Perched on the northeastern shoulder of Mount Rainier, Sunrise welcomes the first morning light into the park. While campgrounds and even golf courses once blighted this ridgetop setting, today's visitors find just a couple of rustic CCC structures built in the 1930s and seemingly endless fields of green splashed with swaths of vibrantly colored wildflowers.

Positioned just at the timberline, Sunrise offers an array of hiking opportunities, from short, nearly flat routes perfect for families and folks short of time, to long meadow and forest rambles that lead to some of the most picturesque places in a park known for its photogenic wonders.

At 6,400 feet, Sunrise is the highest elevation visitor center and trailhead area in the park, so the road frequently remains closed by snow until late June and the meadows of magenta paintbrush, pearly everlasting, and red mountain heather don't explode until mid- to late July. The colorful displays typically continue through August, providing even late summer visitors the opportunity to experience the vivid color palette of the alpine meadows.

6 Sourdough Ridge The historic structures at Sunrise are surrounded by meadows, and the loop (triangle, actu- ally) route around Sourdough Ridge explores the biggest and most varied meadows in the area.

Starting from the north side of the parking lot, the hard-packed trail climbs a gentle 400 feet to the crest of Sourdough Ridge. During the ascent, watch the patches of freshly turned dirt scattered through the meadows. These mounds of soil mark the burrows of hoary marmots—large, brown critters that feed on the abundant vegetation. If you don't see any marmots right away, just listen closely and you'll likely hear their sharp, high-pitched whistles as you walk among their homes.

Follow the ridgetop trail while enjoy- ing the views north all the way to **Glacier Peak** (some 90 miles distant), then turn and descend the third leg of the 1.5-mile triangle back to the trailhead.

❼ Mount Fremont Trail The era of staffed fire lookouts passed long ago. Today, satellites keep an eye on our wildlands during fire season. But those historic watchtowers still provide a valuable service as recreational destina- tions (when they are not in use during emergencies).

NOT TO BE MISSED: *Taking care to keep to the path, walk through meadows filled with delicate wildflowers.* ▸ *Count the peaks from the Mount Fremont lookout tower.* ▸ *Seek solitude at Bench Lake.* ▸ *Walk among the giants in the Grove of the Patriarchs.* ▸ *Transition through several ecosystems in Spray Park.*

The stilted cabin of the **Mount Fremont Lookout** stands not on the true summit of Mount Fremont, but on a secondary knob to the north of the peak. This off-the-summit option boasts a great view of Mount Rainier directly from the tower, and the mountain can be appreciated all the way up and back down the trail to the tower.

The positioning of the lookout also provides excellent views to the north. On clear days, Glacier Peak, **Mount Stuart**, and even **Mount Baker** can be seen. If the air is too hazy for those dis- tant views, watch the north side of the ridge—mountain goats frequently rest on the slope as it drops off just past the trail's end.

Along the way, you'll be able to peer down in the wild **Huckleberry Creek Basin**, which is frequented by the White River elk herd as well as some of the region's black bears.

NORTHWEST CORNER

The northwest corner of Mount Rainier National Park offers some of the most secret, remote, and pristine wilderness experiences in the park. The best chance for solitude in the park can be found here, on the trails high above the **Carbon River** or beyond the shores of **Mowich Lake.**

This is also one of the best places to encounter shy wildlife. Black bears frequent the berry-rich meadows and mountain goats scamper through the rocky slopes above the subalpine fields.

The **Carbon River Road**, unfortu- nately, disappeared during the floods of 2006 and is no longer open to vehicles. It is now a popular trail for hiking as well as mountain biking.

Mount Rainier and its reflection

❽ Spray Park Alan L. Bauer, a noted northwest photographer, naturalist, and author who is intimately familiar with Mount Rainier, describes the Spray Park area as the best of the park's fantastic meadows.

"Along the hike you get great views, access to a beautiful waterfall, and gradual transitions through a series of ecosystems," he says. "The trail climbs from forest to subalpine meadow, and finally to alpine meadow. If you want—and you are prepared for it—you can climb up into the true high alpine zone, too."

It's the meadows, especially the transition zone from subalpine (starts just below timberline) to alpine (open fields above timberline), that really make Spray Park special.

The trees fade away as the trail climbs, leading the fortunate visitor on a path through a world of sparkling blue ponds and emerald green heathers and grasses interrupted by splashes of color from a variety of wildflowers.

The 3-mile walk to Spray Park leads from the shores of Mowich Lake to seemingly endless open meadows of heather and alpine blossoms. (Please respect the plant life and stay on the trails.)

❾ Tolmie Peak Lookout Start with a stroll along the shores of Mowich Lake, then climb gently into the adjacent lake basin (**Eunice Lake**) where the first grand views of Tolmie Peak and its lookout tower are found.

The trail climbs steeply from Eunice Lake to the crown of Tolmie Peak, but the constant views of the destination, and the towering hulk of Mount Rainier, make the trip bearable. The views from the summit make the 3.5-mile trek (one way) totally worthwhile.

A water-carved sculptured trunk along Second Beach

OLYMPIC

Olympic National Park holds many of the world's best remaining old-growth temperate rain forests—cathedrals of Sitka spruce, western hemlock, bigleaf maples, and western red cedar which fill the river valleys on the west side of the main body of the park. The richness of these places exceeds imagination. Moss coats every surface, lichens drape from every limb. Trees here can grow to be 35 feet or more around the base. The park is truly rife with secrets to be discovered.

Above those majestic emerald valleys stand rugged glacier-covered peaks and jagged rocky ridges. Farther west of the forested valleys runs the coastal strand of Olympic National Park, where you'll find the longest undeveloped stretch of wilderness beach in the lower 48 states. And on the east side of the park are more deep valleys filled with massive Douglas firs and sprawling rhododendron jungles.

Year-Round Visitor Center

▪ Olympic National Park Visitor Center

At the park entrance, 3002 Mount Angeles Road, Port Angeles

Seasonal Visitor Centers

▪ Hurricane Ridge Visitor Center

On Hurricane Ridge Road, 17 miles south of Port Angeles

▪ Hoh Rain Forest Visitor Center

US 101, 31 miles south of Forks

360-565-3130, nps.gov/olym

As a result, you'll find fewer ferns, less moss, and far more rhododendrons growing on the east side. In fact, some of the rhododendron bushes here grow to enormous size, towering 20 to 30 feet over the forest floor.

They also grow in massive jungles, filling entire valleys. Come spring, these turn vibrant pink when the "rhodies," as locals say, explode into bloom.

SOUTHEAST CORNER

President Theodore Roosevelt protected Olympic as a national monument in 1909, and his distant cousin President Franklin D. Roosevelt designated it as a national park in 1938. The United Nations recognized the unique nature of the park and designated it as a World Heritage site in 1981.

US 101 runs north parallel to **Hood Canal** and **Olympic**, providing access to the many valleys that radiate out from the park's center. The eastern half of the park receives around 25 to 30 inches of rain annually, less than a quarter of the rainfall on the west side.

❶ Staircase Rapids Loop This trail provides the rewarding opportunity to explore a "dry-side" river valley. Just inside the park's southeast boundary, this easy route follows the upper **North Fork Skokomish River** upstream from the **Staircase Campground**.

The trail rolls along the cool eaves of an emerald forest and beside the gin-clear waters of the wild river. Rainbow trout hunt the cold depths of the river pools, devouring insects, which live and breed in the waterways. Overhead, kingfishers, bald eagles, and ospreys are frequently seen as they patiently hunt the trout. In the woods along the riverbanks, black-tailed deer and large Roosevelt elk graze.

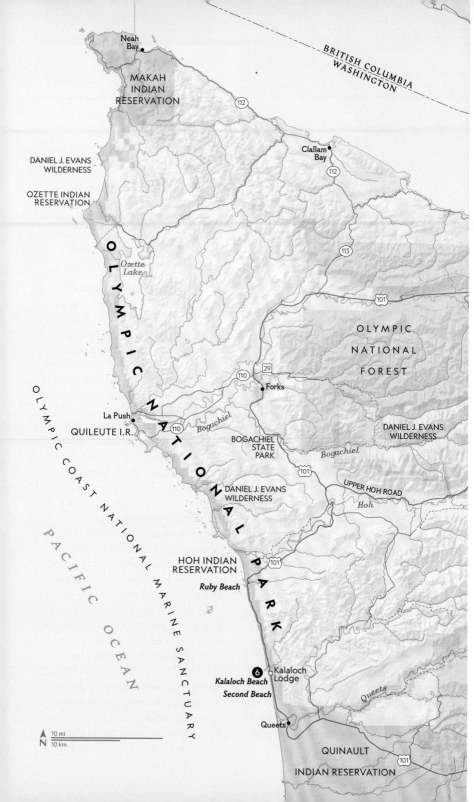

BRITISH COLUMBIA
WASHINGTON

Neah
Bay

MAKAH
INDIAN
RESERVATION

Clallam
Bay

112

112

DANIEL J. EVANS
WILDERNESS

113

OZETTE INDIAN
RESERVATION

101

Ozette
Lake

OLYMPIC
NATIONAL
FOREST

29

110

Forks

La Push

110

Bogachiel

DANIEL J. EVANS
WILDERNESS

QUILEUTE I.R.

BOGACHIEL
STATE
PARK

Bogachiel

101

UPPER HOH ROAD

DANIEL J. EVANS
WILDERNESS

Hoh

HOH INDIAN
RESERVATION

101

Ruby Beach

PACIFIC OCEAN

OLYMPIC COAST NATIONAL MARINE SANCTUARY

6 Kalaloch
Lodge

Kalaloch Beach

Second Beach

Queets

Queets

QUINAULT

INDIAN RESERVATION

101

N
10 mi
10 km

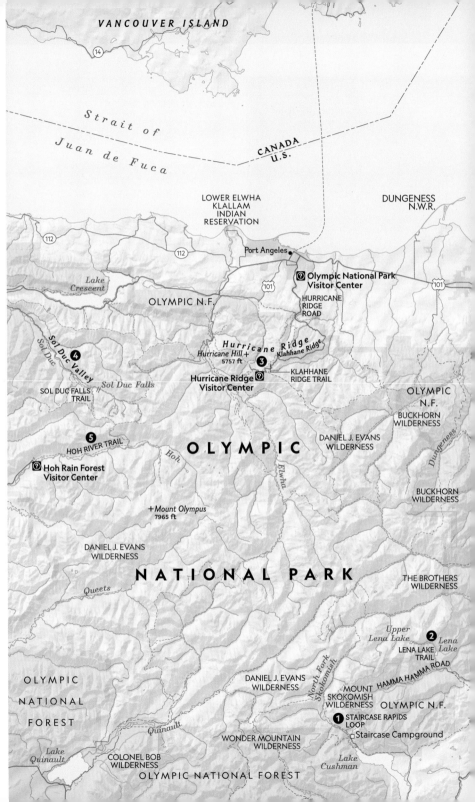

VANCOUVER ISLAND

14

Strait of

Juan de Fuca

CANADA
U.S.

LOWER ELWHA
KLALLAM
INDIAN
RESERVATION

DUNGENESS
N.W.R.

112

112

Port Angeles

Olympic National Park
Visitor Center

101

101

Lake
Crescent

OLYMPIC N.F.

HURRICANE
RIDGE
ROAD

Sol Duc Valley ④

Hurricane Ridge

Sol Duc

Hurricane Hill +
5757 ft

Klahhane Ridge

③

SOL DUC FALLS
TRAIL

Sol Duc Falls

Hurricane Ridge
Visitor Center

KLAHHANE
RIDGE TRAIL

OLYMPIC
N.F.

BUCKHORN
WILDERNESS

⑤
HOH RIVER TRAIL

O L Y M P I C

Hoh Rain Forest
Visitor Center

Hoh

Elwha

DANIEL J. EVANS
WILDERNESS

Dungeness

BUCKHORN
WILDERNESS

+ Mount Olympus
7965 ft

N A T I O N A L   P A R K

THE BROTHERS
WILDERNESS

DANIEL J. EVANS
WILDERNESS

Queets

Upper
Lena Lake

② Lena
Lake

LENA LAKE
TRAIL

HAMMA HAMMA ROAD

OLYMPIC

NATIONAL

FOREST

Lake
Quinault

Quinault

North Fork Skokomish

DANIEL J. EVANS
WILDERNESS

MOUNT
SKOKOMISH
WILDERNESS

OLYMPIC N.F.

① STAIRCASE RAPIDS
LOOP

□ Staircase Campground

COLONEL BOB
WILDERNESS

WONDER MOUNTAIN
WILDERNESS

Lake
Cushman

OLYMPIC NATIONAL FOREST

Petroglyphs along the park's Pacific coast

All of these critters, and a slew of smaller species, provide ample opportunities for hikers to enjoy a wildlife encounter along this quiet, gentle 3-mile loop.

❷ **Lena Lake Trail** To experience the blooming rhododendron forests, hike the Upper Lena Lake trail in May or early June. The best of the rhodies are found on the trail's lower section.

The path leaves the **Hamma Hamma** road and climbs 1,200 feet through a mix of old-growth and second-growth forest to Lower Lena Lake (3 miles one way).

"I love the climb through the rhody forests into the woodland lake basin," says Robert Moody, senior air quality specialist for Olympic Region Clean Air Agency (ORCAA), which protects the air quality for Olympic National Park and all the lands surrounding it on the Olympic Peninsula.

The trail starts in **Olympic National Forest,** as most of the area trails do, and it enters the national park just past **Lower Lena Lake.** The trail to the upper lake runs another 4 miles into the park, climbing 2,800 feet along the way to the alpine

lake above. The entire trail runs 7.3 miles and ascends to 4,500 feet.

HURRICANE RIDGE ROAD

To enjoy the high peaks of the Olympics with the least amount of pain, make use of the park's primary roadway: the Hurricane Ridge Road. Towering over **Port Angeles,** Hurricane Ridge runs parallel to the **Strait of Juan de Fuca,** providing a unique opportunity to enjoy views north and south.

Looking south from the summit of Hurricane Ridge, visitors see the park's central wilderness and the glacier-covered top of **Mount Olympus.** Turning north provides views across the strait to Victoria, British Columbia, and the interior peaks of Canada's Vancouver Island.

Just past the park's visitor center atop Hurricane Ridge, the road ends at the base of **Hurricane Hill.** A short, family-friendly trail leads up the small grade, climbing through brilliant subalpine flower meadows.

Going higher brings better scenery, with magnificent views of the interior

NOT TO BE MISSED: *Wander through enormous rhododendron forests on the Lena Lake Trail.*
▸ *Experience fantastic views both north and south from Hurricane Ridge Road.* ▸ *Traverse the switchbacks of the Klahhane Ridge Trail.* ▸ *Listen for the bugling call of Roosevelt elk.*
▸ *Hike the iconic Hoh River Trail for an unforgettable rain forest encounter.* ▸ *Head west to the coast and count the seals.*

Olympics and the valley carved by the mighty **Elwha River** coming into clearer view with each passing footstep.

❸ Klahhane Ridge Trail For deeper immersion into the alpine environment, pull off the Hurricane Ridge Road 3 miles below Hurricane Ridge (15 miles from the start of the road in Port Angeles) to the Switchback Trailhead for the Klahhane Ridge Trail (you can also start from the Hurricane Ridge Visitor Center).

This 5-mile round-trip wild path climbs a series of switchbacks through steep fields of wildflowers before cresting the knife-edged Klahhane Ridge at 6,000 feet. The north face of the ridge drops away in vertical cliffs, while the south slopes down in near-vertical meadows.

Marmots whistle merrily in the meadows as you wander past the lupines and other alpine plants. Views north and south are worth the sweat expended to reach the ridge top.

THE RAIN FORESTS

The temperate rain forests of the Olympic Peninsula support more biomass per acre of land than any other ecosystem on the planet.

The magnificent old-growth hemlocks, Sitka spruces, and red cedars account for a great deal of that. But the endless layers of moss, lichen, ferns, and other evergreen materials that blanket every surface, usually several feet deep, also make up a significant portion of the biomass total. All that greenery sprouts from rich soils fed by up to 150 inches of rainfall annually.

Of course, not all living things in the verdant world of the Olympic rain forests grow out of the soil. Vast herds of

Temperate Hoh Rain Forest

Sol Duc Falls

Roosevelt elk (the largest unmanaged herd in the Pacific Northwest, see sidebar opposite) call the cathedral forests home. If you're traveling here in September, listen for the bugling to locate them, but beware—they are dangerous, so keep a distance of 50 yards at minimum.

Small black-tailed deer also roam these woods, as do mountain lions, which are the one large predator left to hunt the ungulates.

❹ Sol Duc Valley To experience the broadest range of beauty found in these forests, venture up the Sol Duc Valley from the **Lake Crescent** area of US 101 (which partially circles the park, following the east, north, and west sides).

The **Sol Duc Falls Trail** pierces a magnificent old-growth forest alongside the **Sol Duc River.** The path leads to one of the most scenic waterfalls in the Olympics—a low, thundering cascade that drops into a narrow gorge. The falls make a great destination for a 1.8-mile round-trip walk.

❺ Hoh River Trail The iconic rain forest hike, however, starts just a few miles south on US 101. The Hoh River Trail leads deep into the heart of the ethereal rain forest.

Enjoy a walk of just a few hundred yards, or push up to the very shoulders of **Mount Olympus** (17.4 miles one way). Regardless of the length of the adventure, the Hoh River Trail provides an unforgettable experience in a valley that defines temperate rain forests. The entire valley plays host to massive old-growth western red cedar, Douglas fir, bigleaf maple, and Sitka spruce.

| THE COAST

Olympic's coastal strand includes more than 60 miles of wilderness beach, though in truth, it's not exactly what most people think beaches should look like. The Pacific Ocean does roll up on some sandy strips, but most of the park's coastline boasts stretches of rocky strands separated by jagged headlands.

Just offshore from these cobblestone beaches rise an array of "sea stacks"— rocky remnants of the former coastline before the tides carved it away. Generally speaking, the north end is rocky and the sea stacks are to the south.

The rocky knobs rising from the surf tend to be popular hangouts for seabirds such as rhinoceros auklets, tufted puffins, and brown pelicans, as well as marine mammals including seals and sea lions. Occasionally, black bears venture out of the coastal forests to wade or swim over to the close-in sea stacks at low tide to hunt for young birds and sea mammals.

❻ **Kalaloch Beach** Though some of the more remote sections of this national

Sea stars

park provide the best wilderness experiences, they can be hard to reach.

To get a great taste of Olympic's wild beaches and the powerful Pacific that grinds them down, take US 101 south from the Hoh River to meet the coast at **Ruby Beach,** a mix of sand and smooth cobble-like stones, with a heavy layer of driftwood at the foot of the bluffs.

From here, travel 10 miles south to Kalaloch where the **Kalaloch Lodge** provides great overnight accommodations in the main building itself or in small cabins dotting the bluffs above the waves of the Pacific pounding on rocky Kalaloch Beach.

LOCAL INTELLIGENCE

President Theodore Roosevelt protected what is now Olympic National Park in 1909 with national monument status primarily because he wanted to ensure the survival of a unique species of elk found primarily in the rain forest valleys on the west side of the park. By 1912, the elk numbers on the Olympic Peninsula had dwindled to fewer than 150 animals. The national monument (and later national park) designation kept hunters from taking those last few animals.

Today, the elk thrive and rightfully bear the name of their protector— Roosevelt elk are the largest species of elk, perhaps because of their ready access to rich and plentiful food sources. They graze on the lichens, ferns, and shrubs from the rain forest as well as meadow grasses that blanket the valleys.

Awestruck among the redwood giants

REDWOOD

At least some of what makes Redwood National and State Parks famous can easily be seen from a highway. That may not be entirely a good thing, though. US 101 passes through the northern California park for miles, in places winding among dense groves of coast redwoods, the enormous, awe-inspiring tree species (the world's tallest) for which the area is named. Many times along this route, a driver pulls over, the family hops out to stare upward and take a few photos, and the trip continues north to Oregon or south to San Francisco.

That hypothetical family may have seen some redwoods, but it certainly did not see the park or its secrets. Redwood National and State Parks—as its name indicates, the park is managed jointly by the National Park Service and California State Parks—is composed of several alluring sections, stretching more than 65 miles along the California coast.

SOUTHERN PARK

Entering the park from the south, stop at the **Thomas H. Kuchel Visitor Center** north of US 101 for maps and advice. If driving a recreational vehicle or pulling a trailer, ask which park roads are not recommended for large vehicles.

Continue about 3 miles on Davison Road to **Elk Meadow,** where sightings of Roosevelt elk are common. From the parking lot here, the 2.75-mile loop of the **Trillium Falls Trail** (rated as moderate) leads through a shady landscape of ferns and magnificent redwoods to a small, pretty waterfall. Elk are often seen from the viewing bridge.

Year-Round Visitor Centers
- **Crescent City Information Center**
  111 Second Street, Crescent City
- **Hiouchi Visitor Center**
  On US 199, Hiouchi
- **Prairie Creek Visitor Center**
  Off US 101, along Newton B. Drury Scenic Parkway
- **Thomas H. Kuchel Visitor Center**
  On US 101, Orick

Seasonal Visitor Center
- **Jedediah Smith Visitor Center**
  Within Jedediah Smith Campground, off US 199

707-465-7335, nps.gov/redw

❶ Lyons Ranch Trail Continuing on Bald Hills Road another 15 miles, stop at the **Redwood Creek Overlook** for a vista of not only the creek watershed but also, on a clear day, the Pacific Ocean 6 miles west. This is also "a great place to still see the scars of pre-national-park logging as well as continuing efforts towards reforestation," says Candace Tinkler, the park's chief of interpretation and education.

Continue to the start of the Lyons Ranch Trail, in an oak-and-grassland environment different from the rest of the park and a favorite among park staff.

"Once you are actually in the Bald Hills it is a place little touched by modern times," shares Tinkler.

❷ Newton B. Drury Scenic Parkway Back on US 101, it's about 3 miles north to this 10-mile paved road, which is the best off-highway choice for RVs and leads to some of the park's most visited attractions. "The parkway also hosts more miles of strolls and hikes in

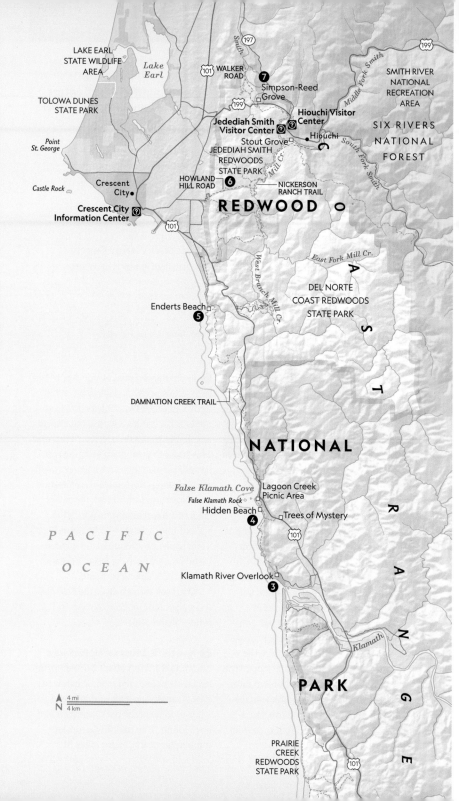

LAKE EARL
STATE WILDLIFE
AREA

Lake Earl

Smith

197

101 WALKER
ROAD

TOLOWA DUNES
STATE PARK

199

7
Simpson-Reed
Grove

**Hiouchi Visitor
Center**

SMITH RIVER
NATIONAL
RECREATION
AREA

Middle Fork Smith

199

SIX RIVERS
NATIONAL
FOREST

**Jedediah Smith
Visitor Center**

Point
St. George

Stout Grove

Hiouchi

JEDEDIAH SMITH
REDWOODS
STATE PARK

South Fork Smith

Castle Rock

Crescent
City

**HOWLAND
HILL ROAD**
6

NICKERSON
RANCH TRAIL

**Crescent City
Information Center**

101

REDWOOD

O

Mill Cr.

East Fork Mill Cr.

DEL NORTE
COAST REDWOODS
STATE PARK

C
O
A
S
T

Enderts Beach
5

West Branch Mill Cr.

DAMNATION CREEK TRAIL

NATIONAL

False Klamath Cove

Lagoon Creek
Picnic Area

False Klamath Rock

Hidden Beach
4

Trees of Mystery

101

R
A
N

PACIFIC

OCEAN

Klamath River Overlook
3

Klamath

G

PARK

E

N 4 mi
N 4 km

PRAIRIE
CREEK
REDWOODS
STATE PARK

101

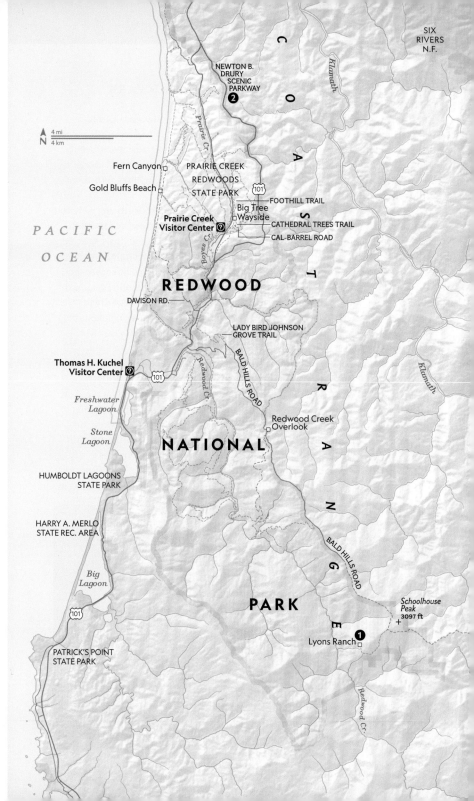

SIX
RIVERS
N.F.

Klamath

NEWTON B.
DRURY
SCENIC
PARKWAY
2

C O A S T

Prairie Cr

4 mi
4 km

Fern Canyon

PRAIRIE CREEK
REDWOODS
STATE PARK

Gold Bluffs Beach

(101)

FOOTHILL TRAIL

Big Tree
Wayside

**Prairie Creek
Visitor Center** ⓘ

CATHEDRAL TREES TRAIL

CAL-BARREL ROAD

Boyes Cr

PACIFIC

OCEAN

REDWOOD

DAVISON RD.

LADY BIRD JOHNSON
GROVE TRAIL

**Thomas H. Kuchel
Visitor Center** ⓘ

(101)

Redwood Cr

BALD HILLS ROAD

Klamath

*Freshwater
Lagoon*

*Stone
Lagoon*

Redwood Creek
Overlook

NATIONAL

HUMBOLDT LAGOONS
STATE PARK

R
A
N
G
E

HARRY A. MERLO
STATE REC. AREA

*Big
Lagoon*

BALD HILLS ROAD

(101)

PARK

*Schoolhouse
Peak
3097 ft*

Lyons Ranch **1**

PATRICK'S POINT
STATE PARK

Redwood Cr

old-growth forest than any other area in Redwood National and State Parks," says Tinkler.

Ted Humphry, a park volunteer, enjoys a 2.2-mile loop walk made up of the **Cathedral Trees** and **Foothill Trails.** "Visitors see different redwood forests, from the big valley-floor trees along Foothill, to the smaller redwoods on the Cathedral hillside, to the big bays and maples and alders along Boyes Creek at the transition from forest to prairie."

Those traveling with pets can enjoy a wonderful wander together among the giant trees. Park your vehicle at the bottom of **Cal-Barrel Road**, just off the Drury Scenic Parkway, and head up this steep and narrow unpaved road for minutes, or hours, of quiet contemplation beneath the huge redwoods. Note: No matter how well behaved, all pets must stay on the roads and be kept on a leash no longer than 6 feet in length.

For more information on including your pet on your visit to Redwood, pick up a "Bark Ranger" brochure at any park visitor center.

NORTHERN PARK

Aside from the redwoods—certainly worth a trip in themselves—the park includes unspoiled beaches, grassland, beautiful streams, and mixed evergreen forests of Douglas fir, Sitka spruce, and western hemlock.

As staff members like to say, Redwood is "more than tall trees," and the park's "more" includes hiking, whale-watching, beach strolling, and stunning ocean sunsets. Ranger-guided tidepool explorations, kayaking the Smith River, and mountain biking in the **Mill Creek Watershed Area** are also highlights of the northern part of the park.

3 Klamath River Overlook About 3 miles north of the Klamath River bridge on US 101, turn west for the short side trip to this spot, with its viewing platform above the Pacific. On a calm summer day you can view the mouth of the Klamath as it meets the ocean.

This is a place to watch bald eagles and ospreys, California sea lions swimming in

Sunset at Enderts Beach

LOCAL INTELLIGENCE

Time your trip: Many locals believe September and October are the best months to visit Redwood National and State Parks. Not only do the summer months have more vacationers, but the coastal areas of the park then are often foggy (though sites inland a few miles are sunnier). Also, it rains a lot from November through April. May and June, though, are best for seeing wildflowers and blooming shrubs such as rhododendron.

the surf, and gray whales as they migrate up and down the coast between Alaska and Baja California.

4 Hidden Beach Over the next 8 miles of US 101 you'll reach access points for two short hikes recommended by Humphry: "A favorite easy walk is from the **Lagoon Creek Picnic Area** to Hidden Beach. From the Lagoon Creek approach, you also view the **False Klamath Rock** rookery in spring and summer," hosting seabirds and sea lions.

5 Enderts Beach Road Check the schedule for low tide and visit Enderts Beach, off US 101 just south of **Crescent City.** Explore the rocks of the intertidal zone for a staggering array of sea stars, sea anemones, crabs, chitons, barnacles, and other life-forms in an environment that rivals a rain forest in its diversity.

NOT TO BE MISSED: *Leave the car and hike into the tall trees on the Trillium Falls Trail.* ▸ *Experience the park with your (leashed) pet on the unpaved Cal-Barrel Road.* ▸ *Spot sea creatures with a ranger at Enderts Beach.* ▸ *Absorb the beauty of the immense redwoods at Stout Grove.* ▸ *Walk the short trail into Simpson-Reed Grove.*

---

6 Howland Hill Road East of Crescent City is one of the park's most stunning drives: Howland Hill Road, a winding, unpaved route through redwood groves (not recommended for large vehicles). For persons with limited mobility, this is an opportunity to drive through a wonderful forest landscape away from the better known park scenic drives.

For hikers, the fairly easy, 1-mile **Nickerson Ranch Trail** off Howland Hill Road follows **Mill Creek,** which provides a sunny corridor lined with a diversity of plants and habitats for a variety of birds.

Continuing east on Howland Hill brings you to **Stout Grove,** arguably the most beautiful grove of redwoods in the park, with a flat, 0.5-mile trail. The open aspect here makes the trees easier to see than at most areas.

7 Simpson-Reed Grove Michael Poole, park staff member, calls the nearby Simpson-Reed Grove "my favorite of all the short redwood walks." It is reached by turning north on Walker Road off US 199 between Crescent City and Hiouchi.

"I like that Simpson-Reed is a more complete-looking old-growth forest," Poole says. "Not only are there redwoods, but I like to tell people to look for the nurse logs [fallen, decaying trunks that serve as habitat for saplings], as well. They are everywhere, with nice big trees growing on them."

MORE PARK SECRETS

View of the Arctic Divide near Anaktuvuk Pass

GATES OF THE ARCTIC

ARCTIC ISOLATION I 907-692-5494 I *nps.gov/gaar*

Located entirely north of the Arctic Circle, Gates of the Arctic National Park and Preserve sets aside some of Alaska's most pristine wilderness, and it can't help being secret. The mountains of the **Brooks Range** soar to the north, while millions of ponds dot valleys where waterfowl like swans, geese, cranes, loons, gyrfalcons, short-eared owls, and montane shorebirds nest in endless summer sunlight. On land, porcupine caribou, musk ox, Dall sheep, grizzlies, black bears, moose, and wolves make their home.

Upon first arrival, visitors may feel that no humans have ever set foot in Gates of the Arctic: There are no roads, no trails, and no campsites. Thousands of archaeological sites, however, testify to the people who have lived and traveled in the area for over 13,000 years. For example, take a floatplane to **Agiak Lake** to explore hundreds of rock cairns that line the valley for nearly a mile. These guided caribou into the lake, where Nunamiut Inuit hunters in kayaks hunted them with lances. Today a number of established outfitters will introduce you to this vast region via plane or boat.

GLACIER BAY
ISLANDS & INLETS **I** 270-758-2180 **I** *nps.gov/glba*

Just over 200 years ago, Glacier Bay was almost completely covered by ice. Since then, the receding glaciers have revealed a dynamic landscape of rugged mountains and temperate rain forest along Alaska's Inside Passage. Marine life is the highlight: harbor porpoises, Steller sea lions, and humpback, minke, and killer whales are all present in the park's waters.

The vast majority of Glacier Bay National Park and Preserve's visitors arrive on cruise ships, and few venture into the many small inlets and coves. For a semi-secret adventure, rent a kayak in Bartlett Cove and explore the **Beardslee Islands,** a complex of about two dozen small islands in the lower part of the bay. Take care not to get stranded by the tides that can rise and fall up to 25 feet—at low tide, some of the areas of the Beardslees are very shallow or exposed mudflat.

"Anyone seeking a short adventure can pick their own island, pitch a tent, and experience the sights and sounds of Glacier Bay's wilderness firsthand," invites Tom VandenBerg, former supervisory park ranger. "Bald Eagles, black bears, harbor seals, and humpback whales are all common in this beautiful area." Whale-watching is particularly productive at **Point Adolphus,** opposite the mouth of Glacier Bay. It's best experienced by kayak, which puts you on their level.

KATMAI
ALASKA IN CONCENTRATE **I** 907-246-3305 **I** *nps.gov/katm*

With 2,200 brown bears and 15 volcanoes—some steaming—Katmai is like Alaska in concentrate. Here you'll find the **Valley of Ten Thousand Smokes,** named for its landscape of once fuming fumaroles, and you might be able to snap that iconic photo of a bear catching salmon in a waterfall at **Brooks Camp** —the square-mile area where as many as 100 bears can roam during peak activity periods.

Rangers function as "bear traffic control," closing trails and bridges to avoid close human encounters with animals that can weigh up to 900 pounds.

"Those visiting should be prepared to be surprised," says Amber Kraft, the park's interpretation and education program manager. "Sockeye salmon swimming upstream are surprised to be snagged by a brown bear. Spruce grouse are surprised by a pouncing lynx. Hikers are surprised by the changing landscape and astonishing views. Visitors on ranger-led culture walks are surprised by how much they learn about those who have lived in this place for more than 5,000 years. And people are often surprised by a bear dozing on a walking path."

KENAI FJORDS

COASTAL FJORDS I 907-422-0500 I *nps.gov/kefj*

With over half of the park covered in ice, Kenai Fjords National Park offers some of the most remarkable scenery in southern Alaska. The **Harding Icefield** and its nearly 40 outflowing glaciers envelop more than 700 square miles of the **Kenai Mountains.** The deep coastal fjords carved by the glaciers form rare estuary ecosystems found in only six locations in the world.

Skip the crowds in Aialik Bay and kayak through **Northwestern Fjord,** which is less exposed to the Gulf of Alaska than many of the park's other bays and fjords. It is, says park ranger Shauna Potocky, "an ideal location for a guided kayak adventure, with an array of glacier types."

Paddling through the fjord offers the chance to see some of the area's famed wildlife, including Harbor seals, as well as nesting sites for such seabirds as pigeon guillemots and the rare Kittlitz's murrelet. "This location and its logistics require being prepared and understanding how to travel safely," warns Potocky. Hiring a guide is strongly recommended.

KOBUK VALLEY

CARIBOU MIGRATIONS I 907-442-3890 I *nps.gov/kova*

Framed by the Baird Mountains to the north and the Kobuk Sand Dunes to the south, Kobuk Valley National Park protects 1.7 million acres well above the Arctic Circle in Alaska. The broad **Kobuk River Valley** presents a stunning landscape of open woodland and thick tundra.

"The largest caribou herd in the state, with just over 250,000 animals, travels through the park during its yearly migrations in spring and fall, as it has for at least 10,000 years," says Maija Katak Lukin, superintendent of the Western Arctic National Parklands.

Humans have also had a long presence in Kobuk Valley, with the Inupiat people protecting the region for some 12,000 years. "This is our home, we take care of it," says elder Hannah Loon, originally from Selawik. With no trails, no roads, and no ranger stations in the park, getting in and out of Kobuk Valley requires plenty of planning and local knowledge.

Hardy paddlers with their own boats and backcountry survival skills may try a seven-day trip down the **Kobuk River** between the villages of Ambler and Kiana. The slow and easy river, edged in spruce forest, winds through the park for 61 miles. Near Kavet Creek, a 2- to 3-mile trek from the river brings hikers to a mostly secret spot: the 100-foot-high **Great Kobuk Sand Dunes,** the largest active dune field in Arctic North America.

LAKE CLARK

BEARS, FISH & VOLCANOES I 907-781-2218 I *nps.gov/lacl*

Inaccessible by any road, Lake Clark National Park and Preserve protects 4 million acres of dynamic wilderness in south-central Alaska, including two active volcanoes: **Mount Iliamna** and **Mount Redoubt**. The **Chigmit Mountains**, the northernmost in the **Aleutian Range**, is divided from the **Alaska Range** by **Lake Clark Pass.**

Most visitors stick to the coastal areas along the **Cook Inlet** for bear viewing, but an adventurous few strike inland via small plane to experience the broad and beautiful **Tlikakila River.** Originating in Lake Clark Pass and fed by a series of glaciers, the brown, fast-moving river hosts memorable multi-day rafting and kayaking trips through towering mountains and glacially braided curves.

Throughout the summer, the park's lakes and rivers offer great fishing (license required). And in fall, once the temperatures drop below freezing at night and the glacial silt load in the river clears out, a significant number of sockeye salmon run up the river all the way to the glacier—attracting the interest of grizzly bears.

Caribou swimming the Kobuk River

LASSEN VOLCANIC

HYDROTHERMAL HEAVEN | 530-595-4480 | *nps.gov/lavo*

The largest hydrothermal area in the continental United States west of Yellowstone, this northeastern California park is sprinkled with seething steam vents, bubbling mudpots, and boiling pools. Lassen Peak blew its top in 1915 and continued to erupt into 1922—the last eruption in the lower 48 before Mount Saint Helens exploded in 1980. While the mountain that dominates Lassen Volcanic National Park has quieted down, it's still considered an active volcano.

Bumpass Hell Trail, with its convenient location and boardwalk past hissing volcanic phenomena, is understandably a visitor hot spot. But travelers often overlook the fascinating sulfur-scented secret known as **Devils Kitchen.**

Tucked into the Warner Valley's upper reaches, this trail isn't all boardwalks, so in some places you'll find yourself stepping on the hard-packed crusty ground, with steam thumping below the surface, mud boiling around you, and the aroma of questionable cooking wafting through the air. Just don't stray from the established trail. Take this seriously: One wrong step and your foot could sink through thin crust and plunge into scalding mud.

Devils Kitchen

NORTH CASCADES

PARTNER IN PROTECTION I 360-854-7200 I *nps.gov/noca*

Less than three hours from Seattle, Washington's North Cascades National Park preserves a wide array of biodiversity, from its western temperate rain forest to its eastern dry ponderosa pine ecosystem. More than 300 glaciers can be found in the park's jagged, comparatively young mountains, with dramatic landscapes spread over 9,000 feet of vertical relief.

Experienced backcountry travelers in search of solitude can take numerous trails, such as the **Bridge Creek Trail** into the Upper Stehekin Valley, in the park's southern section. The narrow, forested area is surrounded by 7,000- to 9,000-foot glaciated peaks, crowned by 9,220-foot Goode Mountain. A side trip along the **Goode Ridge Trail** takes hikers into a spectacular horseshoe surrounded by giant ridges that reveal the park's mountainous grandeur.

Some 680,849 acres of the North Cascades is protected by the national park in partnership with **Ross Lake National Recreation Area** and **Lake Chelan Recreation Area,** forming a complementary suite of protected lands united by a contiguous wilderness overlay.

WRANGELL–ST. ELIAS

WILDERNESS & INDUSTRY I 907-822-7250 I *nps.gov/wrst*

At more than 13 million acres, Wrangell–St. Elias in southcentral Alaska is the United States' largest national park. Here, four major mountain ranges come together, combining volcanoes, coastal mountains, and more than 3,100 individual glaciers into a protected place bigger in area than the country of Switzerland. This is Alaska wilderness so untamed that experienced hikers often set off to make their own trails.

While many visitors are drawn to Wrangell–St. Elias to escape the daily grind of the lower 48 states, it is little known that the park ties its history to American industry. Now a scenic cluster of red and white buildings, the mill town of Kennecott supported the world's most productive copper mine a century ago.

Hoping to supply copper for everything from electrical wires to cars, the wealthy Morgan and Guggenheim families invested in the mine despite its location on a remote, snow-covered mountain. It was a Warren Buffett–style move: When the vein ran out in 1938, the mine had made $100 million in net profits and enriched the heritage of this monumental park.

Today, guided history tours lead visitors through the enormous old **Kennecott Mill** (summer only). Other interesting, ranger-led walks and talks are also available in season.

ILLUSTRATIONS CREDITS

INDEX

Boldface indicates illustrations.

NATIONAL PARK TRUST.

TREASURE FOREVER.

National Park Trust, a nonprofit dedicated to preserving parks today and creating park stewards for tomorrow, is very pleased to be a partner in the production of this book. The Park Trust is the only national land trust with a comprehensive mission of completing our national parks through land acquisition and creating a pipeline of future park stewards by providing kids with their first park experiences. Since 1983, the Park Trust has protected land in 28 states; the U.S. Virgin Islands; and Washington, D.C., benefiting over 50 national park units. In addition, each year, the Park Trust provides 25,000 underserved kids with educational park trips through their nationally recognized Buddy Bison Programs and Kids to Parks Day. Kids to Parks Day is an annual day of outdoor play that inspires more than one million kids and families to explore their parks, public lands, and waters across the country. To learn more, visit *parktrust.org*.

Since 1888, the National Geographic Society has funded more than 13,000 research, exploration, and preservation projects around the world. National Geographic Partners distributes a portion of the funds it receives from your purchase to National Geographic Society to support programs including the conservation of animals and their habitats.

National Geographic Partners
1145 17th Street NW
Washington, DC 20036-4688 USA

Get closer to National Geographic explorers and photographers, and connect with our global community. Join us today at nationalgeographic.com/join

For rights or permissions inquiries, please contact National Geographic Books Subsidiary Rights: bookrights@natgeo.com

Library of Congress Control Number: 2012953600

ISBN: 978-1-4262-2085-2 (2nd ed.)

Printed in China

20/RRDH/1

The information in this book has been carefully checked and to the best of our knowledge is accurate. However, details are subject to change, and the publisher cannot be responsible for such changes, or for errors or omissions.